ESSENTIALS

OF

NEW TESTAMENT GREEK

·The· M ꞇo·

ESSENTIALS

OF

NEW TESTAMENT GREEK

BY

JOHN HOMER HUDDILSTON, A.B. (Harv.),
Ph.D. (Munich)

PROFESSOR OF GREEK IN THE UNIVERSITY OF MAINE

*Author of "Greek Tragedy in the Light of Vase-Paintings," "Lessons
from Greek Pottery," etc.*

New York
THE MACMILLAN COMPANY
LONDON: MACMILLAN & CO., Ltd.
1905

PREFACE.

THE publication of the Revised Version of our English New Testament, in 1881, marked the beginning of a new interest in Bible study. Since that time not only the English, but the Greek and Hebrew have been studied with a zeal quite new. The sources are being more carefully examined to-day than ever before. Students are becoming more and more awake to the great importance of being able to judge of a certain passage for themselves rather than accepting without doubt or question whatever the authorities say in regard to it.

Can anything be done to bring the language of the New Testament within the reach of a larger number of Bible students? Through the great maze of grammatical difficulties that surround the language, can a way be mapped out along which the student may work, and, without sacrificing essentials, gain the same end that usually requires many months of hard study? Can the absolutely essential parts of the language, as used by the New Testament writers, be set forth in small space? This little book is an attempt to answer these questions, and I believe that it lies within the power of the earnest Sunday-school worker or other Bible student to acquire a reading knowledge of New Testament Greek, provided only a substantial part of one's time is thus devoted for a few months.

In my teaching of elementary classes in Garrett Biblical Institute, I have been accustomed to begin my work with the first list of verbs in Bradley and Horswell's New Testament Word Lists, Part I. All of these words occur several hundred times, and furnish the student thus at the very first with a substantial hold on what proves one of the main difficulties in Greek or any other language, — the vocabulary. The work was in part inductive. Those words that presented fewest difficulties of form, and which at the same time were of the most frequent occurrence, were presented first. The second declension was introduced before the first, as being altogether simpler and more easily comprehended by those who had not made the acquaintance of an inflected language. I aimed to keep rare adjectives and tenses of the verb till a later time. The optative mood, which does not occur in the Johannean writings, was omitted entirely from the elementary work. Each lesson was accompanied with illustrative exercises taken as far as possible from the New Testament.

The present volume has grown out of this plan of work. It represents the results of class-room experience. The work has been tried in manuscript form, both with my classes and with private students, and has, therefore, the advantage, so important in this class of books, of having been given a practical test.

Part I. includes the thirty-two lessons, which will afford sufficient preparation for the reading of the Greek, the first letter of John, the Beatitudes and the Lord's Prayer from Matthew, the chapter on the Prodigal Son from Luke, and the thirteenth of First Corinthians. These selections are given in Wescott and Hort's reading and are followed by notes and vocabulary. Of the epistle there is given a translation of three chapters, two literal and one quoted from the Revised Version. This translation may serve for retranslation in case the reading is taken up inductively apart from the lessons. In Part II. are found the essentials of the grammar, embracing, in the first part, the alphabet, table of consonants, vowel and euphonic changes, in the second part, the declension of nouns, pronouns, adjectives, participles, the conjugation of verbs, the optatives of the New Testament, a table of about eighty irregular verbs, and the special study in the classes of verbs and the most common irregular verbs.

In all verbal forms the aim has been to confine the forms given, to New Testament usage. In the third part of the grammar the main features of the syntax are illustrated with quotations from the New Testament Greek. The prepositions also are discussed somewhat and accompanied with sentences illustrating New Testament peculiarities.

I have made the explanations in the lessons so full that much progress may be made by private study, without a teacher. The lessons as arranged represent but one way of applying the Word Lists. The Greek text, the convenient form of declensions and conjugations, afford opportunity for the teacher to exercise his own judgment in putting the student in control of the elementary work.

I wish here to acknowledge my great indebtedness to Professors Bradley and Horswell for the use of their Word Lists, which they so very kindly put at my disposal. Without the great labour which they had already performed, my work would have been either impossible or the labour of producing it would have been very greatly increased.

I wish especially to express my great indebtedness to Rev. Charles Horswell, Ph.D., Professor of Hebrew in Garrett Biblical Institute, for invaluable assistance. Without his suggestion the work would not have been begun, nor completed without his encouragement and co-operation. Whatever of merit this little book may have, it owes much to his rare scholarship and his wide experience as a teacher of the New Testament language. For no errors, however, which the work may contain is he at all responsible. For valuable assistance in correction of the proof I have to express my thanks to Mr. E. A. Bechtel, A.M., and Mr. W. W. Bishop, A.M., Instructors in Classics in Northwestern University. The proof has been read, in part, also, by Professor Milton S. Terry, D.D., Garrett Biblical Institute, and by Professor Henry A. Buttz, D.D., Drew Theological Seminary. I owe much to the valuable suggestions of these well-known scholars.

J. H. HUDDILSTON.

NORTHWESTERN UNIVERSITY,
    EVANSTON, ILL., May 29, 1895.

PREFACE TO SECOND EDITION.

———◆———

ASIDE from the corrections of typographical errors, few changes have been introduced in this new edition. My time since the publication of the book has been so occupied in other lines of study that it has been impossible for me to enlarge certain parts of the grammar which the favourable reception of the work would have warranted.

I am under special obligation to Professor John Humphrey Barbour, Middletown, Conn., who has very kindly gone over the whole work and favoured me with his valuable criticism.

J. H. H.

BERLIN, GERMANY,
    August, 1896.

CONTENTS.

———

INTRODUCTION.

My purpose is to offer here a few considerations on two questions. 1. Why was the New Testament written in *Greek?* 2. What are the main points of difference between this Greek and that of the classical period?

Every one knows that Greek was not a native of Palestine, but that in some way this exotic plant found root there, and, to the exclusion of the native language, became the organ of the everlasting Gospel. How then did this occur?

It will first be necessary to understand something about the languages which were used in the countries to the east from the Mediterranean, prior to and contemporary with the advent of the Greek. All of this part of Asia, including the countries from Assyria on the north to Arabia on the south, had one separate and distinct family or branch of languages, — the Semitic. Of this primitive Semitic nothing is left us. Long before the curtain of history rises, the early language had assumed marked grammatical and lexigraphical peculiarities among the various peoples. Accordingly we know nothing of the parent speech except through the tongues of these early nations. The Assyrians (whose language is known from cuneiform inscriptions) and the Aramaeans, who comprised a large part of the population of Assyria and Babylon and to whose language, the Aramaic, we shall refer later, represented the most northern group of the Semitic. South of these we find the Hebrews of Canaan, in whose language the most considerable portion of the Old Testament was written, and akin to them the Phoenicians, whose language is known to us imperfectly and through inscriptions only. Further south the Arabic and Ethiopic make up what is sometimes termed the South Semitic. Of these three groups, the North, the Middle, and the South Semitic, we shall confine our considerations to the first two; for here it is that we have to look for the language of the Jews. Their Hebrew was early exposed to the dialects of the surrounding tribes and especially open to Aramaic influences on the north. Indeed as early as 700 B.C. we read that the messengers of the king Hezekiah requested the ambassador of the king of Assyria to speak to them in Aramaic, "for we understand *it*" (ii. Kings 18 : 26). The Jews would not long retain their language in its early purity beside that of another people who, as a conquering nation, were continually insinuating themselves into their life and politics. The result was that long before the breaking up of the Jewish kingdom in 586 B.C., the Hebrew had departed considerably from its original integrity. During the long years of captivity in Babylon and throughout the Babylonian empire, the Aramaic, which was the official language of the Babylonian court, must have become quite as much a part of the Hebrews as their native tongue. The books of the Old Testament written after the exile, Ezra and Daniel, are known as the Aramaic books, owing to the fact that considerable portions of them are in the Aramaic. We must not understand, however, that this large admixture of Aramaic is due wholly to the years of exile in Babylon. It has been the accepted view since the time of Jerome that in this period the Israelites ceased to speak and write Hebrew and turned to the use of the Aramaic only. Hence the term Chaldee, so often used to signify the speech of the Jews, as though the language of the Chaldees — the Aramaic — was introduced into Palestine by the returned exiles, and that subsequent to this the Hebrew died out and the Chaldee or Aramaic took its place. In recent years scholars have generally parted with this view, and have attempted to show that the change was more gradual. This seems by all means the most probable. A people retains its language long after its institutions and customs have ceased to exist. A conquering nation rarely succeeds in supplanting the language of the conquered. Slowly and gradually do the forces work that bring in the elements of a new speech. The English, for example, has not after five centuries entirely displaced the Celtic of Ireland, nor has Welsh ceased to be a very important factor in the literature and life of the United Kingdom, notwithstanding the fact that more than 500 years have passed since Edward built his castles on the Welsh frontier.

We must conclude therefore that for centuries the Aramaic gradually gained in popularity over the Hebrew, until the latter became at last the language of scholars and the learned few, while to the great mass of Jews the Aramaic was the only language known. This change must have occurred before the time of Christ; for we find then that the common people no longer understood the Hebrew of the Scriptures, but used instead versions known as Targums, written in Aramaic. This then is the language of Palestine at the time of Christ, and the same which in the New Testament is called Hebrew.

A great distinction, however, must be made between this Jewish-Aramaic and the Hebrew. The literature of each is sacred, but of the Hebrew we have left us the scant remains of the Old Testament only, while the former has extant a vast literature of the Talmud, Targums, and interpretative works, and has lived on in a more or less changed condition till the present time, and forms the basis of the language much used by the Jews to-day throughout the world.

At the close of the fourth century B.C., Alexander of Macedon crossed the historic Hellespont, overturned the Persian empire at Arbela, destroyed the famous city of ancient Tyre, overran all western Asia, even crossing into Egypt, where he founded the world's new metropolis bearing his own name (332 B.C.). It is hard to measure the results of this conquering of the world. By no means the least important of the many that might be described was the spread of Greek letters and Greek civilization. This noble language

of ancient Hellas, so rich and beautiful, so full of power and sweetness, was destined to work far greater results in the minds and hearts of men than the brief rule of Alexander and his successors. They soon passed away, and the Greek kingdom in Asia ceased to exist; but the Greek language which came with them still remained and spread with great rapidity throughout this whole territory, revealing to these Semitic races a new world of beauty and power. Although Greece soon fell under the conquering hand of Rome, Greek art and Greek letters took captive her captor. Rome was then the world, while through all her borders the language of Greece became the speech of trade and intercourse. Greek was even the language of the Roman court, and Roman boys were taught their Homer along with their native Vergil. The wide use of Greek at that period can be best compared with the English of to-day. It may be said with little hesitancy that, at the time of Christ, Greek was known in all parts of the Roman world. What more fitting language than this in which to send forth the Gospel of peace ?

In Palestine there was of course a Greek population which existed alongside of the Jewish, and which became more numerous and distinct with the spread of Roman civilization. Of these two languages, Greek and Aramaic, we must suppose that a considerable part of the population knew enough for conversation at least. It is necessary to turn only to Alsace-Lorraine with its French and German, or to Wales with its Welsh and English, to find in modern times such a fusion of

two tongues as must have existed in Palestine at the beginning of our era.

The question as to whether Christ and his disciples knew and spoke Greek has been one that has long been debated. Some of the most illustrious of modern critics have been found on either side. It is not for me to enter upon it here, but simply to state my belief. It is more than probable, from what has been stated in regard to the two languages of Palestine at this period, that Greek, as well as Aramaic, must have fallen upon the ears of our Lord and his first followers from their earliest boyhood, and that all of them grew up in continual association with two languages. A few examples of this native speech are left us; Mark 5 : 41 and Mark 7 : 34 may be referred to. Instances when we may conclude that Greek was used by Christ are, Mark 7 : 26, 27, and John 12 : 23. Matthew, from his duty as a tax-collector, would have required both languages, while Luke, the most cultured of the evangelists, exhibits marked power in his use of Greek. There was but one way of reaching " all nations " and sending to them the new message. There never could have been any doubt in the mind of Luke, Mark, or John regarding the language they should employ in writing their histories of our Lord's life and works. Matthew appears to have written first in the Aramaic, but no doubt followed this immediately with a Greek version. A parallel to this may be observed in the case of the historian Josephus (A.D. 38–103), who wrote his history of the Jews first in Hebrew (Aramaic), and afterwards in Greek. It is not necessary to note

concerning Paul that " all who are at Rome " and the
"church at Corinth " and " the churches throughout
Asia " could have been addressed in no language but
the Greek.

A considerable portion of the population at Alexandria was Jews, for whom the Greek had displaced
their native Aramaic, and as early as 275 B.C. they
had so far forgotten the tongue of their fathers that
they required a Greek translation of the Old Testament. This was made at Alexandria by Jewish-Greeks,
and is known as the Septuagint or the translation of
the LXX. For the Jews scattered throughout the
world in Cappadocia, Cyprus, Phrygia, Rhodes, Greece,
and Rome the Septuagint became the Bible. So
general was its use even in Palestine that the evangelists quote quite as frequently from the Greek version
as from the Hebrew. Paul, himself a Hebrew and
reared according to the strictest sect of the Pharisees,
often agrees more nearly with the Septuagint when he
quotes from the Old Testament.

After the fall of Jerusalem the Jewish population of
Rome, Alexandria, Antioch, and other seaport towns,
rapidly increased. Then, as now, the Jews were a
commercial people ; Greek was the one language of
commercial intercourse. Thus we see this wonderful
language served as a common bond to hold together
Jew and Gentile, Greek and Roman. Then it was
that men were for the first time united by one speech
and made, so to speak, into one family. With the
overturning of old, worn-out kingdoms, and the breaking down of ancient myth and fable of the pagan world,

a new soil was prepared ready for new seed, — the Gospel of love.

Secondly, we come to consider the characteristics of the Greek of the New Testament. Does it differ very widely from classical Greek? To this the answer is "yes," and we may well rejoice that it does. Had the language as used by Plato and Demosthenes become the organ of the new message to the world, how different would have been the effect! Imagine the result if the simple grace of our English Bible were to be replaced by the swelling periods of Milton or Bacon. A far simpler language was and is needed by the lowly, and this we shall see the later Greek to be.

The language of the Macedonian Greeks, which was the same as that carried into Asia by Alexander, was essentially the same as that which Plato, Sophocles, and Demosthenes had used. From this wide diffusion, however, many changes were effected in the grammatical structure of the language, and especially in the vocabulary. Much of the rigidness which had characterized it in the hands of the great Athenian writers was cast aside. The language was popularized, so to speak. This new form of the Greek was called Hellenistic Greek, and the people who learned and used it were known as Hellenists. We have had occasion already to refer to the Hellenistic Jews in Alexandria and other cities.

In Palestine, however, as well as in the other Semitic countries, this Hellenistic Greek was greatly corrupted by the native tongue. Hebrew, Aramaic, and Syriac words were being continually introduced

into the Greek. To a large number of people who would use the Greek, it would amount to nothing other than a translation of their native tongue, together with the native idiom. Their thinking was all in Aramaic, while their words were in Greek. The literature of the Hebrew and Aramaic was entirely of a religious nature. The religious fervour of the Jews gave a strong bent to the tone of their language. It was the language of the human heart longing for the kingdom of God and the coming of the Messiah. The words in common, every-day use were the same as those in which had been cast the revelation of God to his chosen people. Even at an early day this must have given a deep religious colouring to the Greek — hitherto a pagan language. The translation, however, of the Old Testament did most to fix the idiom and form of the Greek for the expression of religious ideas. Then it was that Greek meant something to the Jews beyond a convenient means of intercourse for commercial life. For two centuries and a half this Greek Bible worked into the hearts and minds of the dispersed Jews, and the words that before in pagan Greece and Rome had meant little beyond the mortal and perishable of this world, took on a new meaning — fired with the flame of the sacred Hebrew.

When we come to the language of the New Testament, we have crossed a wondrous gulf. To quote from the words of the celebrated Dr. Schaff: "The language of the apostles and evangelists is baptized with the spirit and fire of Christianity, and receives a character altogether peculiar and distinct from secular

Greek. . . .   The Greek was flexible and elastic
enough to admit of a transformation under the inspir-
ing influences of revealed truth.   It furnished the flesh
and blood for the incarnation of divine ideas.   Words
in common use among the classics, or in popular
intercourse, were clothed with a deeper spiritual
significance ; they were transplanted from a lower to
a higher sphere, from mythology to revelation, from
the order of nature to the order of grace, from the
realm of sense to the realm of faith."   It is worth
while to note the word " transformation " in the above.
Here is the key to the whole question.   How rich this
baptism of the pagan words has been may be seen by
comparing the New Testament and the classical sense
of such words as *love, faith, prophet, sin, glory, peace,
joy, mercy.*

The purity of the New Testament Greek differs
very considerably in different authors, and indeed in
one and the same writer we can observe two extremes.
Luke, for example, in the first four verses of his gospel
furnishes a specimen of as pure and elegant Greek as
may be found on the page of any classical author.
Immediately, however, he drops off into the vernacu-
lar, as though aware that he is addressing the many
and not the few.   In considerable portions of his
gospel and the Acts are to be found the harshest
Hebraisms.   This is especially noticeable when he
quotes from the Old Testament.   In all the writers of
the New Testament, the Hebrew of the Old Testament
quotation appears distinctly through the thin veiling
of the Greek.

Of the four evangelists Luke was the best educated, and therefore used the purest Greek. Matthew may be placed next, with Mark last. Concerning John, there is great difference of opinion. Some scholars declare his gospel the most thoroughly Hebrew of the four. It is said to have a Hebrew body with a Greek dress. On the other hand, there are those who maintain for him the purest Greek. The fact is, his short sentences would fall naturally into the idiom of almost any language. Paul's Greek exhibits nearly every variety of classic elegance. However, it does not come within the scope of this article to give the peculiarities of the individual authors.

It is necessary to speak more definitely as regards the linguistic differences between the Greek of the New Testament and that of the period of classical Greek, which we may consider to have closed with Aristotle (B.C. 384–322). 1. The vocabulary of the New Testament furnishes nearly 900 words that are not found in the classical writers. Many of these occur in subsequent authors, as Polybius and Plutarch and in the Septuagint. 2. Compound words are especially common. Rare combinations are used. The etymology always reveals the force of the expression. 3. What is called the doctrinal sense of certain words, as *love*, *hope*, *faith*, introduces a new element quite distinct from anything earlier.

Grammatically, very wide changes from the classical Greek may be noted. 1. The dual number has disappeared entirely. 2. Adjectives of the third declension in -ων (*-ōn*) and -υς (*-us*) are especially rare. Of adjectives in -ης (-ēs) there are but two or three common examples. 3. The comparison of adjectives has been simplified, and is usually done by the use of an adverb, and the positive degree, except in the case of a few adjectives of irregular comparison.

In the verb a great breaking away from classical usage is seen. 1. The optative mood is comparatively rare. It does not occur at all in the writings of John, and is found in the epistles and the Acts more than in the gospels. Except in the optative of *wish* or *desire*, the subjunctive regularly takes the place of this mood. 2. In the uses of the voice and tense the changes are not so marked. In the subjunctive rarely any tense occurs aside from the present and the aorist. 3. It may be observed that in the verbs those in -μι (-mi) tend to break down into the ending in -ω (-ō), while verbs in -ιζω (-idsō) are much more common than in other Greek. 4. The forms in -μι (-mi) in the present system are comparatively rare. Hardly ever does the present subjunctive of these verbs occur, while the second aorist system has few forms in this mood.

The syntax is too difficult a question to discuss here, and so but few points shall be presented. 1. Especially characteristic of New Testament Greek are the various uses of ἵνα (hina), which in classical Greek is confined for the most part to the introduction of *final* clauses. Of this conjunction there are no less than six well-defined uses in the New Testament. 2. While in classical Greek the conjunction ὥστε (hōstĕ) is used with either the indicative or infinitive to denote result, and with nearly equal frequency in both constructions, the indicative occurs but twice in the New Testament. 3. The participle still continues a fundamental form of construction, but shows signs of weakening in such instances as John 11 : 1 and Luke 15 : 1, where the simple imperfect of the verb would have been expected. This form of expression is most common in Luke.

The prepositions present a great variety of uses not inherent in the Greek word, thus betraying Hebrew influence.

These are only a few of the most marked peculiarities of the language of the New Testament, but perhaps enough to show that it is much weakened and simplified as compared with classical Greek. If one adds to the grammatical peculiarities here mentioned the strong colouring in idiom and vocabulary that arises from the Hebrew, a general notion may be formed as to the structure of this language.

To know thoroughly the real force and value of this language, a wide familiarity with Semitic — especially Hebrew and Aramaic — is indispensable. Not only this, but the investigator must know Latin, of the influence of which I have taken no notice, as well as Greek from its earliest beginning in Homer. Such preparation as this few are able to acquire. A student may, however, gain a very satisfactory facility in handling the New Testament language, who knows nothing of any language except his own. Careful, assiduous labour for a few months will put the average student in control of the essentials, and this slight acquaintance will be found to repay one a thousandfold. No one can ever attain to the ability of reading and understanding the grand simplicity and power of John's brief sentences, ringing as they do with the imperishable grandeur of the Greek, without seeing an entirely new power in the Word. Any translation must ever fall far short of rendering the grace and force of the Greek. As a rose when plucked loses its sweetness and the fragrance is soon blown, so perishes in translation that fleeting, indescribable something that makes Greek the noblest of languages.

The following list of books is recommended as representing perhaps the most helpful works for students of the New Testament Greek. Those marked * are particularly valuable for the beginner.

For assistance in making up this list the author has to express his indebtedness to Professor C. F. Bradley, D.D., Garrett Biblical Institute. He has very kindly given me the benefit of his wide knowledge of New Testament bibliography.

TEXT. *The New Testament in the Original Greek (School Edition). Westcott and Hort. Macmillan & Co., New York, 1893. $1.25.

This edition is also published with a lexicon, by the same publishers. $1.90.

LEXICON. *Thayer's Grimm's Wilke, Greek-English Lexicon of the New Testament, "Corrected Edition." Harper & Brothers, New York, 1889. $5.00.

GRAMMAR. *Winer's Grammar of New Testament Greek
(Ninth English Edition). Trans. by Moulton.
T. & T. Clark, Edinburgh, 1882. $3.60.

CONCORDANCE. *Bruder's Concordance of All the Words
in the Greek New Testament (Fourth Edition).
Leipzig, 1888. 25 M.

    A new edition of this monumental work, which will
include the readings of Westcott and Hort, is to be
published.

Bagster's Englishman's Greek Concordance of the New
Testament. London, 1883. £1, 1s.

*Bradley and Horswell's New Testament Word Lists.
Greek-English. Series I. and II. Garrett Biblical
Institute, Evanston, Ill. 35 cents each.

*Burton's Syntax of the Moods and Tenses in New Testa-
ment Greek. Chicago University Press (Second
Edition). $1.50.

*Buttman's Grammar of the New Testament. Trans. by
Thayer. W. F. Draper, Andover, Mass. $2.75.

Hatch's Essays on Biblical Greek. Macmillan & Co.,
New York. $2.75.

Robinson's Greek Harmony of the Gospels. Ed. by M. B.
Riddle. Houghton, Mifflin & Co., Boston, 1885.
$2.00.

*Schaff's Companion to the Greek Testament and English
Version (Fourth Edition). Harper & Brothers, New
York, 1892. $2.75.

Simcox's (W.H.) The Language of the New Testament.
Thomas Whitaker, New York, 75 cents. By the
same author, The Writers of the New Testament.
Same publishers and price.

Terry's Biblical Hermeneutics. Hunt and Eaton, New
York. $4.00.

*Thayer's Books and their Use, A Lecture, to which is added a list of books for students of the New Testament Greek. Houghton, Mifflin & Co., Boston. 75 cents.

An exceedingly helpful little volume.

Trench's Synonyms of the New Testament (Eleventh Edition). Macmillan & Co., New York, 1890. $3.50.

*Warfield's An Introduction to the Textual Criticism of the New Testament. Whitaker, New York. 75 cents.

Westcott's Introduction to the Study of the Four Gospels (Seventh Edition, American Edition). Macmillan & Co., New York. $2.25.

*Westcott and Hort's The New Testament in the Original Greek. 2 vols. Harper & Brothers, New York.

Vol. I. includes the text. Vol. II. has an Introduction to Textual Criticism and an Appendix. Price per vol. $2.00. Complete $3.50.

SUGGESTIONS TO THE STUDENT.

———————◆———————

1. All vocabularies must be thoroughly mastered. Writing the words several times will greatly help to fix them in the mind. Pronouncing the Greek aloud is helpful.

2. The acquisition of forms (*i.e.* declensions and conjugations) must keep pace with the matter of a vocabulary.

3. It is recommended that at least thirty lessons be mastered before the reading of the Greek text is attempted.

4. Care should be taken in learning points of syntax that occur in the lessons.

5. When the text is finally begun, the table of irregular verbs (§ 88) should be committed to memory. Also the verb forms in §§ 90–110 should be carefully studied.

6. When the Greek Testament is taken up, the syntax in Part III. may be studied to best advantage. At no time should the student fail to keep up the review of Part II.

7. Finally, learn words, words, words. Only steady application and continual review will bring satisfactory results.

PART I. — LESSONS: TEXT

ESSENTIALS OF
NEW TESTAMENT GREEK.

LESSON I.

1. VOCABULARY.

ἀκούω, *I hear.* θέλω, *I wish, will.* λέγω, *I say.*
γινώσκω, *I know.* λαλέω, *I speak.* πιστεύω, *I believe.*
ἔχω, *I have.* λαμβάνω, *I take.* ποιέω, *I do, make.*

a. Each of these words occurs more than 200 times in
the New Testament, and some of them 1500 times.

2. Notes on the Vocabulary.

a. ἀ-κού-ω, ä-koú-ō, *I hear;* cf. ACOUSTIC. α = *a* in
father; κ = hard *c*, as in *can;* ου is a diphthong composed of ο and υ (English *o* and *u*) and pronounced like
ou in *group;* ω = *ō* in *note.* The mark (') over the initial
vowel of this word is called the breathing. Note the turn
from right to left. This is called the *smooth* breathing,
and it does not affect the sound of the vowel. The mark
(') over the ου is the *acute* accent. The ending -ω equals
I in English.

b. γι-νώ-σκω, gĭ-nó-skō, *I know.* γ = hard *g*, as in
get; ι = *i* in *machine;* ν = *n*; σ = *s*. Observe the same
accent and on the same syllable as in ἀκούω.

B   1

c. ἔ-χω, ĕ-chō, *I have.* ε = *e* in *let*; χ = *ch*, of which there is no equivalent sound in English. It is found in the German *buch.* Cf. *chasm* pronounced in a harsh guttural tone. The accent and breathing, when they occur on the same syllable, are written together, as here. All words beginning with a vowel have a breathing mark.

d. θέ-λω, thĕ-lō, *I will* or *I wish.* θ = *th* in *thin*; λ = *l.*

e. λα-λέ-ω, lä-lĕ-ō, *I speak.* The accent occurs on what syllable of the verb so far?

f. λαμ-βά-νω, läm-bâ-nō, *I take.* μ = *m*; β = *b.*

g. λέ-γω, lĕ-gō, *I say.*

h. πι-στεύ-ω, pĭ-steú-ō, *I believe.* π = *p*; τ = *t*; ευ = the diphthong *eu* in *feud.* When the accent comes on a diphthong, it is placed over the second vowel, as here. Cf. ἀκούω.

i. ποι-έ-ω, poi-ĕ-ō, *I do,* or *make*; cf. POET, POETRY. οι is a diphthong pronounced like *oi* in *oil.*

3. Topics for study.

a. The vowels in this lesson are α, ε, ι, ο, υ, ω. The following diphthongs occur: ου, ευ, οι. The consonants are: β = *b*, γ = *g*, θ = *th*, κ = *k*, λ = *l*, μ = *m*, ν = *n*, π = *p*, σ = *s*, τ = *t*, χ = *ch.*

b. In the matter of the accent of verbs the following must be noted. 1. The accent is always *recessive, i.e.* it goes back as far as possible from the last syllable. 2. The last syllable determines the position of the accent. 3. If the last syllable is long, the accent always occurs on the next to the last syllable — the *penult*; otherwise on the third syllable — the *antepenult.* 4. A syllable is long if it has a long vowel or a diphthong in it.

4. In English we have the personal pronouns written generally before the verb and always

separate from the verb. In Greek, on the contrary, the pronouns are often found as an integral part of the verb, forming what is called the *personal* endings. Cf. -ω in the verbs given above. In the case of most verbs the ending -μι of the 1 per. sing. pres. ind. act. is dropped, and the preceding vowel is lengthened in compensation. *E.g.* the primary form of λέγω is λέγ-ο-μι, of ἀκούω is ἀκού-ο-μι : ακου = stem, o = variable vowel, μι = personal ending.

LESSON II.

5. PRESENT INDICATIVE ACTIVE.

Sing.	*Plur.*
1. λέγ-ω, *I say.*	1. λέγ-ο-μεν, *we say.*
2. λέγ-εις,[1] *you say.*	2. λέγ-ε-τε, *ye say.*
3. λέγ-ει, *he, she,* or *it says.*	3. λέγ-ουσι, *they say.*

Observe from the translation appended that the indicative mood has in Greek the same declarative force as in English.

a. ει as in λέγεις is a diphthong and equals *ei* in *height.*

6. Note in the conjugation of λέγω : 1. The theme λεγ- appears unchanged throughout. 2. A vowel occurs after this theme. 3. The

---

[1] *s* at the close of a word, but σ in the middle of a word.

vowel is *o* or *ε* (often written %), called the variable vowel. 4. The variable vowel is followed by an ending, as -μεν, -τε, in the plur., which is called the *personal ending.* See 4.

How many distinct parts has λέγ-ο-μεν?

7. The personal endings of the active voice, primary [1] tenses, are seen in the following :

Sing.   1. -μι, *I.*   *Plur.*   1. -μεν, *we.*
        2. -ς, *thou.*   2. -τε, *ye.*
        3. -σι (τι), *he, she, it.*   3. -νσι, *they.*

8. The variable vowel and the personal ending may be seen in the following :

         ο-μι   ο-μεν
         ε-ς   ε-τε
         ε-σι   ο-νσι

Note that *o* occurs before μι, μεν, and νσι, *i.e.* before μ and ν, ε occurring in all other places.

9. Certain changes take place in these primitive forms, which give the following :

         -ω, *I.*   -ομεν, *we.*
         -εις, *thou.*   -ετε, *ye.*
         -ει, *he, she, it.*   -ουσι, *they.*

These forms must be absolutely mastered.

[1] See § **52** for the meaning of the word *primary.* (Where reference is made to the grammar, a section mark [§] precedes the figure, otherwise the reference is to the first part, — the lessons.)

10. EXERCISES.

I. Translate into English :

1. λαμβάνει, ἀκούει, θέλετε. 2. πιστεύω, λαμβάνουσι, ἔχουσι, ποιέω. 3. λαμβάνετε, θέλεις, πιστεύεις. 4. γινώσκεις, ἀκούουσι, ἔχομεν, λέγετε. 5. θέλουσι, γινώσκετε, πιστεύομεν, ἀκούεις. 6. λαμβάνεις, πιστεύετε, ἀκούει.

II. Translate into Greek :

1. I take, you wish, they know. 2. I have, ye say, they have, we say. 3. You take, he hears, we have. 4. You believe, ye believe, they hear. 5. We know, they know, I say, they do.[1] 6. We wish, we speak,[1] ye do.

Let the student analyze each verb form carefully, pointing out the theme, variable vowel, and the personal ending. Apply also the principles of accent given in **3**, *b*.

[1] It is recommended that the teacher allow the matter of contract verbs to pass unnoticed, till the principles of contraction appear gradually in the lessons. No harm need arise from the student's writing uncontracted forms. The frequent occurrence of these verbs in -εω explains their appearance here.

LESSON III.

THE SECOND OR O–DECLENSION.

11.   VOCABULARY.

ἄρτος, *bread.*

θρόνος, THRONE.

κόσμος, *world,* COSMIC.

λίθος, *stone,* LITHO*graphy.*

λόγος, *word,* LOGIC.

νόμος, *law,* eco NOMY.

ὄχλος, *crowd.*

τόπος, *place,* TOPO*graphy.*

χρόνος, *time,* CHRONO*logy.*

ἄγγελος, ANGEL.

ἄνθρωπος, *man,* ANTHROPO*logy.*

ἀπόστολος, APOSTLE.

ἔρημος, *desert.*

θάνατος, *death,* THANATO*psis.*

κύριος, *Lord.*

The student should learn thoroughly the meanings of the words in each vocabulary, pronouncing each word aloud, so as to be sure to get the proper accent. *The case endings are to be absolutely mastered.* Some of the words in this vocabulary occur 1000 times in the New Testament.

a. ἄρτος, ăr-tŏs. ρ = *r* ; ο = *o* in *on.*

b. In ἄγγελος the first γ is pronounced like *ng.* This is always true of γ when followed by κ, γ. or χ.

c. In ἔρημος, the η = ē, and is pronounced like *e* in *they.*

d. υ in κύριος = *u.* There is no similar sound in English. See § 1. The sound approaches *e* in *key.*

This includes all the vowels in Greek.

12. It is to be observed : 1. All these nouns end in -ος. 2. All these nouns belong to the O-declension. 3. They all have the *acute* accent.

13. All nouns in Greek come under one of three declensions, §§ **16** and **17**. The following is the second or O-declension :

	Sing.	*Plur.*
Nom.	λόγος, *a word.*	λόγοι, *words.*
Gen.	λόγου, *of a word.*	λόγων, *of words.*
Dat.	λόγῳ, *to* or *for a word.*	λόγοις, *to* or *for words.*
Acc.	λόγον, *a word* (obj.).	λόγους, *words* (obj.).
Voc.	λόγε, *O word.*	λόγοι, *O words.*

a. The ending -ῳ in the dat. sing. is for -οι. ο is lengthened to ω, and ι (*iota*) is written underneath. This is called *iota-subscript*, and can never be wanting in the dat. sing. of this declension.

14. Observe from the above that there are five cases in Greek : *Nominative, Genitive, Dative, Accusative, Vocative.* The nominative equals English nominative ; the genitive equals English possessive or the objective with *of ;* the dative corresponds to the English indirect objective, *to* or *for* which anything *is* or *is done ;* the accusative is the English direct objective ; the vocative, which is rarely used, is the case of address. Cf. § **21.**

15. In verbs we noted that the *endings* are especially important as showing the person and number.   So in nouns also the relation of nouns to each other, and to the other parts of the sentence, is denoted by the *case endings*.   While in English we have to depend (for the most part) on prepositions such as *to, for, by, in, at, on, of,* etc., to express case relation, the Greek has this relation expressed by the *endings* of the several cases.

(There are, of course, prepositions in Greek, but these case endings are always observed apart from the prepositions).

16. Observe that the accent on λόγος *remains on the same syllable throughout the declension.* This is the fundamental principle of accent in nouns. , *The accent remains on the same syllable, if possible.*

17. Learn the declension of ἄνθρωπος, § **23**.

a. When the last syllable becomes long, as in the endings -ov, -ῳ, -ων, -οις, -ους (**3**, *b*, 4), the accent cannot remain on the antepenult, but removes to the penult. Cf. the same principle in verbs, **3**, *b*.

b. Final οι, although a diphthong, is considered short in determining the place of accent in the O-declension.

c. The accent of the nominative must be learned by observation.

18.   EXERCISES.

I. 1. ἀποστόλῳ, θρόνων, νόμον, χρόνοις.
2. ἄνθρωποι, κόσμου, λόγοι κυρίου. 3. ὄχλος
ἀνθρώπων, νόμῳ καὶ¹ ὄχλῳ. 4. ἀπόστολος λέγει.
5. ἀπόστολος λέγει λόγον. 6. ἀπόστολος λέγει
λόγον ἀνθρώπῳ. 7. ἄγγελοι ἀκούουσι. 8. κόσμος πιστεύει. 9. λαμβάνετε ἄρτον. 10. ὄχλος
γινώσκει. 11. ἄνθρωποι ἔχουσι νόμους.

II. 1. Of a man, to a throne, words of men.
2. Angels and men, to the world, of a desert.
3. Death of apostles. 4. He takes a stone.
5. Words of man to a world. 6. Ye say to
a crowd. 7. We have a place. 8. An angel
of (the) Lord. 9. We hear law and believe.
10. He has bread for apostles.

LESSON IV.

The O–Declension Concluded.

19.   VOCABULARY.

ἀδελφός, *brother*.	ὀφθαλμός, *eye*, OPHTHALMO-
Θεός, *God*.	*logy*.
λαός, *people*.	υἱός, *son*.
νεκρός, *deceased*, NECRO*logy*.	ὁδός, *way*.
οὐρανός, *heaven*.	δοῦλος, *servant*.

¹ The *acute* accent (´), on a final syllable, is changed to the
grave (`) when other words follow in a sentence.

οἶκος, *house.*   παιδίον, *little child.*
ἔργον, *work.*   πλοῖον, *boat.*
ἱερόν, *temple.*   πρόσωπον, *face.*
ἱμάτιον, *garment.*   σάββατον, SABBATH.
          τέκνον, *child.*

20. *a.* ἀδελφός, ä-dĕĭ-phŏs.   δ = *d* ; φ = *ph* in *phase.*

b. In οὐρανός observe that the breathing occurs on the second vowel of the diphthong.

c. The diphthong υι, as in υἱός, is pronounced like *wee.* The breathing is always *rough* (ʽ), *i.e.* the explosion of breath is so strong as to give an *h* sound. υἱ is, then, pronounced *whee.*

d. Note the rough breathing on ἱμάτιον, hĭ-mǎ-tĭ-ŏn, and ἱερόν, hĭ-ĕ-rŏn, ὁδός, hŏ-dŏs.

e. αι as in παιδίον = *ai* in *aisle.*

21. There are two principal accents in Greek, the acute (ʹ) and the circumflex (ˆ). The acute can occur on any one of the last three syllables, while the circumflex can occur on one of the last two.

22. Learn the declension of υἱός, *son,* § **23**, and note that in every gen. and dat. the acute (ʹ) is changed to a circumflex (ˆ).

23. Learn the declension of δοῦλος, *servant,* § **23**, and observe that the circumflex accent occurs on a *long* syllable only, and when *at the same time* the last syllable is short. When the ultima becomes long, the (ˆ) changes to the (ʹ).

24. Nouns of the O-declension end in -ος masc. (rarely fem.) and -ον neut. The inflection of neuter nouns is the same as that of masculine nouns, except that the nom., acc., and voc. sing. end in -ον, and the same cases in the plur. end in -ἄ. Cf. δῶρον, gift, § 23.

25. All adjs. in Greek are declined, and agree in gender, number, and case with the words they modify. The definite article the, ὁ, is an adj. and is declined; e.g. ὁ δοῦλος, the servant; τοῦ δούλου, of the servant; τὸ τέκνον, the child; τῷ τέκνῳ, to the child; τὰ τέκνα, the children; τῶν λόγων, of the words. Learn the masc. and neut. (ὁ and τό) of the article, § 24.

26.   EXERCISES.

I. 1. τῷ λόγῳ καὶ τοῖς λόγοις. 2. τῶν δούλων καὶ τῷ παιδίῳ. 3. τὸ σάββατον τοῖς ἀνθρώποις. 4. ὁ κύριος τοῦ σαββάτου. 5. ὁ ἀδελφὸς γινώσκει τὸ τέκνον. 6. ὁ λαὸς ἔχει τοὺς νόμους. 7. λαμβάνετε ἄρτον καὶ ἱμάτια. 8. οἱ ἀπόστολοι ἀκούουσι τῶν παιδίων.[1] 9. ἐν (in) τῷ ἱερῷ λέγομεν. 10. τὸν κύριον τοῦ κόσμου γινώσκετε.

II. 1. In (ἐν) the temple and in the boat. 2. To the people and of the people. 3. The

---

[1] Verbs of *hearing* may be followed by the genitive case, as the case of the direct object.

eyes of the servant.   4. For the work and for
the garments.   5. Ye hear the people.[1] 6. The
apostle knows the law.   7. I speak to the ser-
vants, and they hear.   8. The Lord has a
temple in Heaven.   9. We have the garments
for the children.   10. The son of God knows
the world.

LESSON V.

THE PRESENT PASSIVE INDICATIVE.

27.   VOCABULARY.

ἀγαπάω, *I love.*	ἐγείρω, *I raise up.*
βάλλω, *I throw.*	κρίνω, *I judge.*
βλέπω, *I see.*	πέμπω, *I send.*
γράφω, *I write,* GRAPHic.	στέλλω, *I send.*
διδάσκω, *I teach,* DIDACTic.	σώζω, *I save.*

a. In σώζω, save, ζ is a double consonant, *ds*, and
pronounced like *dz* in *adze.*

28. The passive voice, as in English, represents the subject as being acted upon. The
personal endings of the passive distinguish it
from the active.

Following are the primary pass. endings:

Sing. 1. -μαι, *I.*   *Plur.* 1. -μεθα, *we.*
       2. -σαι, *you.*   2. -σθε, *ye.*
       3. -ται, *he.*   3. -νται, *they.*

[1] See footnote, p. 11.

a. The variable vowel ⁰/ₑ is found as in the active voice. Before μ and ν, o occurs, and before all other endings ε is found.

29. The following is the conjugation of the pres. pass. ind. of λύω, *I loose:*

Sing.	Plur.
1. λύ-ο-μαι, *I am loosed.*	1. λυ-ό-μεθα, *we are loosed.*
2. λύ-ει, *you are loosed.*	2. λύ-ε-σθε, *ye are loosed.*
3. λύ-ε-ται, *he is loosed.*	3. λύ-ο-νται, *they are loosed.*

a. Observe that the 2 per. sing. λύει is for λύεσαι. σα is dropped, and ε and ι form the diphthong ει. η may be found instead of ει.

b. The same principle of accent is to be noted as in **3**, *b.* αι is considered short in the personal endings, hence the accent occurs on the antepenult.

30.   EXERCISES.

I.   1. βάλλει, βάλλεται, πέμπεις, πέμπε-σθε.   2. κρίνει, κρίνεται, διδάσκω, διδάσκομαι. 3. λαμβάνετε, λαμβάνεσθε, ἀκούουσι, ἀκούονται. 4. στελλόμεθα, βλέπουσι, γράφομεν.   5. σώζετε, ἐγείρουσι, πιστεύομεν, γράφεται.   6. οἱ ἄνθρωποι κρίνονται.   7. ἐγειρόμεθα εἰς (into) τὸν οὐρανόν. 8. γράφεται ἐν (in) τῷ νόμῳ.   9. ὁ υἱὸς ἀνθρώπου σώζεται.   10. ἐν τῷ ναῷ[1] λέγει καὶ ἀκούεται. 11. οἱ ἀπόστολοι εἰς τὸν κόσμον στέλλονται. 12. πιστεύομεν εἰς (on) τὸν κύριον καὶ σωζό-μεθα.

―――――
[1] *Temple.*

II. 1. He sees and is saved. 2. You believe
and are saved. 3. We judge and are judged.
4. They send and are sent. 5. He raises up
the dead. 6. It is written in the laws. 7. We
see the brethren. 8. The son of man is judged.
9. The Lord hears in the temple. 10. I speak
and am heard. 11. We are saved and are raised
up into Heaven. 12. Ye take the bread.
13. They know that (ὅτι) the Lord saves men.

We have so far met in the vocabularies 52 words, which
give more than 400 different forms by their inflection.

LESSON VI.

Imperfect Indicative Active.

31.   VOCABULARY.

ἄγω, *lead.*   καλέω, *call.*
βαπτίζω, BAPTIZE.   μαρτυρέω, *bear witness,*
ἐσθίω, *eat.*   MARTYR.
ζάω, *live.*   μέλλω, *am about.*
ζητέω, *seek.*   μένω, reMAIN.

For the tenses of the indicative mood see
§§ 50 and 52. The uses and meanings of the
various tenses will be explained as we advance.

32. The imperfect indicative represents an
act as *going on* in time past, — continued, accustomed, or repeated action ; *e.g.* ἔγραφον, *I was
writing;* ἔλυον, *I was loosing;* ἐβάπτιζε, *he was
baptizing.*

33. All active secondary tenses (§ 52) have the same personal endings, as follows :

Sing.		Plur.	
1.	-ν	1.	-μεν
2.	-ς	2.	-τε
3.	none	3.	-ν or -σαν

34. The imperfect indicative of λύω :

Sing.	Plur.
1. ἔ-λυ-ο-ν, *I was loosing.*	ἐ-λύ-ο-μεν, *we were loosing.*
2. ἔ-λυ-ε-ς, *you were loosing.*	ἐ-λύ-ε-τε, *ye were loosing.*
3. ἔ-λυ-ε, *he was loosing.*	ἔ-λυ-ο-ν, *they were loosing.*

35. Observe : 1. The variable vowel ⁰/ₑ as in the present tense.   2. The ε before the stem λυ.   This is called *augment*.

36. The *secondary* tenses, besides having different endings from the primary, have also an *augment.* This augment is of two forms.   1. If the verb begins with a consonant, ε is prefixed — *syllabic* augment.   2. In the case of verbs beginning with a vowel, this vowel is lengthened to the corresponding long vowel (except α gives η) — *temporal* augment.   In diphthongs made with ι the first vowel is lengthened, and ι appears as iota subscript.   Other diphthongs do not ordinarily have the augment ; *e.g. ἀκούω, hear ; ἤκουον, I was hearing ; ἄγω, lead ; ἦγον, I was leading ; ἐσθίω, eat ; ἤσθιον, I was eating.*

37. EXERCISES.

I. 1. ἔβαλλον, ἔκρινε, ἐγράφετε. 2. ἐκρίνομεν, ἠκούομεν, ἔβλεπον. 3. πιστευόμεθα καὶ ἐγράφομεν. 4. ἤγειρες, ἠσθίετε, ἐγινώσκετε. 5. ἐμένομεν ἐν τῷ πλοίῳ. 6. ἦγες τὰ τέκνα. 7. ἤσθιον τὸν ἄρτον. 8. οἱ ἀπόστολοι ἐβάπτιζον τοὺς ἀνθρώπους. 9. εἶχον¹ τοὺς δούλους ἐν τῷ οἴκῳ.

II. 1. We were hearing. 2. He was believing. 3. They were taking. 4. You were saying. 5. Ye were beholding. 6. They were raising up. 7. He was judging. 8. I was eating the bread. 9. He was leading the sons of men. 10. We saw the face of the Lord. 11. The God of Heaven saves the children of men. 12. Ye were remaining in the law.

LESSON VII.

IMPERFECT INDICATIVE PASSIVE.

38. VOCABULARY.

αἰτέω, *ask for*.
ἀκολουθέω, *follow*.
γεννάω, *beget*.
δοξάζω, *glorify*.
ἐρωτάω, *ask* (a question).

θεωρέω, *see, observe*, THEORY.
κηρύσσω, *preach, announce*.
πείθω, *persuade*.
πληρόω, *fill*, PLENty.
κράζω, *cry*.

¹ ἔχω is an exception to the principle stated in **36**, 2, and takes the syllabic augment. ἔεχον is contracted to εἶχον, § 6, 7.

a. In δοξάζω, *glorify*, occurs the double consonant ξ, from κ + σ, and pronounced like *ks* in *ricks.*

39. The personal endings in the secondary tenses of the indicative passive are:

	Sing.			*Plur.*	
	1.	-μην		1.	-μεθα
	2.	-σο		2.	-σθε
	3.	-το		3.	-ντο

40. The conjugation of λύω is:

Sing.   *Plur.*

1. ἐ-λυ-ό-μην, *I was being loosed.*   1. ἐ-λυ-ό-μεθα
2. ἐ-λύ-ου, *you were . . .*   2. ἐ-λύ-ε-σθε
3. ἐ-λύ-ε-το, etc.   3. ἐ-λύ-ο-ντο

a. In the 2 per. sing. -εσο changes to -ου, σ drops between the two vowels, and εο contracts to ου, § 5, 7.

Review the present and imperfect indicative active and passive of λύω, § 56.

41. The personal endings of the verb give us the following:

a. The *person* of the verb.
b. The *number* of the verb.
c. The *tense*, whether primary or secondary, and by this whether past or not.
d. The *voice* of the verb.
e. The mood to some extent, as we shall see later on.

c

42. The changes in the endings that are to be particularly noted are :

ACTIVE.	PASSIVE.
-ομι = -ω	-εσαι = -ει or -ῃ
-εσ = -εις	-εσο = -ου
-εσι = -ει	
-ονσι = -ουσι	

The importance of mastering the personal endings of the verb, and, indeed, the whole matter of the verb, cannot well be overestimated. It is safe to say that the student who has thoroughly learned the detail of the verb given thus far has mastered the greater part of the difficulty in the regular verb, and has gone far towards gaining a reading knowledge of the New Testament.

The student should now be familiar with more than 800 different forms.

43.   EXERCISES.

I. 1. ἤγετο καὶ ἦγε. 2. ἐβαπτίζετο, βαπτίζε-ται. 3. ἐδιδάσκετο ἐν τῷ ἱερῷ. 4. ἐκρινόμεθα. 5. στέλλεται καὶ ἐστέλλεσθε. 6. ἐσῴζου. 7. ἐν τῷ οἴκῳ ἐδοξάζετο. 8. ὁ κύριος ἠκούετο. 9. οἱ ἀπόστολοι εἰς τὸν οὐρανὸν ἔβλεπον. 10. τὰ τέκνα ἔκραζε.[1]

[1] A neuter plural nom. takes a verb in the singular in Greek.

II. 1. We believed and were saved. 2. Ye were glorified. 3. He was preaching to the men. 4. The son of man was being glorified. 5. I was judging and I was being judged. 6. The world trusted in (εἰς) the Lord. 7. The angel of Heaven was heard. 8. We persuade the sons of men. 9. The law was taught in the temple. 10. The work of man is judged.

LESSON VIII.

First or A–Declension.

44. VOCABULARY.

ἀρχή, ἡ, *beginning*, ARCHAIC.
γραφή, ἡ, *scripture, writings.*
ἐντολή, ἡ, *commandment.*
ζωή, ἡ, *life*, ZOÖLOGY.
παραβολή, ἡ, PARABLE.
συναγωγή, ἡ, SYNAGOGUE.
φωνή, ἡ, *voice*, PHONO*graph.*
ψυχή, ἡ, *soul*, PSYCH*ology.*
ἁμαρτία, ἡ, *sin.*

ἐκκλησία, ἡ, *church* ; cf. EC-CLESIASTICAL.
ἐξουσία, ἡ, *power*.
καρδία, ἡ, *heart* ; cf. CAR-DIAC.
ἐπαγγελία, ἡ, *promise.*
οἰκία, ἡ, *house.*
σοφία, ἡ, *wisdom*, SOPH-*istry.*

Most of these nouns occur as many as 100 times in the New Testament.

a. ψ in ψυχή, *soul*, is a double consonant, pronounced like *ps* in *lips*. This now gives us all the letters in Greek. Learn the classification of consonants in § 2.

b. Observe the gender of the nouns in the vocabulary. In what letters do the nouns end ? Cf. §§ 18 and 19.

45. The following paradigms of ἀρχή and σοφία will serve as models for the remaining nouns of this form :

ἀρχή, *beginning.*		σοφία, *wisdom.*	
Stem αρχᾱ-		Stem σοφιᾱ-	
Sing.	*Plur.*	*Sing.*	*Plur.*
N. V. ἀρχή	ἀρχαί	σοφία	σοφίαι
G. ἀρχῆς	ἀρχῶν	σοφίας	σοφιῶν
D. ἀρχῇ	ἀρχαῖς	σοφίᾳ	σοφίαις
A. ἀρχήν	ἀρχάς	σοφίαν	σοφίας

46. Observe : 1. The stem ends in *ā*, hence the term A-declension. 2. The case endings are somewhat similar to those already learned in the O-declension : (*a*) the dat. sing. must have *iota-subscript;* (*b*) the acc. sing. ends in -ν ; (*c*) the gen. plur. in -ων ; (*d*) -οι of the second = -αι of the first, and -οις of the second = -αις of the first. 3. That nouns having -η in the nominative retain -η throughout the sing., and nouns with ια in the nominative retain the *a* in all cases of the sing.

47. Nouns that have the acute accent on the last syllable (the *ultima*) are called oxytones ; *e.g.* ἀρχή, ζωή. Rule of accent : *All oxytones of the first and second declension have the circumflex accent in all genitives and datives.*

48. Learn the fem. of the art.[1] ἡ (§ **24**), and compare this with the case endings of ἀρχή.

49.   EXERCISES.

I. 1. αἱ ἁμαρτίαι ἀνθρώπων. 2. ἡ ἐντολὴ ζωῆς. 3. ἡ ἐξουσία τῆς ἐκκλησίας. 4. ὁ κύριος λέγει παραβολήν. 5. ἐντολὴν γράφω. 6. ἐν ἀρχῇ ὁ λόγος ἠκούετο. 7. ὁ ὄχλος τὴν φωνὴν ἤκουε. 8. αἱ γραφαὶ ἐγράφοντο. 9. οἱ ἀπόστο-λοι τὴν ἐπαγγελίαν τοῖς ἀνθρώποις ἔπεμπον. 10. ἐν τῷ κόσμῳ ἡ ἁμαρτία μένει. 11. τὴν ἐξου-σίαν ὁ υἱὸς ἀνθρώπου ἔχει. 12. ἡ φωνὴ ἐν τῇ ἐρήμῳ[2] ἔκραζε.

II. 1. In the synagogue. 2. In the heart of men. 3. I hear a voice. 4. The soul is saved. 5. The parable was spoken in the temple. 6. He sent the bread of life to men. 7. The church has power. 8. They were speaking a parable in the synagogue. 9. It is written in the scriptures. 10. We have a promise of the Lord. 11. Men preached wisdom to the world. 12. In the beginning we heard the word.

---

[1] The forms of the article ὁ, ἡ, οἱ, αἱ, are called *proclitics* (προ-κλίνω, *lean forward*), since they have no accent, and are pronounced as part of the following word.

[2] ἔρημος is a fem. noun in -ος.

LESSON IX.

A-Declension Continued.

50.   VOCABULARY.

ἀγάπη, ἡ, *love*.

ἀλήθεια, ἡ, *truth*.

βασιλεία, ἡ, *kingdom*.

γῆ, ἡ, *earth*, GEology.

γλῶσσα, ἡ, *tongue*, GLOSSAry.

δικαιοσύνη, ἡ, *righteousness*.

δόξα, ἡ, *glory*.

εἰρήνη, ἡ, *peace*.

ἡμέρα, ἡ, *day*, epHEMERAL.

θάλασσα, ἡ, *sea*.

κεφαλή, ἡ, *head*.

μαθητής, ὁ, *disciple*.

προφήτης, ὁ, PROPHET.

χαρά, ἡ, *joy*.

ὥρα, ἡ, *hour*.

Most of these nouns occur more than 100 times in the New Testament.

51. The following paradigms furnish models for other nouns of this declension :

δόξα, ἡ, *glory*.		προφήτης, ὁ, *prophet*.	
Stem δοξᾱ-		Stem προφητᾱ-	
Sing.	*Plur.*	*Sing.*	*Plur.*
N. V. δόξα	N. V. δόξαι	N. προφήτης	N. V. προφῆται
G. δόξης	G. δοξῶν	G. προφήτου	G. προφητῶ,
D. δόξῃ	D. δόξαις	D. προφήτῃ	D. προφήταις
A. δόξαν	A. δόξας	A. προφήτην	A. προφήτας
		V. προφῆτα	

52. Learn ὥρα and σοφία. § 22.

53. Observe: 1. When ε, ι, or ρ precedes *a*
of the nom. sing., *a* is retained throughout the
sing.; and when other letters precede *á*, as in
δόξα, the *a* is changed in the gen. and dat. sing.
to η.　2. -αι of the nom. plur., as in the endings
of the verb, is considered short in determining
the accent.

54. Feminine nouns of the first declension
end in ᾰ, ᾱ, or η; masculine nouns, in -της or
·ας. The gen. of masc. nouns is ου, as in the
O-declension. Masc. nouns in -της have ᾰ in the
voc. sing.

a. γῆ, ἡ, *earth*, is contracted from γέα, § 6, 6. The
circumflex is found throughout.

55. The following table shows the case end·
ings of the A-declension:

Fem. Sing.			*Masc. Sing.*	
N.V. ᾱ	or ᾰ	η	N. ᾱ-ς	η-ς
G. ᾱ-ς or η-ς		η-ς	G. ᾱ-ιο = ου	
D. ᾱ-ι or η-ι		η-ι	D. ᾱ-ι	η-ι
A. ᾱ-ν or ᾰ-ν		η-ν	A. ᾱ-ν	η-ν
			V. ᾱ	ᾰ or η

Masc. and Fem. Plur.

N.V. α-ι
G. ω-ν for α-ων
D. α-ις
A. ᾱ-ς for α-νς

56. Observe that *all* nouns have the same plural in the first declension. If *o* be substituted for *a* in this table of endings, the first declension will be seen to differ but little from the second.

57. The following are the principles of *nominal* accent :

1. There are three kinds of accent : the acute (´), the circumflex (ˆ), and the grave (`).

2. The acute can occur on any one of the last three syllables ; the circumflex on either of the last two ; the grave on the last.

3. The acute can stand on a syllable either *long* or *short;* the circumflex can occur on a long syllable only ; *i.e.* a syllable in which there is a long vowel or a diphthong.

4. The accent in the nominative must be learned by observation.

5. The accent tends to remain on the same syllable on which it occurs in the nominative.

6. When the *ultima* is *short,*

a. The antepenult if accented has the acute.
b. The penult if accented has the acute, unless it be long; in this case the circumflex must occur.
c. The ultima if accented must have the acute.

7. When the *ultima* is *long,*

a. The antepenult cannot be accented.
b. The penult if accented must have the acute.
c. The ultima may have either the acute or the circumflex.

Nouns of the first and second declensions include about seventy-five per cent of the nouns in the New Testament. The importance, therefore, of mastering the vocabularies and forms thus far given can be easily appreciated.

58.   EXERCISES.

I. 1. ἔχομεν εἰρήνην καὶ ἀγάπην. 2. ἀκούομεν ἀπὸ[4] τῆς ἀρχῆς. 3. οἱ προφῆται τὴν δόξαν ἔχουσιν.[1] 4. ἡ δικαιοσύνη καὶ ἡ ἀλήθεια ἐν τῷ κόσμῳ ἔμενον. 5. ἤκουον τὴν ἀγγέλου φωνήν. 6. ἔλεγε ἐν παραβολαῖς. 7. ὁ προφήτης ἔγραφε τὴν ἐντολήν. 8. τοῖς ἀνθρώποις χαρὰν ἐπέμπετε. 9. ἐν τῇ ἀληθείᾳ μένομεν. 10. τὴν σοφίαν ἐν παραβολαῖς ἐκήρυσσεν. 11. ἐν τῇ γῇ καὶ ἐν τῇ θαλάσσῃ ἐδόξαζες τὸν κύριον. 12. τοῖς μαθηταῖς τοῦ κυρίου πιστεύουσιν.[2]

II. 1. We remain in the truth. 2. The hour is announced. 3. Ye have joy in your[3] hearts. 4. We see the beginning of righteousness. 5. The way, the truth, and the life. 6. Joy and peace, love and glory. 7. They were remaining in the synagogue. 8. They speak in parables. 9. It is taught in the Scriptures. 10. The kingdom of God and his[3] righteousness.

[1] *Movable ν*, for which see § **11**.
[2] The dative often follows πιστεύω, where our *believe* requires the objective case with *in*. See lexicon.   [3] Use the article.
[4] *From*.

LESSON X.

Adjectives of the Vowel Declensions.

59.   VOCABULARY.

ἀγαπητός, *beloved.*

ἄλλος, *other.*

αἰώνιος, *eternal;* cf. AEON.

δίκαιος, *righteous.*

ἐκεῖνος, *that one.*

ἕτερος, *another.*

ἔσχατος, *last.*

ἴδιος, *one's own,* IDIOM.

κακός, *evil.*

καλός, *good.*

μέσος, *middle.*

μόνος, *only, alone,* MONO-
theism.

οὗτος, *this one.*

πιστός, *faithful.*

πρῶτος, *first.*

60. Learn the declension of καλός, *good,* ἴδιος, *one's own,* and μικρός, *small, little,* § **25.**

Observe that the masc. and neut. are in the second declension, while the fem. is in the first declension.

61. Note that when ι or ρ precedes the final vowel of the stem, as in ἴδιος and μικρός, the fem. has *ā* in the nom. sing. Cf. **53,** 1.

62. οὗτος, *this one,* and ἐκεῖνος, *that one,* are demonstrative pronouns, but are declined for the most part as adjectives in -ος.

a. οὗτος refers to somebody or something near at hand or present, while ἐκεῖνος refers to that which is more remote — at a distance.

63. Learn the paradigm of οὗτος, § **26**.

Observe : 1. The rough breathing of the nom. masc. and fem. sing. and plur. appears in all other forms as τ.   2. The vowel of the penult varies as the vowel in the ultima.   3. The accent remains on the penult.

64. All substantives used with οὗτος and ἐκεῖνος must have the article ; *e.g.* οὗτος ὁ ἄνθρωπος or ὁ ἄνθρωπος οὗτος, *this man*. Observe that the pronoun must come *before* the article or *after* the nom.   This is called the *predicate* position.   Any other position of an adj. would be the *attributive* position.

65.   EXERCISES.

I. 1. ἡ ἐσχάτη ἡμέρα.   2. οὗτος ὁ λόγος.
3. ἐν τῷ οἴκῳ ἐκείνῳ.   4. οἱ δίκαιοι καὶ οἱ κακοὶ κρίνονται.   5. παιδία, ἐσχάτη ὥρα ἐστίν.   6. ἡ ἐντολὴ ζωὴ αἰώνιός [1] ἐστιν (is).   7. οἱ καλοὶ μόνοι σώζονται.   8. αὕτη ἐστὶ ἡ πρώτη καὶ μεγάλη [2] ἐντολή.   9. ἐκεῖνος δίκαιός ἐστιν.   10. οἱ ἄλλοι τοὺς νόμους ἐδίδασκον.   11. ἐν ἐκείναις ταῖς ἡμέραις κακοὶ προφῆται ἠκούοντο.

II. 1. The first, last; and the last, first.
2. That disciple knows the Scriptures.   3. In

---

[1] An adj. that has the masc. and fem. alike. Such are called adjs. of two endings.   [2] *Great.*

the last day.   4. His own (use art. for *his*)
know the truth.   5. These children are saved.
6. This is the work of God.   7. This commandment I write to the brethren.   8. Beloved, we
have another promise.   9. On the first day he
preached in the synagogue.   10. This one knows
the law and the prophets.

LESSON XI.

PERSONAL PRONOUNS AND εἰμί, *I am.*

66.   VOCABULARY.

ἀγαθός, *good.*	εἰς, prep., *into* (with acc.).
ἅγιος, *holy.*	ὅλος, *whole.*
ἀλλά, conj., *but.*	ὅτι, conj., *because, that.*
αὐτός, *he, himself.*	οὐ,[2]
γάρ,[1] conj., *for.*	οὐκ, } *not.*
δέ,[1] conj., *moreover, but.*	οὐχ,
ἐγώ, *I.*	πονηρός, *wicked.*
εἰμί, *I am.*	σύ, *thou, you.*

Each of the words in this vocabulary, except
the adjectives, occurs more than 1000 times in
the New Testament.

[1] Words that cannot come first in a sentence are called *post-
positives.* γάρ and δέ are such.

[2] οὐ before consonants; οὐκ before vowels; οὐχ before the
rough breathing.

67. The personal pronouns in Greek are : ἐγώ, *I ;* σύ, *thou ;* and αὐτός, αὐτή, αὐτό, *he, she, it.*

68. Learn the declension of ἐγώ and σύ, § **40**. Observe : 1. That the short forms of ἐγώ in the sing. have no accent. These are *enclitics.*[1] The meaning of the dissyllabic forms does not differ from the monosyllabic. The former are more emphatic.

2. The endings -*ου*, -*οι* = ῳ, and -*ων*, -*ας* are common with the endings of the two declensions. Associate the meaning of ὑμεῖς with its initial vowel.

69. Learn the declension of αὐτός, § **26**, *a.*
Observe that, except in the forms αὐτός, αὐτή, sing., and αὐτοί, αὐταί, plur., we have the declension of the article ὁ with the prefix αυ-.

70. Observe the following for the uses of αὐτός :

1. αὐτὸς ὁ ἄνθρωπος or ὁ ἄνθρωπος αὐτός, *the man himself.* αὐτός is in the predicate position, **64**.

---

[1] An *enclitic* gives up its accent for the preceding word. If the preceding word has the (′) on the antepenult or the (^) on the penult, it receives an additional accent on the ultima; *e.g.* ἱμάτιόν μου, *my garment,* οἶκός μου, *my house.* What is the difference between an *enclitic* and a *proclitic?*

71. 1. ὁ αὐτὸς ἄνθρωπος, *the same man.*
When the article *precedes* αὐτός, the meaning
is always *the same.*

2. When used alone, as κρίνουσιν αὐτόν, *they
judge him,* it is the simple personal pronoun of
the third person.

72. The use of conjunctions and prepositions
is an important thing in inflected languages.

1. καί is the ordinary copulative conjunction,
joining words, phrases, and clauses.

2. δέ is an adversative, *but,* in a mild way.
It often has little meaning beyond *and, indeed.*

3. ἀλλά is the strongest adversative, a very
emphatic *but.*

4. γάρ expresses a reason, as καὶ γὰρ ἀκούουσι
means *and* (I say this) *for they are listening.*

5. εἰς, *into,* always occurs with the accusative, and denotes motion, either expressed or
implied.

73. We noticed that the primary active ending -μι, as in ἀκού-ο-μι, was dropped, and the ο
preceding was lengthened to ω. There are
some verbs that do not drop this μι, and that
do not have the variable vowel %. Verbs that
drop the μι belong to the ω-conjugation, and
verbs that do not drop the μι belong to the
μι-conjugation.

These make up what are called the ω-conjugation and the μι-conjugation. Of the latter is εἰμί, *I am.* The following is the pres. ind. :

Sing.		Plur.	
εἰμί, *I am.*		ἐσμέν, *we are.*	
εἶ, *thou art.*		ἐστέ, *ye are.*	
ἐστί, *he, she,* or *it is.*		εἰσί, *they are.*	

a. εἰμί is for ἐσ-μί; εἶ is for ἐσ-σί; εἰσί for ἐσνσί. The root εσ- may be compared with *is.*

b. All the forms in the pres. ind. of this verb, except εἶ, are enclitic, 68, 1, note.

74. EXERCISES.

I. 1. ἐγὼ δέ εἰμι. 2. σὺ γὰρ εἶ ἐν τῷ ἱερῷ. 3. αὐτὸν δὲ ἐκρίνομεν. 4. αὐτοὶ ἡμεῖς οὐ κρινόμεθα. 5. τοῦτό ἐστι τὸ ἔργον τοῦ θεοῦ. 6. ἀλλὰ οὐ λόγοις ὑμεῖς σώζεσθε. 7. ἐν αὐτῷ δὲ ζωὴ αἰώνιός ἐστιν. 8. ὑμεῖς ἐστε τὰ τέκνα τοῦ θεοῦ. 9. ὁ προφήτης εἶ σύ. 10. καὶ λέγει αὐτῷ ὁ Ἰησοῦς. 11. ἡ ἀλήθεια οὔκ ἐστιν ἐν ἡμῖν. 12. πιστεύετε γὰρ ὅτι ἐγώ εἰμι. 13. ἐγώ εἰμι ἡ ὁδὸς καὶ ἡ ἀλήθεια καὶ ἡ ζωή. 14. σάββατον δέ ἐστιν ἐν ἐκείνῃ τῇ ἡμέρᾳ.

II. 1. But you know me. 2. I glorify Him. 3. Moreover, we speak the truth. 4. Ye are in the world. 5. Darkness [1] is not in Him. 6. And these things we write to you. 7. Jesus himself was not baptizing, but his disciples. 8. Beloved,

[1] ἡ σκοτία.

we are the children of God.   9. He hears my
words and does not do them.   10. And this is
the witness of him.   11. He himself is the life.
12. On (ἐν) the same day he was speaking to
the people.   13. Thou art the son of God.

LESSON XII.

DEPONENT VERBS.

75.   VOCABULARY.

ἀπέρχομαι, *go away.*	ἐξέρχομαι, *go out.*
ἀποκρίνομαι, *answer.*	ἔρχομαι, *come, go.*
γίνομαι, *be, become.*	ἦν, *was.*
διέρχομαι, *go through.*	οἶδα, *I know.*
δύναμαι, *am able, can.*	ὅς, *who.*
εἰσέρχομαι, *enter.*	πορεύομαι, *go.*
προσέρχομαι, *come to.*	

76. Deponent verbs have the *form* of the
middle, § **47**, or the passive, but the *sense* of
the active.

77. Note in the vocabulary above that there
are many verbs that are composed of ἔρχομαι +
something.   These are compound verbs; and
the forms ἀπό, *away*, διά, *through*, εἰς, *into*, ἐκ,
out of, πρός, *to*, are prepositions.   In this verb
of motion the preposition, it will be seen, gives

the *direction* to the motion. So in most verbs
compounded with prepositions, the idea of the
verb is only modified by the preposition.

When the preposition ends in a vowel, as
ἀπό, διά, the final vowel is dropped before a
verb that begins with a vowel; *e.g.* διέρχομαι
is for δια + ερχομαι.[1]

78. The imperfect indicative of εἰμί, *am*, is as
follows :

Sing.	Plur.
1. ἦν (ἤμην), I was.	1. ἦμεν (ἤμεθα), we were.
2. ἦς (ἦσθα), thou wert.	2. ἦτε, ye were.
3. ἦν, he was.	3. ἦσαν, they were.

a. The forms in parentheses need not be learned at
present, as they occur but seldom. ἤμην, 16 times; ἤμεθα,
3 times; ἦσθα, twice.

79. οἶδα, *I know*, is an irregular verb, but
conjugated in one tense regularly, as follows :

Sing.	Plur.
1. οἶδα, I know, etc.	1. οἴδαμεν, we know, etc.
2. οἶδας	2. οἴδατε
3. οἶδε	3. οἴδασι

80. Learn the paradigm of ὅς, ἥ, ὅ, § 27.

This pronoun it will be noticed is declined
like the article, except initial τ and the nominative forms ὅς, ἥ, ὅ, ἅ.

---

[1] On the same principle, when these compound verbs receive
the augment the final vowel of the preposition is dropped; *e.g.*
ἀποστέλλω, *I send*, ἀπέστελλον, *I was sending*. The prepositions
περί and πρό retain their final vowel. Cf. note, p. 58.

81.   EXERCISES.

I. 1. ὑμεῖς οὐκ οἴδατε αὐτόν. 2. ἔρχεται ὁ
Φίλιππος καὶ λέγει τῷ Ἀνδρέᾳ. 3. ἐν τῷ κόσμῳ
ἦν καὶ ὁ κόσμος αὐτὸν οὐκ ἐλάμβανεν. 4. ἡ ἐντολή
ἐστιν ὁ λόγος ὃν ἀκούετε. 5. ἡ ὥρα ἔρχεται.
6. οὐ γράφω ὑμῖν ὅτι οὐκ οἴδατε τὴν ἀλήθειαν
ἀλλὰ ὅτι οἴδατε αὐτήν. 7. ὃ ἀκούω ἀπ' ἀρχῆς
γινώσκω. 8. καὶ αὕτη ἐστὶν ἡ ἐπαγγελία ἣν
αὐτὸς ἐπαγγέλλεται.[1] 9. καὶ οἶδας ὅτι ἡ ἁμαρτία
ἐν αὐτῷ οὐκ ἐστίν. 10. ἐγὼ δὲ τὸν νόμον οἶδα.
11. ὁ δὲ καιρός[3] ἐστιν ἐν ᾧ τὴν ἐξουσίαν λαμβάνομεν. 12. τίς γὰρ οὐκ οἶδε ὅτι ἡ ἐσχάτη ἡμέρα
ἔρχεται ;[2]

II. 1. We know that we are saved. 2. Ye
enter the synagogue. 3. They are becoming
the children of God. 4. In the beginning was
the Word. 5. The Word was with (πρός, acc.)
God. 6. The truth, moreover, is glorified in
Him. 7. I know that His commandment is life
everlasting. 8. What I say to you was from
the beginning. 9. The life which we live is
eternal. 10. On that day was the Sabbath.
11. Whom He knows the world does not
know.

[1] ἐπαγγέλλομαι, I announce.
[2] See § 14 for the punctuation in Greek.
[3] Time.

LESSON XIII.

Present Active Subjunctive and Infinitive.

82.   VOCABULARY.

αἴρω, *take away.*
ἀμήν, *verily.*
ἀποθνήσκω, *die.*
ἀποστέλλω, *send.*
γέ, *indeed, at least.*
δέχομαι, *receive.*
διά, prep. with gen., *through;*
  with acc., *on account of.*
εἰ, conj., *if.*
ἐκ, prep. with gen., *out of, of.*
ἔτι, adv., *still, yet.*

ἤδη, adv., *now, already.*
ἵνα, conj., *in order that.*
μετά, prep. with gen., *with;*
  with acc., *after.*
μή, *not.*
νῦν, adv., *now.*
οὔπω, adv., *not yet.*
παρακαλέω, *beseech.*
περί, prep. with gen.,
  concerning; with acc.,
  around.

πῶς, adv., *how.*

83. The terms *primary* and *secondary* apply to the tenses of the indicative only.

The subjunctive mood, as in English, denotes a doubt or a contingency. Unlike the English, however, the subjunctive in Greek is very common. There are but two tenses that are usually found, the *present* and the *aorist.* The perfect is very rare.

84. The pres. subjv. act. of λύω is:

	Sing.		*Plur.*	
1.	λύ-ω		1.	λύ-ω-μεν
2.	λύ-ῃς		2.	λύ-η-τε
3.	λύ-ῃ		3.	λύ-ω-σι

85. The pres. subjv. of εἰμί is :

Sing. 1. ὦ *I may be*   Plur. 1. ὦ-μεν *we may b*
       2. ᾖ-ς   2. ἦ-τε
       3. ᾖ   3. ὦ-σι

86. Note that the pres. subjv. of εἰμί is the same as the personal endings of the regular verb ; and while the indicative has the variable vowel %ₑ, the subjunctive has the corresponding long vowel ᵂ/η.

a. The personal endings are those of the primary active indicative.

87. The subjunctive follows ἵνα, *in order that*.

Examine the following :

ἔρχεται ἵνα ἀκούῃ, *he comes that he may hear*.
πιστεύομεν ἵνα μὴ ἁμαρτάνωμεν, *we believe in order that we may not sin*.

88. Rule of syntax : *Clauses of purpose take the subjunctive with ἵνα. The negative is μή.*

89. The following forms illustrate the present active infinitive :

λύ-ειν,   ἀκού-ειν,   ἔχ-ειν,   μέν-ειν,
to loose.   *to hear*.   *to have*.   *to abide*.

-ειν = ε + ending -εν of pres. inf. For -εεν contracting to -ειν, see § **6**, 7.

90. The participle is very common in Greek, and it is necessary to master its uses as soon as possible. -ων is the ending of the pres. act. nom. masc. sing. ; *e.g.* :

> ὁ λέγων, *the one saying, he who says.*
> ὁ αἴρων, *the one taking away, he who takes away.*
> ὁ ἀκούων, *the one hearing, he who hears.*

The article and participle in this use are equivalent, as is seen, to a dependent clause in English.

91.   EXERCISES.

I. 1. οὗτος ἔρχεται ἵνα λέγῃ περὶ τῆς ἀληθείας. 2. ἀμὴν, ἀμὴν λέγω ὑμῖν ὅτι ἡ ὥρα οὔπω ἐστίν. 3. δέχεται ἡμᾶς ἵνα ἔτι ζῶμεν.[1] 4. πῶς γε δύναται σώζειν ; 5. μετὰ ταῦτα αὐτοῖς λέγει. 6. τὰς ἁμαρτίας ἡμῶν αἴρει. 7. ἐκ τοῦ θανάτου εἰς τὴν ζωὴν ἐγειρόμεθα. 8. ὁ μένων ἐν αὐτῷ ἔχει ζωὴν αἰώνιον. 9. ὁ ἀγαπῶν[1] τὸν ἀδελφὸν αὐτοῦ ἐν τῇ ἀγάπῃ μένει. 10. ἐγὼ δὲ ἔρχομαι ἵνα τὸν κόσμον σώζω.

II. 1. They baptize in order that they may glorify God. 2. Already we become the children of Him. 3. Ye are able to know the truth. 4. How can He take away our sins ? 5. Through Him they are saved and have eternal life. 6. After these things they go away

---

[1] For ζάωμεν, § 5, 2.

into the desert.   7. He comes that He may
save sinners (ἁμαρτωλός).   8. I am willing to
hear the Gospel.   9. Veriiy, verily the one loving his brother is not a servant.   10. Ye are
not able to hear my word.   11. That one was
from the beginning and truth is in Him.

LESSON XIV.

PRESENT PASSIVE SUBJUNCTIVE AND INFINITIVE.

92.   VOCABULARY.

ἅμα, adv., *at the same time.*   ἤ, conj., *or.*
ἀντί, prep. with gen., *instead*   καθώς, adv., *just as.*
    of.   καινός, *new.*
ἀπό, prep. with gen., *from.*   λοιπός, *remaining.*
ἀσπάζομαι, *salute.*   οὖν, adv., *therefore.*
δαιμόνιον, DEMON.   πρός, prep. with acc., *to,*
ἐάν, conj., *if.*   *toward.*
εὐαγγέλιον, *gospel.*   προσκυνέω, *worship.*
εὑρίσκω, *find.*   τηρέω, *keep.*

93. The pres. pass. subjv. of λύω is :

   Sing. 1. λύ-ω-μαι   *Plur.* 1. λυ-ώ-μεθα
        2. λύ-η   2. λύ-η σθε
        3. λύ-η-ται   3. λύ-ω-νται

94. Observe : 1. The long vowel ᵂ/η, as in
the active.   2. The personal endings are the
pass. primary endings of the indicative.   3. -η
of 2 per. sing. is for -ησαι.

95. The subjunctive is used in exhortation.

Examine the following :

εὑρίσκωμεν τὴν ἀλήθειαν, *let us find the truth.*
μὴ ἀγώμεθα εἰς τὴν ἁμαρτίαν, *let us not be led in sin.*

96. Rule of syntax : *The first person plural (of the subjunctive) may be used to express an exhortation.   The negative is μή.*

97. Examine the following :

ἐὰν κρίνω δὲ ἐγώ, *if I, moreover, judge.*
ἐὰν μὴ λέγωμεν τὴν ἀλήθειαν, *if we say not the truth.*

Rule of syntax : *The subjunctive follows ἐάν (= if) ; the negative is μή.*   Cf. § **124**.

98. The pres. pass. inf. may be seen in the following verbs :

λύ-ε-σθαι,   ἀκού-ε-σθαι,   κρίν-ε-σθαι,
to be destroyed.   *to be heard.*   *to be judged.*

What is the pres. pass. inf. ending ?

99. Examine the following :

ὁ κριν-ό-μενος, *the one being judged.*
ὁ ἀκου-ό-μενος, *the one being heard.*

This ending -μενος is the passive participle ending in nom. masc. sing, as -ων is in the active. The ending -ος is declined like καλός, § **25**.

What was said in **90** about the sense of the active participle applies equally to the passive.

100.   EXERCISES.

I. 1. ἀσπαζώμεθα τοὺς ἀδελφούς. 2. καθὼς ἐκεῖνος δίκαιός ἐστιν ὦμεν δίκαιοι ἡμεῖς. 3. ἐν τῷ μέσῳ ἐκήρυσσε λέγων ὅτι ἔρχεται εἰς τὰ ἴδια. 4. μένετε ἐν ἐμοὶ καὶ ἐγὼ ἐν ὑμῖν. 5. ἐγὼ οὐκ εἰμὶ μόνος ὅτι αὐτὸς μετ᾽ ἐμοῦ ἐστιν. 6. βλέπει τὸν κύριον ἐρχόμενον πρὸς αὐτὸν καὶ · λέγει αὐτῷ Οὗτός ἐστιν ὁ αἴρων τὰς ἁμαρτίας τοῦ κόσμου. 7. εἰ ὑμεῖς μένετε ἐν τῷ λόγῳ ἐμοῦ, μαθηταί μού ἐστε καὶ γινώσκετε τὴν ἀλήθειαν. 8. ἐὰν δὲ κρίνω ἐγώ, τὴν ἀλήθειαν κρίνω. 9. ἐὰν ἐγὼ δοξάζω ἐμαυτόν (*myself*), ἡ δόξα μου οὐδέν (*nothing*) ἐστιν.

II. 1. Let us keep this commandment. 2. Let us receive the truth. 3. If, therefore, we are the children of God, let us do His works. 4. Let us believe that through Him we have eternal life. 5. They were willing to receive the Gospel. 6. He who believes is saved and has eternal life. 7. Let us not speak concerning these things. 8. A new commandment write I unto you. 9. If we say that we have not sin, the truth is not in us. 10. He preaches the Gospel of the kingdom of God.

LESSON XV.

Third Declension : Neuter Nouns in ă.

101.   VOCABULARY.

αἷμα, τό, *blood* ; cf. HEMOR-
   RHAGE.
θέλημα, τό, *will.*
ὄνομα, τό, *name* ; cf. NOMI-
   NATE.
πνεῦμα, τό, *spirit.*
ῥῆμα, τό, *word* ; cf. RHETORIC.
σπέρμα, τό, *seed.*

στόμα, τό, *mouth.*
σῶμα, τό, *body.*
νύξ,[1] ἡ, *night.*
πούς, ὁ, *foot.*
πῦρ, τό, *fire,* PYROtechnics.
σάρξ, ἡ, *flesh.*
φῶς, τό, *light,* PHOTOgraphy.
χείρ, ἡ, *hand,* CHIROgraphy.

102. The third declension is ordinarily called
the *consonant declension* from the fact that the
stem of the nouns usually ends in a consonant.
A few nouns, as we shall see later, end in a
close vowel, ι or υ, or in the diphthong ευ.

103. It is necessary in declining a noun of
this declension to have the *stem.* This is determined by dropping the genitive ending -ος.

104. The nominative is formed from the stem
in various ways. The *nominative,* therefore, is
not easily determined till we know the *genitive.*

---

[1] These monosyllables have peculiarities of form which will
be explained later. The frequency of their occurrence is the
reason for introducing them thus early.

105. The declension of ὄνομα, *name*, is as follows :

Sing.	*Plur.*
N. A. V. ὄνομα	N. A. V. ὀνόματα
G. ὀνόματος	G. ὀνομάτων
D. ὀνόματι	D. ὀνόμασι

106. Observe the following :

1. The genitive ending is -ος.

2. The dative ends in -ι, as in the first and second declensions. Here, however, it does not appear as *iota-subscript*, but is written in the line.

3. In the plur. ă is the same as in the O-declension, so likewise -ων.

4. The dat. plur. ends in -σι, with which compare -ις of the A- and O-declensions. τ of the stem drops before -σι.

5. The stem is ονοματ-. The nominative is the mere stem, final τ being dropped.[1]

107. Learn the declension of νύξ, *night*, § **28**.

108. Rule of accent : *Monosyllables of the consonant declension accent the ultima in all genitives and datives. -ων of the genitive plural is circumflexed.*

---

[1] The only single consonants that can stand at the close of a word in Greek are ν, ρ, ς. All other letters which would occur here are dropped.

109.   EXERCISES.

I. 1. τὰ ῥήματα ζωῆς αἰωνίου ἔχεις.   2. ὄνομα
ἦν αὐτῷ Ἰωάνης.   3. τοῦτό ἐστι τὸ σῶμά μου.
4. γινώσκεις τὸ θέλημα τοῦ θεοῦ.   5. θέλετε ἄγειν
ἐφ᾽ (against) ἡμᾶς τὸ αἷμα τοῦ ἀνθρώπου τούτου ;
6. οὗτός ἐστιν ὁ βαπτίζων ἐν πνεύματι ἁγίῳ.   7. ἡ
νὺξ ἔρχεται.   8. σπέρμα Ἀβραάμ ἐσμεν.   9. ὁ
λόγος σὰρξ ἐγένετο (became).   10. οὐ τὸ εἰσερχό-
μενον εἰς τὸ στόμα κοινοῖ (defiles) ἄνθρωπον ἀλλὰ
τὸ ἐξερχόμενον ἐκ τοῦ στόματος τοῦτο κοινοῖ
ἄνθρωπον.   11. ὑμεῖς ἐστε τὸ φῶς τοῦ κόσμου.
12. εἰ δὲ ἡ χείρ σου ἢ ὁ πούς σου σκανδαλίζει
(offend) σε ἔκκοψον (cut off) αὐτόν.   13. τὸ φῶς
ἐν τῇ σκοτίᾳ φαίνει.

II. 1. They believe on (εἰς) His name.   2. He
baptizes you, moreover, in the holy spirit.   3. He
is able to save by (ἐν) night and day.   4. Let us
believe on the name of the Lord.   5. The word
becomes flesh.   6. These are the good seed.
7. This is the will of God.   8. He speaks
through the mouth of God.   9. The bread of
life is my flesh.   10. Verily, verily I say to you,
he who believes on His name has eternal life.

LESSON XVI.

THIRD DECLENSION : STEMS IN -ι AND -ερ.

110.   VOCABULARY.

ἀνήρ, ὁ, *man*.

ἀνάστασις, ἡ, *resurrection*.

γνῶσις, ἡ, *knowledge*.

δύναμις, ἡ, *power*, DYNA-
    MITE.

θλίψις, ἡ, *tribulation*.

κρίσις, ἡ, *judgment*.

κτίσις, ἡ, *creation*.

μήτηρ, ἡ, *mother*.

παράκλησις, ἡ, *exhortation*.

πατήρ, ὁ, *father*.

πίστις, ἡ, *faith*.

πόλις, ἡ, *city*.

συνείδησις, ἡ, *conscience*.

111. Above are given the most common nouns
in the New Testament in -ις, stem in -ι. They
are declined as follows :

πόλις, *city*.

Sing.   Stem πολι-.   *Plur.*

Sing.		*Plur.*
N. πόλις		N. V. πόλεις
G. πόλεως		G. πόλεων
D. πόλει		D. πόλεσι
A. πόλιν		A. πόλεις
V. πόλι		

112. The following is to be noted regarding
the declension of this class of nouns :

1. ε takes the place of the final stem vowel ι
in all cases except the nom., acc., and voc. sing.

2. The gen. sing. has -ως, not -ος.

3. The accent in gen. sing. and plur. is irregular, and here the acute accent is found on the antepenult when the ultima is long.

4. ε unites with ι of the dat. sing., and forms a diphthong ει.

5. The acc. sing. adds simply -ν to the stem.

6. In the vocative the mere stem occurs.

7. The nom. plur. -εις is for εες, § **6**, 7.

113. Learn the declension of πατήρ, § **33**, and a.

Observe the following:

1. The nominative ends in -ηρ, while the stem ends in -ερ.

2. The gen. and dat. sing. drop this ε of the stem, and take the accent on the last syllable.

3. Voc. sing. has recessive accent (3, b, 1).

4. The dat. plur. has αρ for ερ.

114. Learn ἀνήρ, *man*, § **33**. Note that whenever ερ of the stem would be followed by a vowel, δ takes the place of the ε. The same peculiarities of accent obtain as in πατήρ, but -ων of the gen. plur. is circumflexed.

115.   EXERCISES.

I. 1. ἐγώ εἰμι ἡ ἀνάστασις καὶ ἡ ζωή. 2. ἡ
πίστις σου σώζει σε. 3. ἐν τῇ δυνάμει τοῦ πνεύματος εἰς Γαλιλαίαν εἰσέρχεται. 4. αὕτη δέ ἐστιν
ἡ κρίσις ὅτι τὸ φῶς ἔρχεται εἰς τὸν κόσμον.
5. γράφω ἐπ' (on) αὐτὸν τὸ ὄνομα τοῦ θεοῦ μου
καὶ τὸ ὄνομα τῆς πόλεως τοῦ θεοῦ μου. 6. ἄνδρα
οὐ γινώσκω. 7. νῦν κρίσις ἐστὶν τοῦ κόσμου
τούτου. 8. ἡμεῖς οἴδαμεν τὸν πατέρα καὶ τὴν
μητέρα. 9. ἐν τῷ κόσμῳ θλίψιν ἔχετε. 10. ἔλε-
γον οὖν αὐτῷ ποῦ (where) ἐστιν ὁ πατήρ σου.
11. ποιῶ τὰ ἔργα τοῦ πατρός μου. 12. ἐν τῇ
ἡμέρᾳ τῆς κρίσεως ἕξομεν (shall have) χαρὰν καὶ
εἰρήνην.

II. 1. The faith which we have saves men.
2. Life is in him who has the spirit of faith.
3. This is my father and my mother. 4. He
who does the will of God abides in the truth.
5. We have power to become the children of
God. 6. He is the resurrection and the life.
7. We are raised from the dead on (ἐν) the day
of judgment. 8. He who hears my word comes
not into judgment. 9. In that city he preached
the Gospel. 10. For those days are tribulation.

LESSON XVII.

Future Indicative.

116.   VOCABULARY.

ἀδικέω, *do wrong.*

ἀδικία, ἡ, *unrighteousness.*

ἄδικος, η, ον, *unrighteous.*

ἀναβλέπω, *look up.*

ἀρνέομαι, *deny.*

ἄρχομαι, *begin.*

θαυμάζω, *wonder at, marvel.*

μισέω, *hate.*

νικάω, *conquer.*

ὁμολογέω, *confess.*

περιπατέω, *walk.*

συνάγω, *gather together.*

ὑπάγω, *go away.*

φανερόω, *make manifest.*

φοβέομαι, *fear.*

φυλάσσω, *guard.*

117. The fut. ind., as in English, denotes what is going to take place.

The following is the fut. ind. act. of λύω :

Sing.	Plur.
1. λύ-σ-ω, *I shall loose,*	1. λύ-σ-ο-μεν, *we shall loose,*
2. λύ-σ-εις etc.	2. λύ-σ-ε-τε, etc.
3. λύ-σ-ει	3. λύ-σ-ου-σι

118. The fut. ind. mid.[1] of λύω is :

Sing.	Plur.
1. λύ-σ-ο-μαι	1. λυ-σ-ό-μεθα
2. λύ-σ-η	2. λύ-σ-ε-σθε
3. λύ-σ-ε-ται	3. λύ-σ-ο-νται

[1] For the middle voice, see §§ **47, 48.** The middle and passive are the same in form, except in the *future* and the *aorist,* which we shall learn later.

119. Observe that the future has primary endings, and differs from the present in the use of σ, with which compare *shall* in the English future. Note that σ appears before the variable vowel %. Hence, while the present is formed by adding % to the stem, the future is formed by adding σ%.

Learn the fut. ind. of εἰμί, § 65.

120. The future of ἀδικέω, *do wrong*, is ἀδική-σ-ω ; of νικάω, *conquer*, is νική-σω ; of μισέω, *hate*, is μισή-σω ; of φανερόω, *make manifest*, is φανερώ-σω. From these forms it can be seen that a *short final vowel must be lengthened before* σ% *of the future.* ε = η, α = η,[1] ο = ω.

121. The future of ἄγω, *lead*, is ἄξω ; of ἄρχο-μαι, *begin*, is ἄρξομαι ; of φυλάσσω, *guard*, stem φυλακ-, φυλάξω. From which it is seen that stems in κ, γ, χ form with σ%, ξ%.

122. The future of βλέπω, *see*, is βλέψω ; of ἀναστρέφω, *turn*, is ἀναστρέψω ; of νίπτω, *wash*, stem νιβ-, is νίψω. Stems in π, β, φ + σ% = ψ%.

123. The future of σώζω, *save*, stem σωδ-, is σώσω ; of πείθω, *persuade*, is πείσω. From which observe that stems in τ, δ, θ would

---

[1] But α after ε, ι, or ρ is not changed to η, but ā. Cf. **53**, 1.

have simple σ% in the future. The consonant drops before the tense sign.

124. The various forms of future stems may be seen by examining the following summary :

Vowel Stems.	*Mute*[1] *Stems.*
-α + σ% = ησ%	
-ε + σ% = ησ%	Labials, π, β, φ + σ% = ψ%
-ο + σ% = ωσ%	Palatals, κ, γ, χ + σ% = ξ%
-υ + σ% = ῡσ%	Linguals, τ, δ, θ + σ% = σ%

Other vowel stems hardly occur.	No stems end in the double consonants ξ, ζ, ψ, nor in σ.

The future of liquid stems, λ, μ, ν, ρ, will be explained in a future lesson. Aside from stems in these four letters, we may now be able to form the future of any regular verb in Greek.

125.   EXERCISES.

I. 1. ἡ πίστις σου σώσει σε. 2. γράψω ταῦτα, παιδία, ὑμῖν. 3. ὁ κόσμος ἡμᾶς μισήσει. 4. πέμψω τὸν υἱόν μου τὸν ἀγαπητόν. 5. οὕτω (*thus*) καὶ ὁ πατὴρ ὁ οὐράνιος ποιήσει ὑμῖν. 6. ἀκολουθήσω σοι, Κύριε. 7. ἀγαπήσεις κύριον τὸν θεὸν ἐν ὅλῃ καρδίᾳ σου καὶ ἐν ὅλῃ τῇ ψυχῇ σου καὶ ἐν ὅλῃ τῇ διανοίᾳ (*mind*) σου · αὕτη ἐστὶν ἡ πρώτη ἐντολή. 8. ὁμολογήσω αὐτοῖς ὅτι οὐ γινώσκω ὑμᾶς. 9. ἐν ἐκείνῃ τῇ ἡμέρᾳ ἐν τῷ ὀνό-

---

[1] See § 2 for the classification of consonants.

E

ματί μου αἰτήσεσθε, καὶ οὐ λέγω ὑμῖν ὅτι ἐγὼ
ἐρωτήσω τὸν πατέρα περὶ ὑμῶν. 10. οὕτως δὲ
ἔσονται οἱ ἔσχατοι πρῶτοι. 11. πείσομεν τὴν
καρδίαν ἡμῶν. 12. οὕτως ἔσται καὶ (*also*) ἐν
ταῖς ἡμέραις τοῦ υἱοῦ τοῦ ἀνθρώπου.

II. 1. There shall be tribulations. 2. We shall
do the truth.   3. He who knoweth the truth
and doeth it shall live.   4. Ye shall be with [1]
me this day.   5. They shall hate us because
we are not of (ἐκ) the world.   6. We shall love
the Lord God with all our heart.   7. I shall do
the will of my father.   8. The son of man shall
believe on (εἰς) the word.   9. They shall bear
witness concerning Him that He is the light.
10. We shall seek Him.   11. There shall be joy
in Heaven because he is saved.   12. He shall
glorify God.

LESSON XVIII.

THIRD DECLENSION : MUTE STEMS.

126.   VOCABULARY.

αἰών, ὁ, *age,* AEON.	καινός, *new.*
ἀλλότριος, *another's, strange.*	κρίμα, τό, *judgment.*
βρῶμα, τό, *food.*	οἰκοδομέω, *build up.*
ἐλπίς, ἡ, *hope.*	πρεσβύτερος, *elder.*
ἕτοιμος, *ready.*	σκοτία, ἡ, *darkness.*
δουλεύω, *be a servant.*	φανερός, *manifest.*

χάρις, ἡ, *grace.*

[1] μετά with Gen.

127. Observe the following:

1. ἐλπίς, *hope*, stem ἐλπιδ-; νύξ, *night*, stem νυκτ-; πούς, *foot*, stem ποδ-; σάρξ, *flesh*, stem σαρκ-; φῶς, *light*, stem φωτ-; χάρις, *grace*, stem χαριτ-.

2. In all these nouns note that the stem ends in a mute (§ **2**), and that the nominative is formed by adding ς to the stem. For the euphonic changes that occur with ς and the mutes, see **124**.

128. In αἰών, *age*, stem αιων-; ἡγεμών, *leader*, stem ἡγεμον-; and χείρ, *hand*, stem χειρ-, we have liquid stems which form the nominative from the mere stem. A short vowel, as in ἡγεμον-, may be lengthened.

a. ἄρχων, *prince, ruler*, has the stem αρχοντ-, but does not add ς for the nominative, which is the mere stem with τ dropped and o lengthened to ω.

129. Learn the declension of χάρις, ἐλπίς, and ἄρχων, § **28**, and αἰών, § **32**.

130. When nouns with stem in τ, δ, or θ preceded by ι or υ are not accented on the ultima, the acc. sing. has ν, the mute being dropped; *e.g.* χάρις, χαριτ-, acc. χάριν; but ἐλπίς, ἐλπιδ-, has acc. ἐλπίδα. Cf. **112**, 5.

131. The voc. sing. is rare and is usually the same as the nom. ἐλπίς, however, has voc. ἐλπί.

132. When -ντ- of the stem would come before -σι of the dat. plur., both the letters are dropped and the preceding vowel is lengthened (ο to ου); *e.g.* ἄρχων, stem αρχοντ-, dat. plur. ἄρχουσι.

133.   EXERCISES.

I. 1. εὑρίσκεις γε χάριν παρὰ τῷ θεῷ. 2. αὐτός ἐστιν ἐν τῷ φωτί. 3. νυνὶ[1] δὲ μένει πίστις, ἐλπίς, ἀγάπη. 4. ἴδετε (*behold*) τὰς χεῖράς μου καὶ τοὺς πόδας μου ὅτι ἐγώ εἰμι αὐτός. 5. ὁ ἐσθίων ἐκ τούτου τοῦ ἄρτου ζήσει εἰς τὸν αἰῶνα. 6. ὁ Ἰησοῦς ἔρχεται εἰς τὴν οἰκίαν τοῦ ἄρχοντος. 7. οὐ γάρ ἐστε ὑπὸ νόμον ἀλλ᾽ ὑπὸ χάριν. 8. καὶ ὁ ἔχων τὴν ἐλπίδα ταύτην ἐπ᾽ (*in*) αὐτῷ σῴζεται. 9. ὁ δὲ δοῦλος οὐ μένει ἐν τῇ οἰκίᾳ εἰς τὸν αἰῶνα, ὁ υἱὸς μένει εἰς τὸν αἰῶνα. 10. χάριτι[2] δὲ θεοῦ εἰμι ὅ εἰμι. 11. σοῦ ἐστιν ἡ βασιλεία καὶ ἡ δύναμις καὶ ἡ δόξα εἰς τοὺς αἰῶνας. 12. χάρις ὑμῖν καὶ εἰρήνη ἀπὸ θεοῦ πατρὸς ἡμῶν καὶ Κυρίου Ἰησοῦ Χριστοῦ.

II. 1. Truth abides forever. 2. Now have we faith and hope. 3. I write these (things) with my hand. 4. The light appears in the darkness.

---

[1] ι may be added to adverbs and pronouns to emphasize them. The accent in all such cases is upon the ι; *e.g.* οὐχ is often οὐχί; νῦν, νυνί.   [2] Cf. § 157.

5. We are saved by faith.   6. He who has love in his heart has grace.   7. We are not under the law, but under grace.   8. By the grace of God we are what we are.   9. Behold my hands and feet.

LESSON XIX.

End of first term

THIRD DECLENSION : NEUTER NOUNS, STEMS IN εσ- ;
    MASCULINE NOUNS, STEMS IN ευ-.

134.   VOCABULARY.

ἀρχιερεύς, ὁ, *chief priest.*	ἱερεύς, *priest,* HIERArchy.
βασιλεύς, ὁ, *king.*	μέλος, τό, *member.*
γένος, τό, *race.*	μέρος, τό, *part.*
γραμματεύς, ὁ, *scribe.*	οὖς, τό, *ear.*
γυνή, *woman.*	πλῆθος, τό, *multitude.*
ἔθνος, τό, *nation.*	σκότος, τό, *darkness.*
ἔθος, τό, *custom,* ETHICS.	τέλος, τό, *end.*
ἔλεος, τό, *pity.*	ὕδωρ, τό, *water,* HYDROlogy.

Neuter nouns with the nominative in -ος and the stem in -εσ form an important class of nouns of the third declension. The most common examples are given above.

135. Learn the declension of γένος, *race* (§ **30**). Observe the following.

1. In the gen. and dat. sing. the σ of the stem is dropped between the two vowels, and γένεος contracts into γένους.

2. In all cases of the plur. the σ of the stem is dropped; γένεα, γενέων are contracted to γένη, γενῶν; see §§ 5, 8 and **6**, 6.

136. Learn the declension of βασιλεύς, *king* (§ **31**), with which compare the vowel stem of πόλις.

137. For some irregular nouns of the third declension, as γυνή, *woman*, θρίξ, *hair*, οὖς, *ear*, πούς, *foot*, ὕδωρ, *water*, χείρ *hand*, see § **34**. Only such forms are given as occur in the New Testament.

138.　　　　　EXERCISES.

I. 1. ἀλλ᾽ οὔπω τὸ τέλος ἐστίν. 2. σὺ εἶ βασιλεὺς Ἰουδαίων. 3. τὸ εὐαγγέλιον ὃ κηρύσσω ἐν τοῖς ἔθνεσι. 4. οὐκ ἔχεις μέρος μετ᾽ ἐμοῦ. 5. οἱ δὲ ἀρχιερεῖς καὶ οἱ πρεσβύτεροι ἔπεισαν (*persuaded*) τοὺς ὄχλους. 6. εἰς τὰ ἔθνη πορευόμεθα. 7. οὐκ ἔχομεν βασιλέα. 8. ἐν ἑνὶ (*one*) σώματι πολλὰ[1] μέλη ἔχομεν. 9. χάρις ἀπὸ Ἰησοῦ Χριστοῦ, ὁ ἄρχων τῶν βασιλέων τῆς γῆς. 10. καὶ ἔπαισε (*struck*) τὸν τοῦ ἀρχιερέως δοῦλον· ἦν δὲ ὄνομα τῷ δούλῳ Μάλχος. 11. ἔμελλεν Ἰησοῦς ἀποθνήσκειν ὑπὲρ (*for*) τοῦ ἔθνους καὶ οὐχ ὑπὲρ τοῦ ἔθνους μόνον. 12. χάρις, ἔλεος, εἰρήνη ἀπὸ θεοῦ πατρὸς καὶ Χριστοῦ Ἰησοῦ τοῦ Κυρίου ἡμῶν.

[1] *Many.*

II. 1. Ye are not in the darkness. 2. This one is the king of the Jews. 3. For we know in (ἐκ) part. 4. The scribes and the chief priests will say this. 5. They know that he is not the king of this world. 6. A great multitude will follow him (dat.). 7. We have a part in the kingdom of God. 8. I say to you brethren that the end is not yet. 9. We shall make him king.

LESSON XX.

FIRST AND SECOND AORIST INDICATIVE.

139. VOCABULARY.

ἁγιάζω, *sanctify*.
δοκέω, *seem, think*.
θεάομαι, *behold*.
καθαρίζω, *purify*.
καταβαίνω, *go down*.
ὁράω, *see*.
παραλαμβάνω, *receive*.
τυφλόω, *blind*.

ἀπέθανον, *I died*.
ἔβαλον, *I threw*.
ἐγενόμην, *I became*.
εἶδον, *I saw*.
εἶπον, *I said*.
εὖρον, *I found*.
ἦλθον, *I went or came*.
παρέλαβον, *I received*.

140. The aorist is the most common tense in Greek to represent what *has taken place*. Thus, *I loosed, I did loose,* or *I have loosed* would most likely be expressed in Greek by one word, ἔ-λυ-σα, the aor. ind. act. of λύω.

141. The aorist indicative of λύω is :

	ACTIVE.	MIDDLE.
Sing. 1.	ἔ-λυ-σα *I loved.*	ἐ-λυ-σά-μην *reflet*
2.	ἔ-λυ-σα-ς	ἐ-λύ-σω (for ἐ-λύ-σα-σο)
3.	ἔ-λυ-σε	ἐ-λύ-σα-το
Plur. 1.	ἐ-λύ-σα-μεν	ἐ-λυ-σά-μεθα
2.	ἐ-λύ-σα-τε	ἐ-λύ-σα-σθε
3.	ἔ-λυ-σα-ν	ἐ-λύ-σα-ντο

a. In 2 pers. sing. ind. mid. σ drops between the two vowels α ο, and these contract to ω, § **5**, 1.

142. Observe the following on the formation of the aorist :

1. The augment as in the imperfect.
2. The tense suffix is σα, which changes to σε in 3 per. sing. act.
3. The personal endings are secondary. ν of 1 per. sing. act. is dropped.

143. Compare the suffix σα with *d* or *ed* in the past tense in English ; *e.g.* :

ἔ-λυ-σα-ς	ἐ-πληρώ-σα-μεν
loose-d-you	*fill - ed - we*

144. The same principles of augment are found in the aor. ind. as in the imperf. ind., **36**, and the same euphonic changes with σα of the aor. as with σ% of the fut., **120–124**.

145. Not all verbs have the aorist in σα, which is called the *first aorist*, but form the tense on the simple stem of the verb by the use of the variable vowel %. This is called the *second aorist*.

146. The 2 aor. ind. of βάλλω, *throw*, theme or stem βαλ-, is:

		ACTIVE.	MIDDLE.
Sing.	1.	ἔ-βαλ-ο-ν	ἐ-βαλ-ό-μην
	2.	ἔ-βαλ-ε-ς	ἐ-βάλ-ου (for ἐ-βάλ-ε-σο)
	3.	ἔ-βαλ-ε	ἐ-βάλ-ε-το
Plur.	1.	ἐ-βάλ-ο-μεν	ἐ-βαλ-ό-μεθα
	2.	ἐ-βάλ-ε-τε	ἐ-βάλ-ε-σθε
	3.	ἔ-βαλ-ο-ν	ἐ-βάλ-ο-ντο

a. Note that the only difference in form between the 2 aor. and the imperf. of the same verb is a difference in *stem*; *e.g.* ἔ-βαλλ-ον, imperf., has the pres. stem βαλλ-, while ἔ-βαλ-ον, 2 aor., has the simple stem or theme, βαλ-.

147. Few verbs have both aorists. *There is no difference whatever in meaning between a first aorist and a second aorist.*

148. The following 2 aor. are given in the vocabulary: ἀποθνήσκω, theme θαν-, 2 aor. ἀπέθανον; γίνομαι, theme γεν-, 2 aor. ἐγενόμην; ὁράω, theme ιδ-, 2 aor. εἶδον; εὑρίσκω, theme εὑρ-, 2 aor. εὗρον; ἔρχομαι, theme ελθ-, 2 aor.

ἦλθον ; παραλαμβάνω, theme λαβ-, 2 aor. παρέλαβον ; εἶπον has no present.

*Note that the second aorist has the simple
theme of the verb and the %.*

149. The difference in form between a first
aorist and a second aorist may be illustrated by
the following :

1. ἀγαπάω, *love* . . . . 1 aor. ἠ-γαπή-σα-μεν, *love-d-we*
2. λαλέω, *talk* . . . . . 1 aor. ἐ-λάλη-σα-ν,   *talk-ed-they*
3. βάλλω, *throw* . . . 2 aor. ἐ-βάλ-ο-μεν,   *threw-we*
4. λαμβάνω, *take* . . . 2 aor. ἔ-λαβ-ο-ν,   *took-they*

In 1 and 2 the past tense in both the Greek
and the English is formed by *adding* something, — σα, and *d* or *ed*.

In 3 and 4 no *suffix* is found, but the change
is in the *stem* of the verb. βαλλ-, *throw*, βαλ-,
threw ; λαμβάνω, *take*, λαβ, *took*.

150.   EXERCISES.

I. 1. καθὼς ἐκεῖνος περιεπάτησεν.[1] 2. ἔγραψα
ὑμῖν, παιδία, ὅτι γινώσκετε τὸν πατέρα.   3. ἠκούσατε ὅτι ἡ ἐσχάτη ὥρα ἔρχεται. 4. καὶ οὐκ οἶδε
ποῦ (*where*) ὑπάγει ὅτι ἡ σκοτία ἐτύφλωσε τοὺς
ὀφθαλμοὺς αὐτοῦ. 5. εἰς τὰ ἴδια ἦλθεν καὶ οἱ
ἴδιοι αὐτὸν οὐ παρέλαβον. 6. αὐτὸς ἠγάπησεν
ἡμᾶς. 7. ὃ ἐθεασάμεθα ἀπαγγέλλομεν καὶ ὑμῖν.

[1] περί and πρό do not drop the final vowel before the augment.

8. περὶ γὰρ ἐμοῦ ἐκεῖνος ἔγραψεν. 9. ἐθεάσαντο
ἃ ἐποίησεν καὶ ἐπίστευσαν εἰς αὐτόν. 10. Χριστὸς ὑπὲρ ἡμῶν ἀπέθανεν. 11. οὗτός ἐστιν ὑπὲρ
οὗ εἶπον. 12. ἐν τῷ κόσμῳ ἦν καὶ ὁ κόσμος δι᾽
αὐτοῦ ἐγένετο. 13. ἡ γυνὴ εἶπεν Οὐκ ἔχω
ἄνδρα. 14. καὶ ἐν τῷ ἀλλοτρίῳ πιστοὶ οὐκ
ἐγένεσθε.

II. 1. They asked him. 2. They went and
saw where (ποῦ) he was abiding. 3. The word
became flesh. 4. He acknowledged that he is
the Christ. 5. He bore witness, saying that he
saw the spirit. 6. For he sent them to preach
the kingdom of God. 7. And it came to pass
in those days. 8. And I saw and heard.

LESSON XXI.

First and Second Aorist Subjunctive.

151.   VOCABULARY.

ἀληθινός, *true.*   διάνοια, ἡ, *mind.*
ἄνεμος, ὁ, *wind.*   ἐκεῖ, adv., *there.*
ἀνοίγω, *open.*   ἐντεῦθεν, adv., *thence.*
ἀποκτείνω, *kill.*   ἐπεί, conj., *when, since.*
ἀπολύω, *release.*   ἐπερωτάω, *ask* (a question).
ἄρτι, adv., *just now.*   ἐπιθυμία, ἡ, *desire.*
ἀσθενέω, *am sick.*   ἰσχυρός, *strong.*
βίος, ὁ, *life.*   ὅπου, adv., *where.*
διάβολος, ὁ, *devil.*   φόβος, ὁ, *fear.*
          χρεία, ἡ, *need.*

152. The aor. subjv. of λύω :

	ACTIVE.	MIDDLE.
Sing. 1.	λύ-σ-ω	λύ-σ-ω-μαι
2.	λύ-σ-η-s	λύ-σ-η (for λύ-ση-σαι)
3.	λύ-σ-η	λύ-σ-η-ται
Plur. 1.	λύ-σ-ω-μεν	λυ-σ-ώ-μεθα
2.	λύ-σ-η-τε	λύ-σ-η-σθε
3.	λύ-σ-ω-σι	λύ-σ-ω-νται

153. Observe on the aor. subjv. :

1. There is *no augment*.
2. σ is the tense suffix.
3. The personal endings are the same as in the pres. subjv.
4. The aor. stem, λυσ-, is the same as the aor. ind. stem, **141**, and the euphonic changes will be the same as in the aor. ind.

154. Write the aor. subjv. of ποιέω, *do;* φανε-ρόω, *make manifest;* γράφω, *write;* πείθω, *persuade;* ἄγω, *lead;* ἄρχομαι, *begin;* πέμπω, *send;* δέχομαι, *receive.*

155. The 2 aor. subjv. of βάλλω, theme βαλ-, is —

	ACTIVE.	MIDDLE.
Sing. 1.	βάλ-ω	βάλ-ω-μαι
2.	βάλ-η-s	βάλ-η (for βάλ-η-σαι)
3.	βάλ-η	βάλ-η-ται
Plur. 1.	βάλ-ω-μεν	βαλ-ώ-μεθα
2.	βάλ-η-τε	βάλ-η-σθ(
3.	βάλ-ω-σι	βάλ-ω-νται

156. Note that the same principles are observed in the formation of the 2 aor. subjv. as in the 2 aor. ind. (**146–147**).

157. The 2 aor. subjv. of the following may be conjugated : ἦλθον, *I came*, subjv. ἔλθω ; εἶδον, *I saw*, subjv. ἴδω ; ἐγενόμην, *I became*, subjv. γένωμαι.   Observe that the augment does not appear in the subjv.

158. Examine the following :

1. πιστεύωμεν εἰς αὐτόν, *let us believe on Him.*
2. πιστεύσωμεν εἰς αὐτόν, *let us believe on Him.*

Observe that there is no difference in translation between a present subjunctive and an aorist.   The distinction ordinarily made between the present and the aorist is that the present denotes what is *continued* or *extended,* while the aorist expresses a simple act without any reference to a continuance of the same.   In 1 the idea is *Let us continue,* or *keep on having faith in him.*   In 2 the thought is *Let us believe in him now,* or *get belief in him.*

159. In dependent clauses with ἵνα, *in order that,* and ἐάν, *if,* either the pres. or aor. subjv. may be used, with the distinction in **158.**   *The aorist subjunctive does not denote past time, but is present or future with reference to the principal verb.*

160. The 2 aor. part. has the same endings as the present, -ων, -μενος, **90** and **99**, with the accent on -ών. ὁ ἐλθών, *he having come;* ὁ ἰδών, *he having seen;* ὁ εἰπών, *he having said;* ὁ ἀποθανών, *he having died;* ὁ λαβών, *he having received;* ὁ γενόμενος, *he having become.*

161. The 2 aor. inf. also has the endings of the present, -ειν, -σθαι, **89** and **98**, with (ˆ) on the ultima of the active and the (´) on the penult of the middle ἐλθεῖν, *to come;* ἰδεῖν, *to see;* εἰπεῖν, *to say;* ἀποθανεῖν, *to die;* λαβεῖν, *to receive;* γενέσθαι, *to become.*

162.   EXERCISES.

1. ἐὰν εἴπωμεν ὅτι ἁμαρτίαν οὐκ ἔχομεν, ἡ ἀλήθεια οὐκ ἔστιν ἐν ἡμῖν.   2. καὶ αὕτη ἐστὶν ἡ ἐντολὴ αὐτοῦ ἵνα πιστεύσωμεν τῷ ὀνόματι τοῦ υἱοῦ αὐτοῦ, Ἰησοῦ Χριστοῦ.   3. οὗτος ἦλθε εἰς μαρτυρίαν ἵνα μαρτυρήσῃ περὶ τοῦ φωτὸς ἵνα πάντες (*all*) πιστεύσωσιν δι' αὐτοῦ.   4. ἄγωμεν καὶ ἡμεῖς ἵνα ἀποθάνωμεν μετ' αὐτοῦ.   5. ἐλθὼν οὖν ὁ Ἰησοῦς εὗρεν αὐτόν.   6. οὐκ ἦν ἐκεῖνος τὸ φῶς ἀλλ' ἵνα μαρτυρήσῃ περὶ τοῦ φωτός.   7. ἐτύφλωσεν αὐτῶν τοὺς ὀφθαλμοὺς ἵνα μὴ ἴδωσι τοῖς ὀφθαλμοῖς.   8. Λάζαρος[1] ἀπέθανεν καὶ χαίρω (*rejoice*) δι' ὑμᾶς ἵνα πιστεύσητε ὅτι οὐκ ἤμην[2] ἐκεῖ.   9. ἐγὼ οὐκ ἦλθον βαλεῖν εἰρήνην ἐπὶ

---

[1] Learn the capital letters, § **1**.   [2] See **78**.

τὴν γῆν. 10. ἦλθε ὁ υἱὸς τοῦ θεοῦ ἵνα λύσῃ τὰ
ἔργα τοῦ διαβόλου. 11. ἡ ἐπιθυμία τῆς σαρκὸς
καὶ ἡ ἐπιθυμία τῶν ὀφθαλμῶν καὶ ἡ ἀλαζονία
(*vain display*) τοῦ βίου, οὐκ ἔστιν ἐκ τοῦ πατρός,
ἀλλὰ ἐκ τοῦ κόσμου ἐστίν· καὶ ὁ κόσμος παράγεται (*pass away*) καὶ ἡ ἐπιθυμία αὐτοῦ, ὁ δὲ ποιῶν
τὸ θέλημα τοῦ θεοῦ μένει εἰς τὸν αἰῶνα.

LESSON XXII.

IRREGULAR ADJECTIVES OF THE CONSONANT DECLENSION.

163. VOCABULARY.

ἀγοράζω, *buy*.
ἀδύνατος, *impossible*.
ἀκάθαρτος, *unclean*.
ἁμαρτωλός, ὁ, *sinner*.
ἅπας, *all*.
βιβλίον, *book, Bible*.
βούλομαι, *wish*.
ἐλεύθερος, *free*.
μέγας, *great*.
ὅτε, conj., *when*.

οὐδέ . . . οὐδέ, *neither . . . nor*.
οὔτε . . . οὔτε, *neither . . . nor*.
παρά, prep. w. gen., *from the side of*; w. dat., *by the side of*; w. acc., *to the side of*.
πᾶς, *all*.
πολύς, *much, many*.
σπείρω, *sow*.
ψεύστης, ὁ, *liar*.

164. Learn the declension of πολύς, *much*,
and μέγας, *great*, § 36. To be observed:

1. That both these adjectives have two distinct stems, a longer and a shorter form, of
which the former is more frequent.

2. That they are declined, for the most part, in the first and second declension.

165. Learn the declension of πᾶς, *all*, § **36**, and note the following peculiarities :

1. The masc. and neut. are declined in the third declension, while the fem. is declined in the first declension.

2. The stem is παντ-, and the nom. masc. is formed by adding ς, as in mute stems. In the fem. nom. sing. -σα is added. Cf. **127**, 2.

3. ντ- drops before ς of nom. sing. and -σι of the dat. plur. Cf. **132**.

4. The accent in the masc. and neut. sing. is that of monosyllables of the third declension, **108**, while in the plur. it is an exception to the rule.

166.   EXERCISES.

I. 1. πάντα δι᾿ αὐτοῦ ἐγένετο.[1] 2. ταῦτα πάντα ἐλάλησεν ὁ Ἰησοῦς ἐν παραβολαῖς τοῖς ὄχλοις. 3. μεγάλη[2] σου ἡ πίστις. 4. καὶ ἐγένετο φόβος μέγας ἐπὶ[3] πάντας. 5. πᾶς ὁ ἐν αὐτῷ μένων οὐχ ἁμαρτάνει.[3] 6. μετὰ ταῦτα ἤκουσα φωνὴν μεγάλην ὄχλου πολλοῦ. 7. ἔσται γὰρ θλῖψις μεγάλη. 8. πάντες ὑμεῖς υἱοὶ φωτός ἐστε καὶ υἱοὶ ἡμέρας. 9. καὶ πολὺ πλῆθος ἀπὸ τῆς Γαλιλαίας ἠκολού-

---

[1] Cf. **43**, 10, note.   [2] In the pred. position, **64**.   [3] See **167**.

θησεν. 10. τὸ αἷμα Ἰησοῦ τοῦ υἱοῦ αὐτοῦ καθαρίζει ἡμᾶς ἀπὸ πάσης ἁμαρτίας. 11. ἔτι πολλὰ
ἔχω ὑμῖν λέγειν. 12. ταύτην τὴν ἐντολὴν ἔλαβον
παρὰ τοῦ πατρός μου. 13. οὔτε ἐμὲ οἴδατε οὔτε
τὸν πατέρα μου.

LESSON XXIII.

Perfect Indicative Active and Passive.

167. VOCABULARY.

ἀληθῶς, adv., *truly*.	ὅθεν, adv., *whence*.
ἁμαρτάνω, *sin*.	οὕτω,[1] adv., *thus*.
ἀναβαίνω, *go up*.	ποῦ, adv., *where*.
ἄνωθεν, adv., *from above*.	σφάζω, *kill*.
διαθήκη, ἡ, *covenant*.	τελειόω, *fulfil, make per-*
ἑορτή, ἡ, *feast*.	*fect*.
ἔξω, adv. w. gen., *without*.	φίλος, ὁ, *friend*.
ἐπί, prep. w. gen., *upon* ;	ψεύδομαι, *lie*.
w. acc., *to, on, over*.	ὡς, conj., *as, about*.
ἥλιος, ὁ, *sun*.	φιλέω, *love*.

168. The perf. ind. of λύω is :

ACTIVE.   PASSIVE or MIDDLE.
                Sing.

1. λέ-λυ-κα, *I have loosed*,   λέ-λυ-μαι, *I have been loosed* or
2. λέ-λυ-κας   etc.   λέ-λυ-σαι   *have freed for*
3. λέ-λυ-κε   λέ-λυ-ται   *myself*.

                Plur.

   1. λε-λύ-κα-μεν   λε-λύ-μεθα
   2. λε-λύ-κα-τε   λέ-λυ-σθε
   3. λε-λύ-κα-σι   λέ-λυ-νται

[1] But οὕτως before a vowel.

F

169. Observe : 1. That the tense suffix in the act. is -κα, with which compare -σα of the aor. 2. That the 3 per. plur. act. has -σι, which shows the endings to be primary. In the sing. the endings do not appear as primary, but are the same as in the aor. act.   The μι, σι, etc., never occur here.   3. That besides the augment there is the initial consonant of the verb, which extra syllable λε- is called *reduplication.*   4. That the perf. pass. has the reduplication and the primary pass. endings, which are added directly to the theme without the intervention of any tense suffix.

170. The following forms will indicate the perfect of a few verbs :

νικάω, *conquer* . . . . Perf. Act. νε-νίκη-κα
πιστεύω, *believe* . . . Perf. Act. πε-πίστευ-κα
ἀγαπάω, *love* . . . . . Perf. Act. ἠγάπη-κα
αἰτέω, *ask for* . . . . Perf. Act. ᾔτη-κα [1]
τελειόω, *fulfil* . . . . . Perf. Pass. τε-τελείω-μαι
γεννάω, *beget* . . . . . Perf. Pass. γε-γέννη-μαι

It is seen from these examples that a short final vowel is lengthened before -κα or -μαι, as before all tense suffixes, and that a verb beginning with a vowel or a diphthong cannot have the reduplication, but the simple augment.   For the principles of augment and reduplication, see § 77, 1, 2, 3, 4.

[1] See **36**, 2 for this augment.

171. The perfect has many peculiarities, which need not concern the learner at this stage, and can well be left for larger hand-books or the lexicon.

Learn the following perfects of irregular verbs:

ἀκούω, *hear* ...... 2 Perf. Act. ἀκ-ήκο-α
γινώσκω, *know* .... Perf. Act. ἔ-γνω-κα
ὁράω, *see* .... Perf. Act. ἑ-ώρα-κα

172. A few verbs have a second perfect in -α, not -κα, § **54**; *e.g.* γίνομαι, *become*, 2 perf. γέ-γον-α ; ἔρχομαι, *come, go*, 2 perf. ἐλ-ήλυθ-α.

173.   EXERCISES.

I. καὶ ἐν τούτῳ γινώσκομεν ὅτι ἐγνώκαμεν αὐτόν. 2. οἴδαμεν ὅτι ἔχομεν ἃ ᾐτήκαμεν ἀπ' αὐτοῦ. 3. ταῦτα λελάληκα ὑμῖν. 4. πᾶς ὁ ποιῶν τὴν δικαιοσύνην ἐξ αὐτοῦ γεγέννηται. 5. καὶ ἡμεῖς πεπιστεύκαμεν τὴν ἀγάπην ἣν ἔχει ὁ θεὸς ἐν ὑμῖν. 6. αὕτη δέ ἐστιν ἡ κρίσις ὅτι τὸ φῶς ἐλήλυθεν εἰς τὸν κόσμον. 7. τὰ ῥήματα ἃ ἐγὼ λελάληκα ὑμῖν πνεῦμά ἐστιν καὶ ζωή ἐστιν. 8. ὃ ἑωράκαμεν καὶ ἀκηκόαμεν ἀπαγγέλλομεν καὶ ὑμῖν. 9. ἐν τούτῳ ἡ ἀγάπη τοῦ θεοῦ τετελείωται. 10. γράφω ὑμῖν, πατέρες, ὅτι ἐγνώκατε αὐτὸν ἀπ' ἀρχῆς. 11. ἐν τούτῳ ἐστὶν ἡ ἀγάπη, οὐχ ὅτι ἡμεῖς ἠγαπήκαμεν τὸν θεὸν, ἀλλ' ὅτι αὐτὸς ἠγάπησεν ἡμᾶς. 12. αὐτὸς γὰρ ὁ πατὴρ φιλεῖ ὑμᾶς, ὅτι ὑμεῖς ἐμὲ πεφιλήκατε καὶ πεπιστεύκατε ὅτι ἐγὼ παρὰ τοῦ πατρὸς ἐξῆλθον. 13. ψεύστην πεποίηκε αὐτὸν ὅτι οὐ πεπίστευκεν εἰς τὴν μαρτυρίαν ἣν μεμαρτύρηκεν ὁ θεὸς περὶ τοῦ υἱοῦ αὐτοῦ.

LESSON XXIV.

Aorist Passive Indicative and Subjunctive.

174. VOCABULARY.

ἀναγινώσκω, *read*.

αὔριον, adv., *to-morrow*.

βλασφημέω, BLASPHEME.

γενεά, ἡ, *generation*.

διδαχή, ἡ, *teaching*.

ἐγγύς, adv., *near*.

ἰάομαι, *heal*.

κελεύω, *command*.

λυπέω, *grieve*.

πάσχα, τό, indecl., *Passover*.

πόθεν, adv., *whence*.

πρωΐ, adv., *early in the morning*.

σοφός, *wise*.

σταυρόω, *crucify*.

ὑπό, prep. w. gen. and acc., *under*.

φωνέω, *call*.

175. The aor. pass. of λύω is —

	INDICATIVE.	SUBJUNCTIVE.
Sing. 1.	ἐ-λύ-θη-ν	λυ-θῶ
2.	ἐ-λύ-θη-ς	λυ-θῇς
3.	ἐ-λύ-θη	λυ-θῇ
Plur. 1.	ἐ-λύ-θη-μεν	λυ-θῶ-μεν
2.	ἐ-λύ-θη-τε	λυ-θῆ-τε
3.	ἐ-λύ-θη-σαν	λυ-θῶ-σι

176. Observe the following :

1. The suffix for the aor. pass. is θε, which is θη in the ind., and contracts with -ω, -ῃς, etc., of the subjv. with the circumflex. See § **5**, 8 and § **6**, 5.

2. The personal endings in the aor. ind. pass. are the *secondary active*. So likewise in the subjv. are found *not* pass., but act. endings.

177. Before -θε a short final vowel is lengthened; *e.g.* ποιέω, *do*, ἐποιήθην; φανερόω, *make manifest*, ἐφανερώθην.

178. A theme in a mute stem (§ 2) is changed before -θε; *e.g.* ἄγω, *lead*, ἤχθην; πείθω, *persuade*, ἐπείσθην.

$$\kappa, \gamma, \chi + \theta\epsilon = \chi\theta\epsilon$$
$$\pi, \beta, \phi + \theta\epsilon = \phi\theta\epsilon$$
$$\tau, \delta, \theta + \theta\epsilon = \sigma\theta\epsilon$$

179. Some deponent verbs (**76**) have an aor. pass. Such are called *passive deponents; e.g.* πορεύομαι, *go*, ἐπορεύθην, *I went;* ἀποκρίνομαι, *reply*, ἀπεκρίθην, *I replied*.

180. In some verbs there is found a 2 aor. pass. with the suffix ε only; *e.g.* γράφω, *write*, 2 aor. pass. ἐγράφη, *it was written*. See 2 aor. pass. of φαίνω, § 58.

181.   EXERCISES.

1. καὶ ἡ ζωὴ ἐν αὐτῷ ἐφανερώθη.   2. καὶ ἀπεκρίθησαν οἱ μαθηταὶ αὐτοῦ.   3. καὶ ἐξελθὼν ἐπορεύθη εἰς ἕτερον τόπον.   4. ὅτι ἐγγὺς ἦν ὁ τόπος τῆς πόλεως ὅπου ἐσταυρώθη ὁ Ἰησοῦς.   5. ἐὰν δὲ πορευθῶ πέμψω αὐτὸν πρὸς ὑμᾶς.

6. οὐκ ἐξ αἱμάτων οὐδὲ ἐκ θελήματος σαρκὸς
οὐδὲ ἐκ θελήματος ἀνδρὸς ἀλλ᾽ ἐκ θεοῦ ἐγεννή-
θησαν.   7. εἰς (for) τοῦτο ἐφανερώθη ὁ υἱὸς τοῦ
θεοῦ ἵνα λύσῃ τὰ ἔργα διαβόλου.   8. οἴδαμεν ὅτι
ἐὰν αὐτὸς φανερωθῇ ὅμοιοι (like) αὐτῷ ἐσόμεθα.
9. ἀπεκρίθη ὁ Ἰησοῦς καὶ εἶπεν αὐτοῖς τοῦτό ἐστι
τὸ ἔργον τοῦ θεοῦ.   10. οἶδα πόθεν ἔρχομαι καὶ
ποῦ ὑπάγω· ὑμεῖς δὲ οὐκ οἴδατε πόθεν ἔρχομαι
ἢ ποῦ ὑπάγω.

LESSON XXV.

PARTICIPLES.

182.   VOCABULARY.

ἀρνίον, τό, *lamb.*   λογίζομαι, *account.*
δυνατός, *possible, able.*   μικρός, *little.*
ἐκλεκτός, ὁ, *chosen,* ELECT.   πάντοτε, adv., *always.*
ἕνεκα, prep. w. gen., *on account* πλανάω, *lead astray.*
    of.   πρό, prep. w. gen., *be-*
ἐπαύριον, adv., *on the morrow.*   *fore.*
εὐχαριστέω, *give thanks, bless.*   τελέω, *finish.*
κώμη, ἡ, *village.*   τοιοῦτος, *such.*

   χωρίς, adv., as a prep. w. gen., *apart from.*

183. The pres. part. of εἰμί, *I am :*

| | | Sing. | | | Plur. | |
	Masc.	Fem.	Neut.	Masc.	Fem.	Neut.
N.V.	ὤν	οὖσα	ὄν	ὄντες	οὖσαι	ὄντα
G.	ὄντος	οὔσης	ὄντος	ὄντων	οὐσῶν	ὄντων
D.	ὄντι	οὔσῃ	ὄντι	οὖσι	οὔσαις	οὖσι
A.	ὄντα	οὖσαν	ὄν	ὄντας	οὔσας	ὄντα

184. Observe the following :

1. This participle is declined in three genders, sing. and plur. the same as πᾶς, **165**.

2. The stem οντ- becomes ων- in nom. masc. sing., and οὖσα is for ὄντσα in nom. fem. sing. The neut. sing. is the mere stem. Cf. **106**, 5.

185. Learn the pres. act. part. of λύω, § **43**.

Note that the pres. part. act. of any verb in -ω is the present stem of the verb with the pres. part. of εἰμί.

What is the pres. act. part. of ἀκούω, *hear*, λέγω, *say*, κρίνω, *judge*, γινώσκω, *know* ?

Participles are accented like adjectives, not with the recessive accent of verbs.

186. Second aorist participles in -ων (**160**) are declined the same as pres. part. in -ων.

187. The same tense signs are found in the participles as occur in the tenses of the indicative.

	Fut.	*Aor.*	*Perf.*				
ACTIVE.	-σ-	-σα-	-κ-				
MIDDLE.	-σ-	-σα-	No sign but the accent on the penult.	-μένος			
PASSIVE.	-θησ-	-θε-	"	"	"	"	"	"

For the changes before tense suffixes, see **124** and **178**.

188. Learn the aor. act. and pass. part. of λύω, § **43**, and observe the same principles in the formation of the nom. sing. as in the pres. act. part.

In the aor. pass. the form λυθείς, which has irregular accent, is for λυθέντς, **165**, 3. ε is lengthened to ει.

189. All middle and passive participles, except the *aorist* passive, have the ending -μενος.

Pres.   *Fut.*   *Aor.*   *Perf.*

MIDDLE. λυ-ό-μενος λυ-σ-ό-μενος λυ-σά-μενος λε-λυ-μένος

PASSIVE. Same as the middle, except the fut. pass. is λυ-θη-σό-μενος.

190. Examine the following:

1. ἀποκριθεὶς ταῦτα ἀπῆλθεν.

> a. *Having said this*
> b. *When he said this* } *he went away.*
> c. *He said this and*

2. πορευόμενοι δὲ ἡμεῖς ἐκηρύσσομεν.

> a. *Going moreover*
> b. *As we advanced* } *we preached.*
> c. *While we advanced*

3. ἰδὼν δὲ ταῦτα ἐθαύμαζεν.

> a. *Seeing this* (these)
> b. *When he saw this* } *he marvelled.*
> c. *Because he saw this*

191. Observe in these sentences:

1. The participle agrees in number and case with the subject of the verb.

2. While the participle may be rendered into
English by a participle (Ex. 1 *a*, 2 *a*, and 3 *a*),
it more naturally takes the form of a *dependent
clause denoting time or cause.*

3. The tense of the participle is relative to
the tense of the principal verb.

192. Examine the following :

1. τοῖς ἀκούουσι, *to those who hear.*
2. περὶ τοῦ γινώσκοντος, *concerning him who knows.*
3. τὸν γεννήσαντα, *him who has begotten.*
4. ὁ γεγεννημένος, *he who is begotten.*

193. Observe that *the article with the participle* may occur in *any* case, and is equivalent to
a relative clause in English.

The participle is a most common form of verbal expression in Greek, and to understand a few of its many uses
is an essential to even a meagre knowledge of the language.
Some of the most ordinary uses have been here explained ;
and if these models are thoroughly mastered, little difficulty need confront the learner in the narrative passages
of the New Testament.

194.   EXERCISES.

1. ὁ μισῶν τὸν ἀδελφὸν αὐτοῦ οὐκ ἔχει τὴν
ἀλήθειαν.   2. πορευόμενοι δὲ κηρύσσετε λέγοντες
ὅτι ἤγγικεν[1] ἡ βασιλεία τῶν οὐρανῶν.   3. καὶ
ἀποκριθέντες αὐτῷ εἶπον Οὐκ οἴδαμεν.   4. ποιῶ
τὸ θέλημα τοῦ πέμψαντός με.   5. καὶ ἐλθόντες

---

[1] ἐγγίζω, *near.*

εἰς τὴν οἰκίαν εἶδον τὸ παιδίον μετὰ Μαρίας τῆς
μητρὸς αὐτοῦ. 6. ὁ μένων ἐν ἐμοὶ καὶ ἐγὼ ἐν
αὐτῷ οὗτος ἔχει χαρὰν πολλήν. 7. ὁ πέμψας με
δίκαιός ἐστιν. 8. ἀκούσας δὲ ὁ Ἰησοῦς ἐθαύμα-
σεν καὶ εἶπεν τοῖς ἀκολουθοῦσιν,[1] ἀμὴν λέγω
ὑμῖν. 9. ταῦτα ἔγραψα ὑμῖν περὶ τῶν πλανώντων[2] ὑμᾶς. 10. ταῦτα αὐτοῦ λαλοῦντος[3] πολλοὶ
ἐπίστευσαν. 11. πᾶς ὁ πιστεύων ὅτι Ἰησοῦς
ἐστὶν ὁ Χριστὸς ἐκ τοῦ θεοῦ γεγέννηται, καὶ πᾶς
ὁ ἀγαπῶν τὸν γεννήσαντα ἀγαπᾷ[4] τὸν γεγεννημένον ἐξ αὐτοῦ.

LESSON XXVI.

INTERROGATIVE AND INDEFINITE PRONOUNS.

195.   VOCABULARY.

ἀγορά, ἡ, market-place.

ἀγρός, ὁ, field.

διακονέω, minister.

διάκονος, ὁ, minister, DEA-
CON.

θεραπεύω, heal.

θηρίον, τό, wild beast.

μᾶλλον, adv., more, rather.

μαρτυρία, ἡ, witness.

οἶνος, ὁ, wine.

οὐκέτι, adv., not yet, no longer.

ὅταν, conj. w. subj., when.

ποτέ, adv., once, ever.

πρόβατον, τό, sheep.

τότε, adv., then.

ταχέως, adv., quickly.

φεύγω, flee, escape.

[1] For the contraction εου, see § 8.

[2] For ω instead of αο, see § 5, 1.

[3] A participle may be used in the genitive to agree with a
noun, pronoun, or adjective. This construction has *no grammatical* connection with the rest of the sentence, and is called
genitive absolute. A conjunction, as *while, when, because*, must
be used in translating such phrases into English.

[4] See § 8, 1.

196. Learn the declension of the interrogative pronoun τίς, *who?* and τί, *what?* and the indefinite pronoun τὶς, *some one*, and τὶ, *something*, § 41.

Observe the following :

1. Both the interrogative and indefinite pronouns are declined alike.

2. The interrogative pronoun has the acute on the *first* syllable, while the indefinite has the grave on the last syllable, or, in other words, has no accent of its own, and is therefore an enclitic.

197. Examine the following :

1. σὺ τίς εἶ ; *who art thou ?*
2. τίς ἔστιν ὁ ἄνθρωπος ; *who is the man ?*
3. τίνα ζητεῖτε ; *whom do you seek ?*
4. γινώσκετε τί πεποίηκα, *ye know what I have done.*

Note that the interrogative τίς is used in both direct (1, 2, 3) and indirect (4) questions.

198. Examine the following :

1. ἐὰν μή τις γεννηθῇ ἄνωθεν, *unless one shall be born from above.*
2. τινὲς δὲ ἐξ αὐτῶν εἶπον, *certain ones of them said.*
3. καί τις ἀνὴρ χωλός, *and a certain lame man.*
4. ἐάν τι αἰτήσητέ με ἐν τῷ ὀνόματί μου τοῦτο ποιήσω, *If you shall ask anything of me in my name, I shall do it.*

Observe that the indefinite τὶς is enclitic[1] when it is possible.

These pronouns are of the most frequent occurrence in the New Testament, each being found several hundred times.

199. The following are the infinitives of λύω :

	Pres.	*Fut.*	*Aor.*	*Perf.*
ACTIVE.	λύ-ειν	λύ-σ-ειν	λῦ-σαι	λε-λυ-κ-έ-ναι
MIDDLE.	λύ-ε-σθαι	λύ-σε-σθαι	λύ-σα-σθαι	λε-λύ-σθαι
PASSIVE.	λύ-ε-σθαι	λυ-θή-σε-σθαι	λυ-θῆ-ναι	λε-λύ-σθαι

It is to be observed that the ending αι is everywhere *short* in the infinitive, and that the infinitive in -ναι has irregular accent, as well as the perf. pass. in -σθαι.

200. The infinitives of εἰμί, *am*, are εἶναι, *pres.*, and ἔσεσθαι, *fut.* Of οἶδα, *I know*, the infinitive is εἰδέναι, *to know*.

201.   EXERCISES.

1. τί δὲ ὑμῖν δοκεῖ ; 2. ἐάν τις ἀγαπᾷ τὸν κόσμον, οὐκ ἔστιν ἡ ἀγάπη τοῦ πατρὸς ἐν αὐτῷ. 3. ἐάν τι αἰτώμεθα κατὰ (*according to*) τὸ θέλημα αὐτοῦ ἀκούει ἡμῶν. 4. εἴδομέν τινα ἐν τῷ ὀνόματί σου ἐκβάλλοντα δαιμόνια. 5. τί θέλετε ποιήσω ὑμῖν ; 6. ἀποκριθεὶς δὲ ὁ Ἰησοῦς εἶπεν οὐκ οἴδατε τί αἰτεῖσθε. 7. ὑμεῖς δὲ τίνα με λέγετε εἶναι ;

[1] See page 29, note.

ἀποκριθεὶς ὁ Πέτρος λέγει αὐτῷ Σὺ εἶ ὁ Χριστός.
8. ἀγαπητοί, νῦν τέκνα θεοῦ ἐσμεν, καὶ οὔπω
ἐφανερώθη τί ἐσόμεθα. οἴδαμεν ὅτι ἐὰν φανερωθῇ
ὅμοιοι αὐτῷ ἐσόμεθα ὅτι ὀψόμεθα (*shall see*) αὐτὸν
καθώς ἐστιν. 9. καὶ πορευομένων αὐτῶν[1] ἐν τῇ
ὁδῷ εἶπέν τις πρὸς αὐτὸν Ἀκολουθήσω σοι.
10. ὅταν γὰρ ἀσθενῶ τότε δυνατός εἰμι.

LESSON XXVII.

FUTURE AND AORIST OF LIQUID VERBS.

202. VOCABULARY.

ἀποκτείνω, *kill*.
δίκτυον, τό, *net*.
ἐκτείνω, *stretch out*.
ἐπαίρω, *raise up*.
ἐπιτιμάω, *rebuke*.
καθίζω, *sit*.
μακρόθεν, adv., *from afar*.
νυμφίος, ὁ, *bridegroom*.

ὀφείλω, *ought*.
πάσχω, *suffer*.
πειράζω, *tempt*.
πλούσιος, *rich*.
ποτήριον, τό, *cup*.
στρατιώτης, ὁ, *soldier*.
σωτηρία, ἡ, *salvation*.
φρόνιμος, *wise*.

203. The future of μένω, *remain*, is :

		ACTIVE.		MIDDLE.	
Sing.	1.	μενῶ	(μεν-έ-ω)	μενοῦμαι	(μεν-έ-ο-μαι)
	2.	μενεῖς	(μεν-έ-εις)	μενῇ	(μεν-έ-ῃ), § 6, 5.
	3.	μενεῖ	(μεν-έ-ει)	μενεῖται	(μεν-έ-ε-ται)
Plur.	1.	μενοῦμεν	(μεν-έ-ο-μεν)	μενούμεθα	(μεν-ε-ό-μεθα)
	2.	μενεῖτε	(μεν-έ-ε-τε)	μενεῖσθε	(μεν-έ-ε-σθε)
	3.	μενοῦσι	(μεν-έ-ου-σι)	μενοῦνται	(μεν-έ-ο-νται)

[1] See footnote 3, page 74.

Observe: 1. That μένω is a liquid verb (theme ending in λ, μ, ν, or ρ). 2. The suffix for the future is not σ%, but ε%. 3. This short vowel contracts with the variable vowel. See § 5, 7 and 8; § 6, 7; § 7, 2. 4. When one of the uncontracted syllables has an accent, the contracted form *must* have an accent — the circumflex when possible.

204. This contraction may be seen more simply if represented thus: ε% = $^{ου}/_{ει}$; *i.e.* ου occurs before μ and ν, and ει in all other forms.

The present and imperfect indicative of themes ending in ε have the same contraction as the future of liquid verbs. Learn φιλέω, § 59.

205. The fut. ind. of αἴρω (αρ-[1]), *take away*, is ἀρῶ; of ἀποστέλλω (αποστελ-[1]), *send*, is ἀποστελῶ; of ἐγείρω (εγερ-), *raise up*, is ἐγερῶ; of ἐπαγγέλλω (επαγγελ-), *promise*, is ἐπαγγελῶ; of ἀποκτείνω (αποκτεν-), *kill*, is ἀποκτενῶ.

206. Rule: *The future of all liquid verbs is formed by the suffix* ε%.

207. The aor. ind. of μένω is ἔ-μειν-α, subjv. μείν-ω, part. μείν-ας, inf. μεῖν-αι.

---

[1] See § 82, 3 and 4.

The aor. ind. of ἐπαγγέλλω is ἐπήγγειλ-α, subjv.
ἐπαγγείλ-ω, part. ἐπαγγείλ-ας, inf. ἐπαγγεῖλ-αι;
κρίνω, ind. ἔκρῑν-α, subjv. κρίν-ω, part. κρίν-ας,
inf. κρῖν-αι.

208. Rule: *The aorist active and middle of
liquid verbs have no σ, but form the aorist by
lengthening the last vowel in the theme to the
corresponding long vowel. ε, however, changes to
ει, and a to η (except before ε, ι, or ρ).* Cf. **53**, 1.

209.   EXERCISES.

1. ἀποστελεῖ ὁ υἱὸς τοῦ ἀνθρώπου τοὺς ἀγγέ-
λους αὐτοῦ. 2. καὶ αὕτη ἐστὶν ἡ ἐπαγγελία
(*promise*) ἣν αὐτὸς ἐπηγγείλατο ἡμῖν τὴν ζωὴν
αἰώνιον. 3. ὁ ἐγείρας τὸν Ἰησοῦν καὶ ἡμᾶς σὺν
Ἰησοῦ[1] ἐγερεῖ. 4. ἦραν τὸν κύριον ἐκ τοῦ μνη-
μείου[2] καὶ οὐκ οἴδαμεν ποῦ ἔθηκαν (*laid*) αὐτόν.
5. ὁ δεχόμενος ὑμᾶς ἐμὲ δέχεται, καὶ ὁ ἐμὲ δεχόμενος δέχεται τὸν ἀποστείλαντά με. 6. καθὼς
ἐμὲ ἀπέστειλας εἰς τὸν κόσμον κἀγὼ[3] ἀπέστειλα
αὐτοὺς εἰς τὸν κόσμον. 7. ἐὰν ἐν ὑμῖν μείνῃ ὃ
ἀπ᾽ ἀρχῆς ἠκούσατε, καὶ ὑμεῖς ἐν τῷ υἱῷ καὶ (*also*)
ἐν τῷ πατρὶ μενεῖτε. 8. διὰ τοῦτο καὶ ἡ σοφία
τοῦ θεοῦ εἶπεν Ἀποστελῶ εἰς αὐτοὺς προφήτας
καὶ ἀποστόλους. 9. ἦν δὲ ἐγγὺς τὸ πάσχα, ἡ

[1] See § **23**, *a*.   [2] *tomb*.   [3] See § **13**.

ἑορτὴ τῶν Ἰουδαίων. (ἐπάρας) οὖν τοὺς ὀφθαλμοὺς
ὁ Ἰησοῦς καὶ θεασάμενος ὅτι πολὺς ὄχλος ἔρχεται
πρὸς αὐτὸν λέγει πρὸς Φίλιππον Πόθεν ἀγορά-
σωμεν ἄρτους ἵνα φάγωσι (eat) οὗτοι ;

LESSON XXVIII.

Pronouns : Reflexive, Reciprocal.

210.   VOCABULARY.

ἀναπίπτω, *recline, fall down.*   καθαρός, *purified.*
γέμω, *fill.*   κρατέω, *grasp.*
δένδρον, τό, *tree.*   μακάριος, *blessed.*
δῶρον, τό, *gift.*   μισθός, ὁ, *hire, pay.*
ἐλπίζω, *hope.*   μυστήριον, τό, MYSTERY.
ἔξεστι, *it is lawful.*   σός, *thy.*
θυσία, ἡ, *sacrifice.*   φρονέω, *think.*
ἱκανός, *sufficient, able.*   ὥστε, conj., *so that, and so.*[1]

211. Learn the declension of the reflexive
pronouns ἐμαυτοῦ, *myself,* σεαυτοῦ, *thyself,* ἑαυτοῦ, *himself,* § **40**.

Observe : 1. These pronouns occur in the
oblique cases only. 2. They are formed from
the personal pronoun and the intensive αὐτός,
ἐμαυτοῦ = ἐμ + αὐτοῦ ; σεαυτοῦ = σε + αὐτοῦ ; ἑαυτοῦ = ἑ (pron. not found in N. T.) + αὐτοῦ.

212. ἑαυτοῦ is often written in a shorter form
αὑτοῦ, αὑτῷ, etc.

[1] This latter sense *at the beginning* of a sentence.

213. Examine the following :

1. ἐγὼ μαρτυρῶ περὶ ἐμαυτοῦ, *I bear witness concerning myself.*
2. ἐγὼ δοξάζω ἐμαυτόν, *I glorify myself.*
3. ἀπ᾽ ἐμαυτοῦ οὐ λαλῶ, *I speak not of myself.*
4. τί λέγεις περὶ σεαυτοῦ, *what sayest thou concerning thyself.*
5. δοξάσει αὐτὸν ἐν ἑαυτῷ, *he will glorify Him in himself.*
6. αὐτοὶ ἐν ἑαυτοῖς στενάζομεν, *we ourselves groan within ourselves.*

In all these examples the pronoun refers back to the *subject* of the sentence, hence the term *reflexive.*

Note that the 3 per. pron. ἑαυτοῖς may refer (as in Ex. 6) to other than the 3 per.

214. The reciprocal pronoun ἀλλήλων, *of one another*, is found in dat. ἀλλήλοις, and acc. ἀλλήλους. μισοῦσιν ἀλλήλους, *they hate one another.*

215.   EXERCISES.

1. τίνα σεαυτὸν ποιεῖς ; 2. αὐτὸς δὲ Ἰησοῦς οὐκ ἐπίστευσεν αὐτὸν αὐτοῖς. 3. οἱ μαθηταί σου ποιοῦσι ὃ οὐκ ἔξεστιν ποιεῖν ἐν σαββάτῳ. 4. ὥστε μαρτυρεῖτε ἑαυτοῖς ὅτι υἱοί ἐστε τῶν φονευσάντων[1] τοὺς προφήτας. 5. ἀπ᾽ ἐμαυτοῦ οὐκ ἐλήλυθα. 6. ὁ γὰρ πατὴρ ἔχει ζωὴν ἐν

---

[1] φονεύω, *slay.*

G

ἑαυτῷ. 7. ἐὰν εἴπωμεν ὅτι ἁμαρτίαν οὐκ ἔχομεν,
ἑαυτοὺς πλανῶμεν καὶ ἡ ἀλήθεια οὐκ ἔστιν ἐν
ἡμῖν. 8. ἐλπὶς δὲ βλεπομένη οὐκ ἔστιν ἐλπίς,
ὃ γὰρ βλέπει τίς ἐλπίζει; 9. ἀμὴν ἀμὴν λέγω
σοι, ἐὰν μή τις γεννηθῇ ἄνωθεν, οὐ δύναται ἰδεῖν
τὴν βασιλείαν τοῦ θεοῦ, τὸ γεγεννημένον ἐκ τῆς
σαρκὸς σάρξ ἐστιν, καὶ τὸ γεγεννημένον ἐκ τοῦ
πνεύματος πνεῦμά ἐστιν.

LESSON XXIX.

Imperative Mood.

216.　　　　VOCABULARY.

ἀποκαλύπτω, *reveal.*	καλῶς, adv., *well.*
βαστάζω, *touch, bear.*	κλαίω, *weep.*
γαμέω, *marry.*	μετανοέω, *repent.*
γνωστός, *known.*	πλήν, conj., and as a prep. w.
δύο, *two.*	gen., *except.*
εἷς, *one.*	σήμερον, adv., *to-day.*
ἐλάχιστος, *least.*	τέσσαρες, *four.*
καθάπερ, *even as.*	τρεῖς, *three.*
κακῶς, adv., *ill, badly.*	ὕστερον, adv., *afterward.*

217. The pres. imp. of λύω is:

		ACTIVE.	MIDDLE and PASSIVE.
Sing.	2.	λῦ-ε	λύ-ου
	3.	λυ-έ-τω	λυ-έ-σθω
Plur.	2.	λύ-ε-τε	λύ-ε-σθε
	3.	λυ-ό-ντων or	λυ-έ-σθων or
		λυ-έ-τωσαν	λυ-έ-σθωταν

218. The endings of the imp. are :

ACTIVE.		MIDDLE and PASSIVE.	
Sing.	*Plur.*	*Sing.*	*Plur.*
2. θι	τε	2. σο	σθε
3. τω	ντων or τωσαν	3. σθω	σθων or σθωσαν

a. θι of the act. is regularly dropped in verbs like λύω.
b. λύου is for λύ-ε-σο.

219. Examine the following :

> ἀκουέτω, *let him hear.*
> μὴ θαυμάζετε, *marvel not.*

Rule : *The imperative is used to express a command. The negative is* μή.

220. Learn the aor. imp. act., mid., and pass. of λύω, § **56**, and the 2 aor. act. and mid. of λείπω, § **57**.

a. ον in the aor. act. is an irregular ending.
b. θι in aor. pass. becomes τι to avoid a combination of rough [1] mutes.

221. οὐδείς, *no one* (οὐδέ, *nor* + εἷς, *one*), is declined as follows :

οὐδείς	οὐδεμία	οὐδέν
οὐδενός	οὐδεμιᾶς	οὐδενός
οὐδενί	οὐδεμιᾷ	οὐδενί
οὐδένα	οὐδεμίαν	οὐδέν

Cf. εἷς, § **39**.

---

[1] See § **2**.

222.   EXERCISES.

1. λέγει αὐτῷ Φίλιππος ἔρχου καὶ ἴδε.
2. μετανοεῖτε καὶ πιστεύετε ἐν τῷ εὐαγγελίῳ.
3. πορεύθητι πρὸς τὸν λαόν.   4. καλῶς ποιεῖτε
τοῖς μισοῦσιν ὑμᾶς.   5. ὁ δὲ Ἰησοῦς εἶπεν αὐτῷ τί[1]
με λέγεις ἀγαθόν; οὐδεὶς ἀγαθὸς εἰ[2] μὴ εἷς ὁ θεός.
6. οἱ δὲ πάλιν (again) ἔκραξαν Σταύρωσον αὐτόν.
7. ὁ ἔχων ὦτα[3] ἀκούειν ἀκουέτω.   8. ὁ θεὸς φῶς
ἐστι καὶ σκοτία οὐκ ἔστιν ἐν αὐτῷ οὐδεμία.[4] 9. ἔτι
πολλὰ ἔχω ὑμῖν λέγειν, ἀλλ' οὐ δύνασθε βαστάζειν.
10. πάντα δι' αὐτοῦ ἐγένετο, καὶ χωρὶς αὐτοῦ
ἐγένετο οὐδὲ ἕν.   11. μὴ κρίνετε ἵνα μὴ κριθῆτε.
12. ὁ πιστὸς ἐν ἐλαχίστῳ καὶ ἐν πολλῷ πιστός
ἐστιν, καὶ ὁ ἐν ἐλαχίστῳ ἄδικος καὶ ἐν πολλῷ
ἄδικός ἐστιν.   13. μὴ θαυμάζετε, ἀδελφοί, εἰ μισεῖ
ὑμᾶς ὁ κόσμος.

LESSON XXX.

ADJECTIVES IN -ον AND -εσ. — COMPARISON.

223.   VOCABULARY.

ἀληθής, *true.*
ἀσθενής, *weak, sick.*
ἄφρων, *foolish.*

γάμος, ὁ, *marriage, poly*GAMY.
δεσμός, ὁ, *chain, bond.*
διώκω, *persecute, pursue.*

---

[1] The neuter τί often has the sense of *why.*
[2] *If.*   [3] See irregular nouns, § 34.
[4] See § 142.

μονογενής, *only begotten.*
ὀλίγος, *few,* OLIGARchy.
περισσός, *abundant.*
πλήρης, *full.*
προσευχή, ἡ, *prayer.*

σκανδαλίζω, *cause to stumble,* SCANDALIZE.
τρέχω, *run.*
ὑγιής, *whole, healthy,* HYGIENE.

ὕψιστος, *highest.*

224. Learn the declension of ἀληθής, *true* (§ 35), with which compare γένος (§ 30). Observe that there are but two endings — the masc. and fem. being alike.

a. -εις of the acc. plur. is irregular.

See § 35 for the declension of ἄφρων.

225. Examine the following adjectives :

Positive.	Comparative.	Superlative.
1. ἰσχυρός, *strong.*	ἰσχυρό-τερος, *strong-er.*	(ἰσχυρό-τατος), *strong-est.*
2. ἀσθενής, *weak.*	ἀσθενέσ-τερος, *weak-er.*	(ἀσθενέσ-τατος), *weak-est.*
3. σοφός, *wise.*	σοφώ-τερος, *wise-r.*	(σοφώ-τατος), *wise-st.*
4. νέος, *young.*	νεώ-τερος, *young-er.*	(νεώ-τατος), *young-est.*

Observe: 1. That in all these examples something is *added* to make the degrees. -τερος = *r* or *er* and -τατος = *st* or *est.* 2. These are added directly to the stem. 3. When the penultimate vowel is short, as in **3** and **4**, the *o* of the stem becomes ω before -τερος and -τατος.

226. The suffixes may be -ιων (declined like ἄφρων) and -ιστος, but mostly in the irregular adjectives. See § **37**, 2, and learn the adjectives in § **38**.

227. Examine the following adverbs :

Positive.	Comparative.	Superlative.
κακῶς, *badly*.	χεῖρον	(——)
καλῶς, *well*.	κάλλιον	(κάλλιστα)
ταχέως, *quickly*.	τάχιον	(τάχιστα)

It is to be observed : 1. The positive of the adverb ends in ς. How different from the gen. plur. of the adj. ? 2. The comparative of the adverb is the neut. sing. acc. of the adjective. 3. The superlative of the adverb is the neut. plur. acc. of the superlative of the adjective.

228. Examine the following :

μείζονα ἀγάπην ταύτης οὐκ οἴδαμεν, *greater love than this we know not*.

Rule : *The comparative degree is followed by the genitive case.*

229.   EXERCISES.

1. οὗτος δέ ἐστιν πλήρης χάριτος καὶ ἀληθείας.
2. οἴδαμεν ὅτι ἀληθὴς εἶ. 3. ὁ δὲ ὀπίσω [1] μου

---

[1] *After.* Adverbs of position are followed by the genitive.

ἐρχόμενος ἰσχυρότερός μου ἐστίν. 4. ἄφρων,
ταύτῃ τῇ νυκτὶ τὴν ψυχήν σου αἰτοῦσι ἀπό σου.
5. οὐκ ἐστιν δοῦλος μείζων τοῦ κυρίου αὐτοῦ οὐδὲ
ἀπόστολος μείζων τοῦ πέμψαντος αὐτόν. 6. καὶ
δόξα ἐν ὑψίστοις. 7. εἰ ἐμὲ ἐδίωξάν, καὶ ὑμᾶς
διώξουσιν· εἰ τὸν λόγον μου ἐτήρησαν, καὶ τὸν
ὑμέτερον τηρήσουσιν, ἀλλὰ ταῦτα πάντα ποιή-
σουσιν εἰς ὑμᾶς διὰ τὸ ὀνομά μου, ὅτι οὐκ οἴδασιν
τὸν πέμψαντά με. 8. Σάββατόν ἐστι, καὶ οὐκ
ἔξεστίν σοι ἆραι τὸν κράβαττον (bed). ὃς δὲ
ἀπεκρίθη αὐτοῖς ὁ ποιήσας με ὑγιῆ ἐκεῖνός μοι
εἶπεν Ἄρον τὸν κράβαττόν σου καὶ περιπάτει.

LESSON XXXI.

REGULAR VERBS IN μι: δίδωμι, *give*.

230. Of the two conjugations in Greek (see
73) the verbs in -ω are by far the more common.
Still, those that have the older endings -μι, -ς,
etc., form a very substantial part of the ordinary
verbal forms ; *e.g.* ἀφίημι, *forgive;* δείκνυμι,
show; δίδωμι, *give;* εἰμί, *am;* ἵστημι, *set;*
ὄμνυμι, *swear;* τίθημι, *put, place;* φημί, *say.*
These words, it is easily seen, are naturally of
very common use. Hence they are among the
old verbs of the language, and may be called
strong verbs, having, as they do, the strong
endings.

231. The conjugation of these verbs differs from the conjugation of the verbs in -ω, in two systems only — the pres. and 2 aor. systems. In these two systems the verbs in μι have *no* variable vowel %, but the endings are added directly to the theme, § 85.

232. Learn the principal parts of δίδωμι (§ 88) and the pres. and 2 aor. systems, act., §§ 62 and 63. (The mid. and pass. of these systems are very rare.)

233. The most important compounds of δίδωμι are with the following prepositions, παρά, ἀπό, ἐπί.

234. Observe the following on the forms of the verbs in μι:

1. The old endings μι, etc., occur.
2. -ᾱσι ends the 3 per. plur. primary.
3. -σαν, and not ν, is found in the secondary tenses 3 per. plur.

235. Note the following in δίδωμι:

1. The present system has a reduplication, δι-.
2. ἐδίδουν like ἐφίλουν, § 59.
3. κα[1] occurs for σα in the aor. ind. act.

---

[1] Three verbs in Greek have this peculiarity in the aor. act. ind., ἀφίημι, aor. ἀφῆκα; δίδωμι, aor. ἔδωκα; τίθημι, aor. ἔθηκα.

4. For the contraction in the 2 aor. subjv., δόω, δόῃς, etc., see §§ **5**, 12, and **8**, 5.

5. δοῦναι, 2 aor. act. inf., is for δο-εναι.

236. Learn the principal parts of ἀφίημι (ἀπό + ἵημι, stem ἑ), *forgive*, § **88**, and the conjugation, § **66**.

237. The pluperf. act., which is a rare tense, has the suffix κει; and being a secondary tense, secondary endings occur. See § **77**, latter part.

238. Translate the forms of ἀφίημι and δίδωμι in §§ **96** and **101**.

LESSON XXXII.

REGULAR VERBS IN μι : ἵστημι, τίθημι.

239. Examine the following :

ἀφίημι (stem ἑ), ἀφ-ί-η-μι	δίδωμι (stem δο), δί-δω-μι
ἵστημι (stem στᾰ), ἵ-στη-μι	τίθημι (stem θε), τί-θη-μι

Observe that in all these verbs there is a reduplication, in which the vowel is ι. ἵστημι is for σί-στημι.

240. So likewise in some verbs in ω —

γι-(γ)νώ-σκω	γί(γ)νο-μαι
(γνο)	(γεν)

This form of reduplication has to do with the *present system only.*

241. Learn the principal parts and pres. and 2 aor. systems of ἵστημι and τίθημι, §§ **62** and **63**.

242. The most common compounds of ἵστημι are with ἀνά, κατά, ἐπί, ἐξ, σύν, ἀπό, ἀντί.

τίθημι is most common with ἐπί, παρά, and πρός.

243. Translate the forms in §§ **105** and **108**.

244.　　　IMPERSONAL VERBS.

δεῖ, *it is necessary*　　ἔξεστι, *it is lawful.*
δοκεῖ, *it seems (best).*　μέλει, *it concerns.*
　　μεταμέλει, *it repents one.*

τί με δεῖ ποιεῖν ; *what must I do?*
δεῖ ὑμᾶς γεννηθῆναι ἄνωθεν, *ye must be born from above.*

Observe that δεῖ takes the accusative and the infinitive.

SELECTIONS FOR TRANSLATION.

———◆———

FIRST EPISTLE OF JOHN.

Ὁ ΗΝ ΑΠ᾽ ΑΡΧΗΣ, ὃ ἀκηκόαμεν, ὃ 1
ἑωράκαμεν τοῖς ὀφθαλμοῖς ἡμῶν, ὃ ἐθεασάμεθα καὶ αἱ χεῖρες ἡμῶν ἐψηλάφησαν περὶ
τοῦ λόγου τῆς ζωῆς, — καὶ ἡ ζωὴ ἐφανε- 2
ρώθη, καὶ ἑωράκαμεν καὶ μαρτυροῦμεν καὶ
ἀπαγγέλλομεν ὑμῖν τὴν ζωὴν τὴν αἰώνιον
ἥτις ἦν πρὸς τὸν πατέρα καὶ ἐφανερώθη
ἡμῖν, — ὃ ἑωράκαμεν καὶ ἀκηκόαμεν ἀπαγ- 3
γέλλομεν καὶ ὑμῖν, ἵνα καὶ ὑμεῖς κοινωνίαν
ἔχητε μεθ᾽ ἡμῶν· καὶ ἡ κοινωνία δὲ ἡ ἡμε-
τέρα μετὰ τοῦ πατρὸς καὶ μετὰ τοῦ υἱοῦ
αὐτοῦ Ἰησοῦ Χριστοῦ· καὶ ταῦτα γράφομεν 4
ἡμεῖς ἵνα ἡ χαρὰ ἡμῶν[1] ᾖ πεπληρωμένη.

Καὶ ἔστιν αὕτη ἡ ἀγγελία ἣν ἀκηκόαμεν 5
ἀπ᾽ αὐτοῦ καὶ ἀναγγέλλομεν ὑμῖν, ὅτι ὁ
θεὸς φῶς ἐστὶν καὶ σκοτία οὐκ ἔστιν ἐν
αὐτῷ οὐδεμία.   Ἐὰν εἴπωμεν ὅτι κοι- 6

[1] ὑμῶν.

91

νωνίαν ἔχομεν μετ' αὐτοῦ καὶ ἐν τῷ σκότει
περιπατῶμεν, ψευδόμεθα καὶ οὐ ποιοῦμεν
7 τὴν ἀλήθειαν· ἐὰν δὲ ἐν τῷ φωτὶ περιπατῶμεν ὡς αὐτὸς ἔστιν ἐν τῷ φωτί, κοινωνίαν ἔχομεν μετ' ἀλλήλων καὶ τὸ αἷμα
Ἰησοῦ τοῦ υἱοῦ αὐτοῦ καθαρίζει ἡμᾶς ἀπὸ
8 πάσης ἁμαρτίας. Ἐὰν εἴπωμεν ὅτι ἁμαρτίαν οὐκ ἔχομεν, ἑαυτοὺς πλανῶμεν καὶ ἡ
9 ἀλήθεια οὐκ ἔστιν ἐν ἡμῖν. ἐὰν ὁμολογῶ-
μεν τὰς ἁμαρτίας ἡμῶν, πιστός ἐστιν καὶ
δίκαιος ἵνα ἀφῇ ἡμῖν τὰς ἁμαρτίας καὶ
10 καθαρίσῃ ἡμᾶς ἀπὸ πάσης ἀδικίας. Ἐὰν
εἴπωμεν ὅτι οὐχ ἡμαρτήκαμεν, ψεύστην
ποιοῦμεν αὐτὸν καὶ ὁ λόγος αὐτοῦ οὐκ
1 ἔστιν ἐν ἡμῖν.   Τεκνία μου, ταῦτα
γράφω ὑμῖν ἵνα μὴ ἁμάρτητε. καὶ ἐάν
τις ἁμάρτῃ, παράκλητον ἔχομεν πρὸς τὸν
2 πατέρα Ἰησοῦν Χριστὸν δίκαιον, καὶ αὐτὸς
ἱλασμός ἐστιν περὶ τῶν ἁμαρτιῶν ἡμῶν, οὐ
περὶ τῶν ἡμετέρων δὲ μόνον[1] ἀλλὰ καὶ περὶ
3 ὅλου τοῦ κόσμου. Καὶ ἐν τούτῳ γινώσκομεν ὅτι ἐγνώκαμεν αὐτόν, ἐὰν τὰς ἐντολὰς
4 αὐτοῦ τηρῶμεν. ὁ λέγων ὅτι Ἔγνωκα αὐτὸν καὶ τὰς ἐντολὰς αὐτοῦ μὴ τηρῶν ψεύ-

[1] μόνων.

στης ἐστίν, καὶ ἐν τούτῳ ἡ ἀλήθεια οὐκ
ἔστιν· ὃς δ' ἂν τηρῇ αὐτοῦ τὸν λόγον, ἀλη- 5
θῶς ἐν τούτῳ ἡ ἀγάπη τοῦ θεοῦ τετελείωται.
Ἐν τούτῳ γινώσκομεν ὅτι ἐν αὐτῷ ἐσμέν·
ὁ λέγων ἐν αὐτῷ μένειν ὀφείλει καθὼς ἐκεῖ- 6
νος περιεπάτησεν καὶ αὐτὸς περιπατεῖν.

Ἀγαπητοί, οὐκ ἐντολὴν καινὴν γράφω 7
ὑμῖν, ἀλλ' ἐντολὴν παλαιὰν ἣν εἴχετε ἀπ'
ἀρχῆς· ἡ ἐντολὴ ἡ παλαιά ἐστιν ὁ λόγος
ὃν ἠκούσατε. πάλιν ἐντολὴν καινὴν γράφω 8
ὑμῖν, ὅ ἐστιν ἀληθὲς ἐν αὐτῷ καὶ ἐν ὑμῖν,
ὅτι ἡ σκοτία παράγεται καὶ τὸ φῶς τὸ
ἀληθινὸν ἤδη φαίνει.   Ὁ λέγων ἐν τῷ 9
φωτὶ εἶναι καὶ τὸν ἀδελφὸν αὐτοῦ μισῶν ἐν
τῇ σκοτίᾳ ἐστὶν ἕως ἄρτι. ὁ ἀγαπῶν τὸν 10
ἀδελφὸν αὐτοῦ ἐν τῷ φωτὶ μένει, καὶ σκάνδαλον ἐν αὐτῷ οὐκ ἔστιν·[1] ὁ δὲ μισῶν 11
τὸν ἀδελφὸν αὐτοῦ ἐν τῇ σκοτίᾳ ἐστὶν καὶ
ἐν τῇ σκοτίᾳ περιπατεῖ, καὶ οὐκ οἶδεν ποῦ
ὑπάγει, ὅτι ἡ σκοτία ἐτύφλωσεν τοὺς ὀφθαλμοὺς αὐτοῦ.   Γράφω ὑμῖν, τεκνία, ὅτι 12
ἀφέωνται ὑμῖν αἱ ἁμαρτίαι διὰ τὸ ὄνομα
αὐτοῦ· γράφω ὑμῖν, πατέρες, ὅτι ἐγνώκατε 13
τὸν ἀπ' ἀρχῆς· γράφω ὑμῖν, νεανίσκοι, ὅτι

[1] οὐκ ἔστιν ἐν αὐτῷ.

14 νενικήκατε τὸν πονηρόν. ἔγραψα ὑμῖν,
παιδία, ὅτι ἐγνώκατε τὸν πατέρα· ἔγραψα
ὑμῖν, πατέρες, ὅτι ἐγνώκατε τὸν ἀπ᾽ ἀρχῆς·
ἔγραψα ὑμῖν, νεανίσκοι, ὅτι ἰσχυροί ἐστε
καὶ ὁ λόγος [τοῦ θεοῦ] ἐν ὑμῖν μένει καὶ
15 νενικήκατε τὸν πονηρόν.   Μὴ ἀγαπᾶτε τὸν
κόσμον μηδὲ τὰ ἐν τῷ κόσμῳ. ἐάν τις
ἀγαπᾷ τὸν κόσμον, οὐκ ἔστιν ἡ ἀγάπη τοῦ
16 πατρὸς ἐν αὐτῷ· ὅτι πᾶν τὸ ἐν τῷ κόσμῳ,
ἡ ἐπιθυμία τῆς σαρκὸς καὶ ἡ ἐπιθυμία τῶν
ὀφθαλμῶν καὶ ἡ ἀλαζονία τοῦ βίου, οὐκ
ἔστιν ἐκ τοῦ πατρός, ἀλλὰ ἐκ τοῦ κόσμου
17 ἐστίν· καὶ ὁ κόσμος παράγεται καὶ ἡ ἐπιθυμία [αὐτοῦ], ὁ δὲ ποιῶν τὸ θέλημα τοῦ
θεοῦ μένει εἰς τὸν αἰῶνα.

18   Παιδία, ἐσχάτη ὥρα ἐστίν, καὶ καθὼς
ἠκούσατε ὅτι ἀντίχριστος ἔρχεται, καὶ νῦν
ἀντίχριστοι πολλοὶ γεγόνασιν· ὅθεν γινώ-
19 σκομεν ὅτι ἐσχάτη ὥρα ἐστίν. ἐξ ἡμῶν
ἐξῆλθαν, ἀλλ᾽ οὐκ ἦσαν ἐξ ἡμῶν· εἰ γὰρ
ἐξ ἡμῶν ἦσαν, μεμενήκεισαν ἂν μεθ᾽ ἡμῶν·
ἀλλ᾽ ἵνα φανερωθῶσιν ὅτι οὐκ εἰσὶν πάντες
20 ἐξ ἡμῶν.   καὶ ὑμεῖς χρίσμα ἔχετε ἀπὸ τοῦ
21 ἁγίου· οἴδατε πάντες——[1] οὐκ ἔγραψα ὑμῖν

----

[1] καὶ οἴδατε πάντα.

ὅτι οὐκ οἴδατε τὴν ἀλήθειαν, ἀλλ' ὅτι οἴδατε
αὐτήν, καὶ ὅτι πᾶν ψεῦδος ἐκ τῆς ἀληθείας
οὐκ ἔστιν.   Τίς ἐστιν ὁ ψεύστης εἰ μὴ 22
ὁ ἀρνούμενος ὅτι Ἰησοῦς οὐκ ἔστιν ὁ χριστός; οὗτός ἐστιν ὁ ἀντίχριστος, ὁ ἀρνούμενος τὸν πατέρα καὶ τὸν υἱόν. πᾶς ὁ 23
ἀρνούμενος τὸν υἱὸν οὐδὲ τὸν πατέρα ἔχει·
ὁ ὁμολογῶν τὸν υἱὸν καὶ τὸν πατέρα ἔχει.
Ὑμεῖς ὃ ἠκούσατε ἀπ' ἀρχῆς, ἐν ὑμῖν με-
νέτω· ἐὰν ἐν ὑμῖν μείνῃ ὃ ἀπ' ἀρχῆς ἠκού- 24
σατε, καὶ ὑμεῖς ἐν τῷ υἱῷ καὶ [ἐν] τῷ
πατρὶ μενεῖτε. καὶ αὕτη ἐστὶν ἡ ἐπαγγε- 25
λία ἣν αὐτὸς ἐπηγγείλατο ἡμῖν, τὴν ζωὴν
τὴν αἰώνιον.   Ταῦτα ἔγραψα ὑμῖν περὶ 26
τῶν πλανώντων ὑμᾶς. καὶ ὑμεῖς τὸ χρίσμα 27
ὃ ἐλάβετε ἀπ' αὐτοῦ μένει ἐν ὑμῖν, καὶ οὐ
χρείαν ἔχετε ἵνα τις διδάσκῃ ὑμᾶς· ἀλλ'
ὡς τὸ αὐτοῦ χρίσμα διδάσκει ὑμᾶς περὶ
πάντων, καὶ ἀληθές ἐστιν καὶ οὐκ ἔστιν
ψεῦδος,[1] καὶ καθὼς ἐδίδαξεν ὑμᾶς, μένετε
ἐν αὐτῷ. Καὶ νῦν, τεκνία, μένετε ἐν αὐτῷ, 28
ἵνα ἐὰν φανερωθῇ σχῶμεν παρρησίαν καὶ
μὴ αἰσχυνθῶμεν ἀπ' αὐτοῦ ἐν τῇ παρουσίᾳ
αὐτοῦ. ἐὰν εἰδῆτε ὅτι δίκαιός ἐστιν, γινώ- 29

----

[1] ὑμᾶς, ἀλλὰ τὸ . . . ψεῦδος·

σκετε ὅτι[1] πᾶς ὁ ποιῶν τὴν δικαιοσύνην ἐξ
αὐτοῦ γεγέννηται.

1   Ἴδετε ποταπὴν ἀγάπην δέδωκεν ἡμῖν ὁ
πατὴρ ἵνα τέκνα θεοῦ κληθῶμεν, καί ἐσμεν.
διὰ τοῦτο ὁ κόσμος οὐ γινώσκει ἡμᾶς ὅτι
2   οὐκ ἔγνω αὐτόν. Ἀγαπητοί, νῦν τέκνα θεοῦ
ἐσμέν, καὶ οὔπω ἐφανερώθη τί ἐσόμεθα.
οἴδαμεν ὅτι ἐὰν φανερωθῇ ὅμοιοι αὐτῷ ἐσό-
3   μεθα, ὅτι ὀψόμεθα αὐτὸν καθώς ἐστιν. καὶ
πᾶς ὁ ἔχων τὴν ἐλπίδα ταύτην ἐπ᾽ αὐτῷ
ἁγνίζει ἑαυτὸν καθὼς ἐκεῖνος ἁγνός ἐστιν.
4   Πᾶς ὁ ποιῶν τὴν ἁμαρτίαν καὶ τὴν ἀνομίαν
5   ποιεῖ, καὶ ἡ ἁμαρτία ἐστὶν ἡ ἀνομία. καὶ
οἴδατε ὅτι ἐκεῖνος ἐφανερώθη ἵνα τὰς ἁμαρτίας ἄρῃ, καὶ ἁμαρτία ἐν αὐτῷ οὐκ ἔστιν.
6   πᾶς ὁ ἐν αὐτῷ μένων οὐχ ἁμαρτάνει· πᾶς
ὁ ἁμαρτάνων οὐχ ἑώρακεν αὐτὸν οὐδὲ ἔγνω-
7   κεν αὐτόν. Τεκνία, μηδεὶς πλανάτω ὑμᾶς·
ὁ ποιῶν τὴν δικαιοσύνην δίκαιός ἐστιν,
8   καθὼς ἐκεῖνος δίκαιός ἐστιν· ὁ ποιῶν τὴν
ἁμαρτίαν ἐκ τοῦ διαβόλου ἐστίν, ὅτι ἀπ᾽
ἀρχῆς ὁ διάβολος ἁμαρτάνει. εἰς τοῦτο
ἐφανερώθη ὁ υἱὸς τοῦ θεοῦ ἵνα λύσῃ τὰ
9   ἔργα τοῦ διαβόλου.   Πᾶς ὁ γεγεννη-

---

[1] καί.

μένος ἐκ τοῦ θεοῦ ἁμαρτίαν οὐ ποιεῖ, ὅτι
σπέρμα αὐτοῦ ἐν αὐτῷ μένει, καὶ οὐ δύναται ἁμαρτάνειν, ὅτι ἐκ τοῦ θεοῦ γεγέννηται.
ἐν τούτῳ φανερά ἐστιν τὰ τέκνα τοῦ θεοῦ 10
καὶ τὰ τέκνα τοῦ διαβόλου· πᾶς ὁ μὴ
ποιῶν δικαιοσύνην οὐκ ἔστιν ἐκ τοῦ θεοῦ,
καὶ ὁ μὴ ἀγαπῶν τὸν ἀδελφὸν αὐτοῦ. ὅτι 11
αὕτη ἐστὶν ἡ ἀγγελία ἣν ἠκούσατε ἀπ’
ἀρχῆς, ἵνα ἀγαπῶμεν ἀλλήλους· οὐ καθὼς 12
Καὶν ἐκ τοῦ πονηροῦ ἦν καὶ ἔσφαξεν τὸν
ἀδελφὸν αὐτοῦ· καὶ χάριν τίνος ἔσφαξεν
αὐτόν; ὅτι τὰ ἔργα αὐτοῦ πονηρὰ ἦν, τὰ
δὲ τοῦ ἀδελφοῦ αὐτοῦ δίκαια.

Μὴ θαυμάζετε, ἀδελφοί, εἰ μισεῖ ὑμᾶς ὁ 13
κόσμος.   ἡμεῖς οἴδαμεν ὅτι μεταβεβήκα- 14
μεν ἐκ τοῦ θανάτου εἰς τὴν ζωήν, ὅτι ἀγαπῶμεν τοὺς ἀδελφούς· ὁ μὴ ἀγαπῶν μένει
ἐν τῷ θανάτῳ. πᾶς ὁ μισῶν τὸν ἀδελφὸν 15
αὐτοῦ ἀνθρωποκτόνος ἐστίν, καὶ οἴδατε ὅτι
πᾶς ἀνθρωποκτόνος οὐκ ἔχει ζωὴν αἰώνιον
ἐν αὐτῷ μένουσαν.   Ἐν τούτῳ ἐγνώκα- 16
μεν τὴν ἀγάπην, ὅτι ἐκεῖνος ὑπὲρ ἡμῶν τὴν
ψυχὴν αὐτοῦ ἔθηκεν· καὶ ἡμεῖς ὀφείλομεν
ὑπὲρ τῶν ἀδελφῶν τὰς ψυχὰς θεῖναι. ὃς 17
δ’ ἂν ἔχῃ τὸν βίον τοῦ κόσμου καὶ θεωρῇ

H

τὸν ἀδελφὸν αὐτοῦ χρείαν ἔχοντα καὶ
κλείσῃ τὰ σπλάγχνα αὐτοῦ ἀπ' αὐτοῦ,
πῶς ἡ ἀγάπη τοῦ θεοῦ μένει ἐν αὐτῷ;

18 Τεκνία, μὴ ἀγαπῶμεν λόγῳ μηδὲ τῇ
γλώσσῃ ἀλλὰ ἐν ἔργῳ καὶ ἀληθείᾳ.

19 Ἐν τούτῳ γνωσόμεθα ὅτι ἐκ τῆς ἀληθείας
ἐσμέν, καὶ ἔμπροσθεν αὐτοῦ πείσομεν τὴν

20 καρδίαν ἡμῶν ὅτι ἐὰν καταγινώσκῃ ἡμῶν
ἡ καρδία, ὅτι μείζων ἐστὶν ὁ θεὸς τῆς

21 καρδίας ἡμῶν καὶ γινώσκει πάντα. Ἀγαπητοί, ἐὰν ἡ καρδία μὴ καταγινώσκῃ, παρ-

22 ρησίαν ἔχομεν πρὸς τὸν θεόν, καὶ ὃ ἂν
αἰτῶμεν λαμβάνομεν ἀπ' αὐτοῦ, ὅτι τὰς
ἐντολὰς αὐτοῦ τηροῦμεν καὶ τὰ ἀρεστὰ

23 ἐνώπιον αὐτοῦ ποιοῦμεν. καὶ αὕτη ἐστὶν
ἡ ἐντολὴ αὐτοῦ, ἵνα πιστεύσωμεν[1] τῷ ὀνόματι τοῦ υἱοῦ αὐτοῦ Ἰησοῦ Χριστοῦ καὶ
ἀγαπῶμεν ἀλλήλους, καθὼς ἔδωκεν ἐντολὴν

24 ἡμῖν. καὶ ὁ τηρῶν τὰς ἐντολὰς αὐτοῦ ἐν
αὐτῷ μένει καὶ αὐτὸς ἐν αὐτῷ· καὶ ἐν
τούτῳ γινώσκομεν ὅτι μένει ἐν ἡμῖν, ἐκ τοῦ
πνεύματος οὗ ἡμῖν ἔδωκεν.

1 Ἀγαπητοί, μὴ παντὶ πνεύματι πιστεύετε,
ἀλλὰ δοκιμάζετε τὰ πνεύματα εἰ ἐκ τοῦ

1 πιστεύωμεν.

θεοῦ ἐστίν, ὅτι πολλοὶ ψευδοπροφῆται ἐξεληλύθασιν εἰς τὸν κόσμον.   Ἐν τούτῳ 2
γινώσκετε τὸ πνεῦμα τοῦ θεοῦ· πᾶν πνεῦμα
ὃ ὁμολογεῖ Ἰησοῦν Χριστὸν ἐν σαρκὶ ἐληλυθότα[1] ἐκ τοῦ θεοῦ ἐστι, καὶ πᾶν πνεῦμα 3
ὃ μὴ ὁμολογεῖ[2] τὸν Ἰησοῦν ἐκ τοῦ θεοῦ
οὐκ ἔστιν· καὶ τοῦτό ἐστι τὸ τοῦ ἀντιχρίστου, ὃ ἀκηκόατε ὅτι ἔρχεται, καὶ νῦν
ἐν τῷ κόσμῳ ἐστὶν ἤδη.   Ὑμεῖς ἐκ 4
τοῦ θεοῦ ἐστέ, τεκνία, καὶ νενικήκατε αὐτούς, ὅτι μείζων ἐστὶν ὁ ἐν ὑμῖν ἢ ὁ ἐν τῷ
κόσμῳ· αὐτοὶ ἐκ τοῦ κόσμου εἰσίν· διὰ 5
τοῦτο ἐκ τοῦ κόσμου λαλοῦσιν καὶ ὁ κόσμος
αὐτῶν ἀκούει. ἡμεῖς ἐκ τοῦ θεοῦ ἐσμέν· 6
ὁ γινώσκων τὸν θεὸν ἀκούει ἡμῶν, ὃς οὐκ
ἔστιν ἐκ τοῦ θεοῦ οὐκ ἀκούει ἡμῶν. ἐκ
τούτου γινώσκομεν τὸ πνεῦμα τῆς ἀληθείας καὶ τὸ πνεῦμα τῆς πλάνης.

Ἀγαπητοί, ἀγαπῶμεν ἀλλήλους, ὅτι ἡ 7
ἀγάπη ἐκ τοῦ θεοῦ ἐστιν, καὶ πᾶς ὁ ἀγαπῶν
ἐκ τοῦ θεοῦ γεγέννηται καὶ γινώσκει τὸν
θεόν. ὁ μὴ ἀγαπῶν οὐκ ἔγνω τὸν θεόν, 8
ὅτι ὁ θεὸς ἀγάπη ἐστίν. ἐν τούτῳ ἐφανε- 9
ρώθη ἡ ἀγάπη τοῦ θεοῦ ἐν ἡμῖν, ὅτι τὸν

---

[1] ἐληλυθέναι.   [2] λύει.

υἱὸν αὐτοῦ τὸν μονογενῆ ἀπέσταλκεν ὁ
θεὸς εἰς τὸν κόσμον ἵνα ζήσωμεν δι᾿ αὐτοῦ.
10 ἐν τούτῳ ἐστὶν ἡ ἀγάπη, οὐχ ὅτι ἡμεῖς ἠγαπήκαμεν τὸν θεόν, ἀλλ᾿ ὅτι αὐτὸς ἠγάπησεν
ἡμᾶς καὶ ἀπέστειλεν τὸν υἱὸν αὐτοῦ ἱλασμὸν
11 περὶ τῶν ἁμαρτιῶν ἡμῶν.   Ἀγαπητοί,
εἰ οὕτως ὁ θεὸς ἠγάπησεν ἡμᾶς, καὶ ἡμεῖς
12 ὀφείλομεν ἀλλήλους ἀγαπᾶν.   θεὸν οὐδεὶς
πώποτε τεθέαται· ἐὰν ἀγαπῶμεν ἀλλήλους,
ὁ θεὸς ἐν ἡμῖν μένει καὶ ἡ ἀγάπη αὐτοῦ
13 τετελειωμένη ἐν ἡμῖν ἐστίν. ἐν τούτῳ γινώσκομεν ὅτι ἐν αὐτῷ μένομεν καὶ αὐτὸς ἐν
ἡμῖν, ὅτι ἐκ τοῦ πνεύματος αὐτοῦ δέδωκεν
14 ἡμῖν.   Καὶ ἡμεῖς τεθεάμεθα καὶ μαρτυροῦμεν ὅτι ὁ πατὴρ ἀπέσταλκεν τὸν υἱὸν σω-
15 τῆρα τοῦ κόσμου.   ὃς ἐὰν ὁμολογήσῃ ὅτι
Ἰησοῦς [Χριστός] ἐστιν ὁ υἱὸς τοῦ θεοῦ,
ὁ θεὸς ἐν αὐτῷ μένει καὶ αὐτὸς ἐν τῷ θεῷ.
16 Καὶ ἡμεῖς ἐγνώκαμεν καὶ πεπιστεύκαμεν
τὴν ἀγάπην ἣν ἔχει ὁ θεὸς ἐν ἡμῖν.   Ὁ
θεὸς ἀγάπη ἐστίν, καὶ ὁ μένων ἐν τῇ ἀγάπῃ
ἐν τῷ θεῷ μένει καὶ ὁ θεὸς ἐν αὐτῷ [μένει].
17 Ἐν τούτῳ τετελείωται ἡ ἀγάπη μεθ᾿ ἡμῶν,
ἵνα παρρησίαν ἔχωμεν ἐν τῇ ἡμέρᾳ τῆς
κρίσεως, ὅτι καθὼς ἐκεῖνός ἐστιν καὶ ἡμεῖς

ἐσμὲν ἐν τῷ κόσμῳ τούτῳ. φόβος οὐκ 18
ἔστιν ἐν τῇ ἀγάπῃ, ἀλλ᾽ ἡ τελεία ἀγάπη
ἔξω βάλλει τὸν φόβον, ὅτι ὁ φόβος κόλα-
σιν ἔχει, ὁ δὲ φοβούμενος οὐ τετελείωται
ἐν τῇ ἀγάπῃ. Ἡμεῖς ἀγαπῶμεν, ὅτι αὐτὸς 19
πρῶτος ἠγάπησεν ἡμᾶς. ἐάν τις εἴπῃ ὅτι 20
Ἀγαπῶ τὸν θεόν, καὶ τὸν ἀδελφὸν αὐτοῦ
μισῇ, ψεύστης ἐστίν· ὁ γὰρ μὴ ἀγαπῶν
τὸν ἀδελφὸν αὐτοῦ ὃν ἑώρακεν, τὸν θεὸν ὃν
οὐχ ἑώρακεν οὐ δύναται ἀγαπᾶν. καὶ ταύ- 21
την τὴν ἐντολὴν ἔχομεν ἀπ᾽ αὐτοῦ, ἵνα ὁ
ἀγαπῶν τὸν θεὸν ἀγαπᾷ καὶ τὸν ἀδελφὸν
αὐτοῦ.

Πᾶς ὁ πιστεύων ὅτι Ἰησοῦς ἐστὶν ὁ 1
χριστὸς ἐκ τοῦ θεοῦ γεγέννηται, καὶ πᾶς
ὁ ἀγαπῶν τὸν γεννήσαντα ἀγαπᾷ τὸν
γεγεννημένον ἐξ αὐτοῦ. ἐν τούτῳ γινώ- 2
σκομεν ὅτι ἀγαπῶμεν τὰ τέκνα τοῦ θεοῦ,
ὅταν τὸν θεὸν ἀγαπῶμεν καὶ τὰς ἐντολὰς
αὐτοῦ ποιῶμεν· αὕτη γάρ ἐστιν ἡ ἀγάπη 3
τοῦ θεοῦ ἵνα τὰς ἐντολὰς αὐτοῦ τηρῶμεν,
καὶ αἱ ἐντολαὶ αὐτοῦ βαρεῖαι οὐκ εἰσίν,
ὅτι πᾶν τὸ γεγεννημένον ἐκ τοῦ θεοῦ νικᾷ 4
τὸν κόσμον. καὶ αὕτη ἐστὶν ἡ νίκη ἡ
νικήσασα τὸν κόσμον, ἡ πίστις ἡμῶν· τίς 5

ἐστιν [δὲ] ὁ νικῶν τὸν κόσμον εἰ μὴ ὁ
πιστεύων ὅτι Ἰησοῦς ἐστιν ὁ υἱὸς τοῦ
6 θεοῦ ;   Οὗτός ἐστιν ὁ ἐλθὼν δι᾽ ὕδατος
καὶ αἵματος, Ἰησοῦς Χριστός· οὐκ ἐν τῷ
ὕδατι μόνον¹ ἀλλ᾽ ἐν τῷ ὕδατι καὶ ἐν τῷ
αἵματι· καὶ τὸ πνεῦμά ἐστι τὸ μαρτυροῦν
7 ὅτι τὸ πνεῦμά ἐστιν ἡ ἀλήθεια.   ὅτι τρεῖς
8 εἰσὶν οἱ μαρτυροῦντες, τὸ πνεῦμα καὶ τὸ
ὕδωρ καὶ τὸ αἷμα, καὶ οἱ τρεῖς εἰς τὸ ἕν
9 εἰσιν.   εἰ τὴν μαρτυρίαν τῶν ἀνθρώπων
λαμβάνομεν, ἡ μαρτυρία τοῦ θεοῦ μείζων
ἐστίν, ὅτι αὕτη ἐστὶν ἡ μαρτυρία τοῦ θεοῦ
10 ὅτι μεμαρτύρηκεν περὶ τοῦ υἱοῦ αὐτοῦ.   ὁ
πιστεύων εἰς τὸν υἱὸν τοῦ θεοῦ ἔχει τὴν
μαρτυρίαν ἐν αὐτῷ²· ὁ μὴ πιστεύων τῷ
θεῷ² ψεύστην πεποίηκεν αὐτόν, ὅτι οὐ πεπίστευκεν εἰς τὴν μαρτυρίαν ἣν μεμαρτύρη-
11 κεν ὁ θεὸς περὶ τοῦ υἱοῦ αὐτοῦ.   καὶ αὕτη
ἐστὶν ἡ μαρτυρία, ὅτι ζωὴν αἰώνιον ἔδωκεν
ὁ θεὸς ἡμῖν, καὶ αὕτη ἡ ζωὴ ἐν τῷ υἱῷ
12 αὐτοῦ ἐστίν.   ὁ ἔχων τὸν υἱὸν ἔχει τὴν
ζωήν· ὁ μὴ ἔχων τὸν υἱὸν τοῦ θεοῦ τὴν
13 ζωὴν οὐκ ἔχει.   Ταῦτα ἔγραψα ὑμῖν
ἵνα εἰδῆτε ὅτι ζωὴν ἔχετε αἰώνιον, τοῖς

¹ μόνῳ.   ² αὐτῷ | †...†

πιστεύουσιν εἰς τὸ ὄνομα τοῦ υἱοῦ τοῦ
θεοῦ. καὶ αὕτη ἐστὶν ἡ παρρησία ἣν ἔχο- 14
μεν πρὸς αὐτόν, ὅτι ἐάν τι αἰτώμεθα κατὰ
τὸ θέλημα αὐτοῦ ἀκούει ἡμῶν. καὶ ἐὰν 15
οἴδαμεν ὅτι ἀκούει ἡμῶν ὃ ἐὰν αἰτώμεθα,
οἴδαμεν ὅτι ἔχομεν τὰ αἰτήματα ἃ ᾐτήκαμεν ἀπ᾽ αὐτοῦ. Ἐάν τις ἴδῃ τὸν ἀδελφὸν 16
αὐτοῦ ἁμαρτάνοντα ἁμαρτίαν μὴ πρὸς θάνατον, αἰτήσει, καὶ δώσει αὐτῷ ζωήν, τοῖς
ἁμαρτάνουσιν μὴ πρὸς θάνατον. ἔστιν
ἁμαρτία πρὸς θάνατον· οὐ περὶ ἐκείνης
λέγω ἵνα ἐρωτήσῃ. πᾶσα ἀδικία ἁμαρτία 17
ἐστίν, καὶ ἔστιν ἁμαρτία οὐ πρὸς θάνατον.
Οἴδαμεν ὅτι πᾶς ὁ γεγεννημένος ἐκ τοῦ 18
θεοῦ οὐχ ἁμαρτάνει, ἀλλ᾽ ὁ γεννηθεὶς ἐκ
τοῦ θεοῦ τηρεῖ αὐτόν, καὶ ὁ πονηρὸς οὐχ
ἅπτεται αὐτοῦ. οἴδαμεν ὅτι ἐκ τοῦ θεοῦ 19
ἐσμέν, καὶ ὁ κόσμος ὅλος ἐν τῷ πονηρῷ
κεῖται. οἴδαμεν δὲ ὅτι ὁ υἱὸς τοῦ θεοῦ 20
ἥκει, καὶ δέδωκεν ἡμῖν διάνοιαν ἵνα γινώσκομεν τὸν ἀληθινόν· καί ἐσμεν ἐν τῷ
ἀληθινῷ, ἐν τῷ υἱῷ αὐτοῦ Ἰησοῦ Χριστῷ.
οὗτός ἐστιν ὁ ἀληθινὸς θεὸς καὶ ζωὴ αἰώνιος. Τεκνία, (φυλάξατε) ἑαυτὰ ἀπὸ τῶν 21
εἰδώλων. military term.

MAT. 5 : 3–12.

3 Μακαριοι οἱ πτωχοὶ τῷ πνεύματι, ὅτι αὐτῶν
ἐστὶν ἡ βασιλεία τῶν οὐρανῶν.

4 μακάριοι οἱ πενθοῦντες, ὅτι αὐτοὶ παρακληθήσονται.

5 μακάριοι οἱ πραεῖς, ὅτι αὐτοὶ κληρονομήσουσι
τὴν γῆν.

6 μακάριοι οἱ πεινῶντες καὶ διψῶντες τὴν
δικαιοσύνην, ὅτι αὐτοὶ χορτασθήσον-
ται.

7 μακάριοι οἱ ἐλεήμονες, ὅτι αὐτοὶ ἐλεηθή-
σονται.

8 μακάριοι οἱ καθαροὶ τῇ καρδίᾳ, ὅτι αὐτοὶ
τὸν θεὸν ὄψονται.

9 μακάριοι οἱ εἰρηνοποιοί, ὅτι [αὐτοὶ] υἱοὶ
θεοῦ κληθήσονται.

10 μακάριοι οἱ δεδιωγμένοι ἕνεκεν δικαιοσύ-
νης, ὅτι αὐτῶν ἐστὶν ἡ βασιλεία τῶν
οὐρανῶν·

11 μακάριοί ἐστε ὅταν ὀνειδίσωσιν ὑμᾶς καὶ
διώξωσιν καὶ εἴπωσιν πᾶν πονηρὸν καθ᾽

12 ὑμῶν ψευδόμενοι ἕνεκεν ἐμοῦ· χαίρετε
καὶ ἀγαλλιᾶσθε, ὅτι ὁ μισθὸς ὑμῶν
πολὺς ἐν τοῖς οὐρανοῖς· οὕτως γὰρ ἐδίω-
ξαν τοὺς προφήτας τοὺς πρὸ ὑμῶν.

MAT. 6:9–15.

Οὕτως οὖν προσεύχεσθε ὑμεῖς   9

Πάτερ ἡμῶν ὁ ἐν τοῖς οὐρανοῖς·
Ἁγιασθήτω τὸ ὄνομά σου
ἐλθάτω ἡ βασιλεία σου,   10
γενηθήτω τὸ θέλημά σου,
   ὡς ἐν οὐρανῷ καὶ ἐπὶ γῆς·
Τὸν ἄρτον ἡμῶν τὸν ἐπιούσιον   11
   δὸς ἡμῖν σήμερον·
καὶ ἄφες ἡμῖν τὰ ὀφειλήματα ἡμῶν,   12
   ὡς καὶ ἡμεῖς ἀφήκαμεν τοῖς ὀφειλέταις
     ἡμῶν·
καὶ μὴ εἰσενέγκῃς ἡμᾶς εἰς πειρασμόν,   13
   ἀλλὰ ῥῦσαι ἡμᾶς ἀπὸ τοῦ πονηροῦ.

Ἐὰν γὰρ ἀφῆτε τοῖς ἀνθρώποις τὰ παρα- 14
πτώματα αὐτῶν, ἀφήσει καὶ ὑμῖν ὁ πατὴρ
ὑμῶν ὁ οὐράνιος· ἐὰν δὲ μὴ ἀφῆτε τοῖς 15
ἀνθρώποις [τὰ παραπτώματα αὐτῶν], οὐδὲ
ὁ πατὴρ ὑμῶν ἀφήσει τὰ παραπτώματα
ὑμῶν.

LUKE: CHAPTER 15.

Ἦσαν δὲ αὐτῷ ἐγγίζοντες πάντες οἱ 1
τελῶναι καὶ οἱ ἁμαρτωλοὶ ἀκούειν αὐτοῦ.
καὶ διεγόγγυζον οἵ τε Φαρισαῖοι καὶ οἱ 2

γραμματεῖς λέγοντες ὅτι Οὗτος ἁμαρτω-
λοὺς προσδέχεται καὶ συνεσθίει αὐτοῖς.
3 εἶπεν δὲ πρὸς αὐτοὺς τὴν παραβολὴν ταύ-
4 την λέγων Τίς ἄνθρωπος ἐξ ὑμῶν ἔχων
ἑκατὸν πρόβατα καὶ ἀπολέσας ἐξ αὐτῶν ἓν
οὐ καταλείπει τὰ ἐνενήκοντα ἐννέα ἐν τῇ
ἐρήμῳ καὶ πορεύεται ἐπὶ τὸ ἀπολωλὸς ἕως
5 εὕρῃ αὐτό; καὶ εὑρὼν ἐπιτίθησιν ἐπὶ τοὺς
6 ὤμους αὐτοῦ χαίρων, καὶ ἐλθὼν εἰς τὸν οἶκον
συνκαλεῖ τοὺς φίλους καὶ τοὺς γείτονας,
λέγων αὐτοῖς Συνχάρητέ μοι ὅτι εὗρον τὸ
7 πρόβατόν μου τὸ ἀπολωλός. λέγω ὑμῖν
ὅτι οὕτως χαρὰ ἐν τῷ οὐρανῷ ἔσται ἐπὶ
ἑνὶ ἁμαρτωλῷ μετανοοῦντι ἢ ἐπὶ ἐνενήκοντα ἐννέα δικαίοις οἵτινες οὐ χρείαν
8 ἔχουσιν μετανοίας. Ἢ τίς γυνὴ δραχμὰς
ἔχουσα δέκα, ἐὰν ἀπολέσῃ δραχμὴν μίαν,
οὐχὶ ἅπτει λύχνον καὶ σαροῖ τὴν οἰκίαν
9 καὶ ζητεῖ ἐπιμελῶς ἕως οὗ εὕρῃ; καὶ
εὑροῦσα συνκαλεῖ τὰς φίλας καὶ γείτονας
λέγουσα Συνχάρητέ μοι ὅτι εὗρον τὴν
10 δραχμὴν ἣν ἀπώλεσα. οὕτως, λέγω ὑμῖν,
γίνεται χαρὰ ἐνώπιον τῶν ἀγγέλων τοῦ θεοῦ
11 ἐπὶ ἑνὶ ἁμαρτωλῷ μετανοοῦντι.   Εἶπεν
12 δὲ Ἄνθρωπός τις εἶχεν δύο υἱούς. καὶ εἶπεν

ὁ νεώτερος αὐτῶν τῷ πατρί Πάτερ, δός μοι
τὸ ἐπιβάλλον μέρος τῆς οὐσίας· ὁ δὲ διεῖλεν αὐτοῖς τὸν βίον. καὶ μετ᾽ οὐ πολλὰς 13
ἡμέρας συναγαγὼν πάντα[1] ὁ νεώτερος υἱὸς
ἀπεδήμησεν εἰς χώραν μακράν, καὶ ἐκεῖ
διεσκόρπισεν τὴν οὐσίαν αὐτοῦ ζῶν ἀσώτως. δαπανήσαντος δὲ αὐτοῦ πάντα ἐγέ- 14
νετο λιμὸς ἰσχυρὰ κατὰ τὴν χώραν ἐκείνην,
καὶ αὐτὸς ἤρξατο ὑστερεῖσθαι. καὶ πορευ- 15
θεὶς ἐκολλήθη ἑνὶ τῶν πολιτῶν τῆς χώρας
ἐκείνης, καὶ ἔπεμψεν αὐτὸν εἰς τοὺς ἀγροὺς
αὐτοῦ βόσκειν χοίρους· καὶ ἐπεθύμει χορ- 16
τασθῆναι ἐκ τῶν κερατίων ὧν ἤσθιον οἱ
χοῖροι, καὶ οὐδεὶς ἐδίδου αὐτῷ. εἰς ἑαυτὸν 17
δὲ ἐλθὼν ἔφη Πόσοι μίσθιοι τοῦ πατρός
μου περισσεύονται ἄρτων, ἐγὼ δὲ λιμῷ ὧδε
ἀπόλλυμαι· ἀναστὰς πορεύσομαι πρὸς τὸν 18
πατέρα μου καὶ ἐρῶ αὐτῷ Πάτερ, ἥμαρτον εἰς τὸν οὐρανὸν καὶ ἐνώπιόν σου, οὐκέτι
εἰμὶ ἄξιος κληθῆναι υἱός σου· ποίησόν με 19
ὡς ἕνα τῶν μισθίων σου. Καὶ ἀναστὰς 20
ἦλθεν πρὸς τὸν πατέρα ἑαυτοῦ. ἔτι δὲ
αὐτοῦ μακρὰν ἀπέχοντος εἶδεν αὐτὸν ὁ
πατὴρ αὐτοῦ καὶ ἐσπλαγχνίσθη καὶ δρα-

[1] ἅπαντα.

μῶν ἐπέπεσεν ἐπὶ τὸν τράχηλον αὐτοῦ καὶ
21 κατεφίλησεν αὐτόν. | εἶπεν δὲ ὁ υἱὸς αὐτῷ
Πάτερ, ἥμαρτον εἰς τὸν οὐρανὸν καὶ ἐνώπιόν σου, οὐκέτι εἰμὶ ἄξιος κληθῆναι υἱός
σου [· ποίησόν με ὡς ἕνα τῶν μισθίων
22 σου]. εἶπεν δὲ ὁ πατὴρ πρὸς τοὺς δούλους αὐτοῦ Ταχὺ ἐξενέγκατε στολὴν τὴν
πρώτην καὶ ἐνδύσατε αὐτόν, καὶ δότε δακτύλιον εἰς τὴν χεῖρα αὐτοῦ καὶ ὑποδήματα εἰς
23 τοὺς πόδας, καὶ φέρετε τὸν μόσχον τὸν
σιτευτόν, θύσατε καὶ φαγόντες εὐφρανθῶ-
24 μεν, ὅτι οὗτος ὁ υἱός μου νεκρὸς ἦν καὶ
ἀνέζησεν,[1] ἦν ἀπολωλὼς καὶ εὑρέθη. Καὶ
25 ἤρξαντο εὐφραίνεσθαι. ἦν δὲ ὁ υἱὸς αὐτοῦ
ὁ πρεσβύτερος ἐν ἀγρῷ· καὶ ὡς ἐρχόμενος
ἤγγισεν τῇ οἰκίᾳ, ἤκουσεν συμφωνίας καὶ
26 χορῶν, καὶ προσκαλεσάμενος ἕνα τῶν παί-
27 δων ἐπυνθάνετο τί ἂν εἴη ταῦτα· ὁ δὲ εἶπεν
αὐτῷ ὅτι Ὁ ἀδελφός σου ἥκει, καὶ ἔθυσεν
ὁ πατήρ σου τὸν μόσχον τὸν σιτευτόν, ὅτι
28 ὑγιαίνοντα αὐτὸν ἀπέλαβεν. ὠργίσθη δὲ
καὶ οὐκ ἤθελεν εἰσελθεῖν. ὁ δὲ πατὴρ αὐ-
29 τοῦ ἐξελθὼν παρεκάλει αὐτόν. ὁ δὲ ἀποκριθεὶς εἶπεν τῷ πατρὶ αὐτοῦ Ἰδοὺ τοσαῦτα

---

[1] ἔζησεν.

ἔτη δουλεύω σοι καὶ οὐδέποτε ἐντολήν σου
παρῆλθον, καὶ ἐμοὶ οὐδέποτε ἔδωκας ἔρι-
φον[1] ἵνα μετὰ τῶν φίλων μου εὐφρανθῶ·
ὅτε δὲ ὁ υἱός σου οὗτος ὁ καταφαγών σου 30
τὸν βίον μετὰ[2] πορνῶν ἦλθεν, ἔθυσας αὐτῷ
τὸν σιτευτὸν μόσχον. ὁ δὲ εἶπεν αὐτῷ 31
Τέκνον, σὺ πάντοτε μετ᾽ ἐμοῦ εἶ, καὶ πάντα
τὰ ἐμὰ σά ἐστιν· εὐφρανθῆναι δὲ καὶ 32
χαρῆναι ἔδει, ὅτι ὁ ἀδελφός σου οὗτος
νεκρὸς ἦν καὶ ἔζησεν, καὶ ἀπολωλὼς καὶ
εὑρέθη.

1 Cor.: Chapter 13.

Ἐὰν ταῖς γλώσσαις τῶν ἀνθρώπων λαλῶ 1
καὶ τῶν ἀγγέλων, ἀγάπην δὲ μὴ ἔχω, γέγονα
χαλκὸς ἠχῶν ἢ κύμβαλον ἀλαλάζον. κἂν 2
ἔχω προφητείαν καὶ εἰδῶ τὰ μυστήρια
πάντα καὶ πᾶσαν τὴν γνῶσιν, κἂν ἔχω
πᾶσαν τὴν πίστιν ὥστε ὄρη μεθιστάνειν,
ἀγάπην δὲ μὴ ἔχω, οὐθέν εἰμι. κἂν ψω- 3
μίσω πάντα τὰ ὑπάρχοντά μου, κἂν παραδῶ
τὸ σῶμά μου, ἵνα καυχήσωμαι, ἀγάπην δὲ
μὴ ἔχω, οὐδὲν ὠφελοῦμαι. Ἡ ἀγάπη μα- 4
κροθυμεῖ, χρηστεύεται, ἡ ἀγάπη οὐ ζηλοῖ,
οὐ περπερεύεται, οὐ φυσιοῦται, οὐκ ἀσχη- 5

---

[1] ἐρίφιον.　　　　　　　[2] τῶν.

μονεῖ, οὐ ζητεῖ τὰ ἑαυτῆς, οὐ παροξύνεται,
6 οὐ λογίζεται τὸ κακόν, οὐ χαίρει ἐπὶ τῇ
7 ἀδικίᾳ, συνχαίρει δὲ τῇ ἀληθείᾳ· πάντα
στέγει, πάντα πιστεύει, πάντα ἐλπίζει, πάντα
8 ὑπομένει. Ἡ ἀγάπη οὐδέποτε πίπτει. εἴτε
δὲ προφητεῖαι, καταργηθήσονται· εἴτε
γλῶσσαι, παύσονται· εἴτε γνῶσις, καταρ-
9 γηθήσεται. ἐκ μέρους γὰρ γινώσκομεν
10 καὶ ἐκ μέρους προφητεύομεν· ὅταν δὲ ἔλθῃ
τὸ τέλειον, τὸ ἐκ μέρους καταργηθήσεται.
11 ὅτε ἤμην νήπιος, ἐλάλουν ὡς νήπιος, ἐφρό-
νουν ὡς νήπιος, ἐλογιζόμην ὡς νήπιος· ὅτε
γέγονα ἀνήρ, κατήργηκα τὰ τοῦ νηπίου.
12 βλέπομεν γὰρ ἄρτι δι᾽ ἐσόπτρου ἐν αἰνίγ-
ματι, τότε δὲ πρόσωπον πρὸς πρόσωπον·
ἄρτι γινώσκω ἐκ μέρους, τότε δὲ ἐπιγνώ-
13 σομαι καθὼς καὶ ἐπεγνώσθην. νυνὶ δὲ
μένει πίστις, ἐλπίς, ἀγάπη· τὰ τρία ταῦτα,
μείζων δὲ τούτων ἡ ἀγάπη.

ABBREVIATIONS.

acc.	= accusative.		*masc.*	= masculine.
act.	= active.		*mid.*	= middle.
adj.	= adjective.		*neut.*	= neuter.
aor.	= aorist.		*nom.*	= nominative.
art.	= article.		*opt.*	= optative.
cf.	= **confer,** compare.		*part.*	= participle.
dat.	= dative.		*pass.*	= passive.
e.g.	= **exempli gratia,** for the sake of example.		*perf.*	= perfect.
			pers.	= person.
			plur.	= plural.
fem.	= feminine.		*poss.*	= possessive.
fut.	= future.		*pred.*	= predicate.
gen.	= genitive.		*prep.*	= preposition.
impers.	= impersonal.		*pres.*	= present.
ind.	= indicative.		*prin.*	= principal.
indecl.	= indeclinable.		*pron.*	= pronoun.
indir.	= indirect.		*rel.*	= relative.
inf.	= infinitive.		*sc.*	= **scilicet,** understood.
imp.	= imperative.			
imperf.	= imperf.		*sing.*	= singular.
κ.τ.λ.	= καὶ τὰ λοιπά, et cetera.		*subj.*	= subject.
			subjv.	= subjunctive.
lit.	= literally		*voc.*	= vocative.

NOTES.

——◆——

The First Epistle of John.

CHAPTER I.

1. Ο ΗΝ ΑΠ' ΑΡΧΗΣ = ὃ ἦν ἀπ' ἀρχῆς. The breathing and accent are not written on capitals. ὅ, the antecedent of the rel. pron. is often omitted. ἀκηκόαμεν, 2 perf. act. ind. of ἀκούω, prin. parts § 88. A few verbs beginning with α, ε, or ο have what is called *Attic* reduplication; *i.e.* a reduplication which is the first two letters prefixed to the theme. ἀκήκοα = ἀκ-ήκου-α, ν is dropped between two vowels. ἑωράκαμεν, learn prin. parts of ὁράω, § 88. This verb most commonly has both the *temporal* and *syllabic* augment. ὀφθαλμοῖς, § 157. ἡμῶν, lit. *of us.* The pers. pron. is often used for the poss. pron. ἐψηλάφησαν, ψηλαφάω. τῆς the art. may be used with *abstract* nouns in Greek, and ofttimes with concrete nouns, where it cannot be translated.

2. Observe the change in tenses, aor., perf., pres. For τὴν repeated after ζωὴν, see 64. πρὸς, § 159.

3. καὶ ὑμῖν, *also to you*, not as in Eng. *to you also.* ἔχητε, § 119. μεθ', § 12.

4. ᾖ πεπληρωμένη, perf. pass. subjv. See λύω, § 56. The perfects made thus from εἰμί, *am*, and the perf. part. are called *periphrastic* forms.

5. ἔστιν, note the accent. Always emphatic when on the *penult*. οὐδεμία, for the double negative, see § 142.

6. ἐὰν, § 124. εἴπωμεν, learn prin. parts of φημί, § 88.

8. ἑαυτοὺς; for the 3 pers. used for the 1 pers. cf. 213, latter part.

9. ἀφῇ, 2 aor. act. subjv. of ἀφίημι, § 66. For the sense of the aor. here and in καθαρίσῃ, see § 114.

10. For the two acc. cf. § 161.

CHAPTER 2.

1. τεκνία is voc. μὴ ἁμάρτητε, for neg. see § 119. The verb is 2 aor. act. subjv. of ἁμαρτάνω, learn prin. parts § 88. See § 83, 1 for class of verbs.

2. οὐ μόνον . . . ἀλλὰ καὶ, *not only . . . but also*.

3. ἐγνώκαμεν, prin. parts of γινώσκω.

4. μὴ τηρῶν is equal to a condition, *if one does not keep*, hence the neg. μή, § 137.

5. ὃς δ᾿ ἂν τηρῇ, § 126. ἀληθῶς, for the formation of adverbs, cf. 227.

6. μένειν, the inf. depends upon λέγων. See § 131 for the inf. in indirect discourse. αὐτὸς, intensive. περιπατεῖν, after ὀφείλει.

7. εἴχετε, what tense? 37, 9, note.

9. εἶναι, cf. note on v. 6.

12. ἀφέωνται, see under ἀφίημι, § 66. The perf. denotes the completion of the act, and equals here "stand forgiven."

13. τὸν = αὐτόν. τὸν πονηρόν, note the gender. The art. and an adj. are thus often used substantively.

15. μὴ, § 138. τὰ, *i.e.* the *goods* or *affairs* of the world. The general use of the neut. is to be noted.

16. πᾶν τὸ, explained by the following clauses.

18. καὶ νῦν, *even now*. γεγόνασι, 2 perf. act. of γίνομαι. Theme γεν changes to γον. Cf. 2 perf. of λείπω, § 57.

I

19. ἐξῆλθαν = ἐξ-ῆλθον, prin. parts of ἔρχομαι. The 1 aor. vowel α often appears in the place of the 2 aor. variable vowel %. εἰ γὰρ . . . μεθ᾽ ἡμῶν, for the condition, see § 122 and § 123, latter part. φανερωθῶσιν, 175 and 176.

22. εἰ μὴ, *unless, except*, as one word.

23. καὶ, *also*.

24. ὑμεῖς ὃ κ.τ.λ. = τοῦτο ἐν ὑμῖν μενέτω ὃ ἠκούσατε. This is a common construction in John. Not only does the relative clause come before the principal clause, but to make the expression more emphatic a personal pronoun (not used except for emphasis) is thrust before the relative, whose antecedent is dropped. μείνη . . . μενεῖτε, for the fut. and aor. of liquid verbs, see 203–208.

25. ἐπηγγείλατο, ἐπ-αγγέλλομαι.

26. τῶν πλανώντων, 192, 193.

27. τὸ χρίσμα, subj. of μένει. Cf. note on v. 24, above. ἐλάβετε, prin. parts of λαμβάνω. πάντων is neut. αὐτῷ, masc.

28. σχῶμεν, 2 aor. act. subjv. of ἔχω, § 88. μὴ, why not οὐ? ἀπ᾽ αὐτοῦ, *i.e.* shrink in shame *from him*.

29. εἰδῆτε, learn the subjv. of οἶδα, § 68.

CHAPTER 3.

1. ἴδετε, cf. 2 aor. of ὁράω. δέδωκεν, how different from the aor.? κληθῶμεν, prin. parts of καλέω. ἔγνω, prin. parts of γινώσκω. The long vowel ω appears in the 2 aor. ind. where in other verbs we find %.

2. ἐσόμεθα, fut. of εἰμί, § 65. αὐτῷ, § 153. ὀψόμεθα, see ὁράω.

5. ἄρῃ, αἴρω. For the class of verbs, see § 82, 4.

7. μηδεὶς, why not οὐδεὶς? § 138.

8. εἰς τοῦτο, *for this* (*purpose*).

12. Καὶν, Hebrew names of places and names of persons, unless given a Greek ending, are indeclinable. τοῦ πονηροῦ, masc. ἔσφαξεν, σφάττω (σφαγ-), § 82, 2. χάριν, an improper prep. *for sake of.*

14. μεταβεβήκαμεν, μεταβαίνω, prin. parts of βαίνω. μετά has the sense of *over*, a change from one place to another. Note the strong antithesis between the gen. with ἐκ and the acc. with εἰς.

15. μένουσαν goes with ζωὴν. Review pres. act. part. of λύω, § 43.

16. ἔθηκε, § 63 and 235, 3, note. Learn prin. parts of τίθημι. θεῖναι = θε-έναι, 2 aor. act. inf. The 2 *aor.* always has the *simple theme* of the verb.

17. ὃς δ᾽ ἂν ἔχῃ ... θεωρῇ ... κλείσῃ, § 126.

18. ἀγαπῶμεν, for the mood, see § 113.

19. γνωσόμεθα, γινώσκω. αὐτοῦ, for the gen. see § 152. ἡμῶν, § 151.

20. μείζων, see μέγας, § 38. τῆς καρδίας, § 150.

22. ὃ ἂν, cf. ὃς ἂν, above. ἐνώπιον αὐτοῦ, § 152.

23. ὀνόματι, § 155. ἔδωκεν, see note on ἔθηκε, above.

24. οὗ where we should expect ὅ. The relative is often attracted to the case of its antecedent, when the latter is in the gen. or dat. case.

CHAPTER 4.

1. ἐξεληλύθασιν, 2 perf. of ἔρχομαι. Cf. γεγόνασι, 1 Jn. 2: 18.

2. ἐληλυθότα, 2 perf. part. Cf. λελυκώς, § 43. For the participle in indirect discourse, where ὅτι and the indicative are more common, see § 136.

3. τοῦ ἀντιχρίστου, § 147. ἀκηκόατε, cf. note on 1 Jn. 1: 1.

4. ὁ ἐν ὑμῖν, a substantive expression. Note the wide use of the article in Greek.

5. αὐτῶν, § 148.

9. τὸν μονογενῆ, cf. a similar use of the art. and adj. in
1 Jn. 3 : 12. ἀπέσταλκεν, prin. parts of στέλλω. ζήσωμεν,
how different in meaning from ζῶμεν? Cf. 157.

11. ἀγαπᾶν, see § 59 for the inf. of contract verbs. *Iota-
subscript* is regularly omitted here in classical Greek.

12. τεθέαται, θεάομαι, § 77, 4.

15. ὃς ἐάν, § 126, latter part.

19. ἀγαπῶμεν, not ind.

20. εἴπῃ, see under φημί, in table of irregular verbs.

21. ἀγαπᾷ, ind. or subjv.? § 59.

CHAPTER 5.

1. τὸν γεννήσαντα . . . τὸν γεγεννημένον, 192, 193.

2. ὅταν ἀγαπῶμεν, § 127.

3. βαρεῖαι, nom. fem. plur.   Adjs. in -υς are rare.

4. ἡ νίκη ἡ νικήσασα = ἡ νικήσασα νίκη, *the victory
which has conquered.*   See aor. act. part. of λύω, § 43.

6. ὁ ἐλθών, *he who has come*; lit. *the (one) having
come.*   μαρτυροῦν, -υρέον.   Cf. λύω, § 43.

8. ἕν, εἷς, § 39.

10. αὐτῷ = ἑαυτῷ.

13. τοῖς πιστεύουσιν, goes back to ὑμῖν.   Observe the
tense.

14. αἰτώμεθα, the mid. how different from the act.?

15. ἐὰν οἴδαμεν, a rare construction, § 124.   ὃ ἐάν, cf. ὃς
ἐάν, 1 Jn. 4 : 15.

16. ἴδῃ, ὁράω.

18. γεννηθείς, cf. aor. pass. part. of λύω, § 43.

20. ἵνα γινώσκομεν, note the mood.   § 119.

21. φυλάξατε, φυλάττω (φυλακ-), § 82, 1.   ἑαυτά, 213,
latter part.   Why neut. gender?

Mat. 5 : 3–12.

THE BEATITUDES.

3. μακάριοι is in the pred. position, **64**. αὐτῶν, § 147.

4. παρακληθήσονται, **παρακαλέω**. See the fut. pass. of λύω, § 56.

9. υἱοὶ is pred.

10. δεδιωγμένοι, perf. pass. part. of **διώκω**. κ, χ change to γ before μ.

11. καθ᾽, *against*. ψευδόμενοι may be trans. as an adv.

Mat. 6 : 9–15.

THE LORD'S PRAYER.

9. πάτερ, note the case. ὁ = ὅς εἶ. ἁγιασθήτω, **ἁγιάζω** (ἁγιαδ-), see **178** and the aor. pass. imp. of λύω, § 56.

10. ἐλθάτω, note the use of the imperative mood in commands. For the α in this form, cf. note on 1 Jn. 2 : 19. γενηθήτω, **γίνομαι**. ἐπὶ, see under prep. § 164.

11. δὸς, see 2 aor. act. system of **δίδωμι**, § 63.

12. ἄφες, see 2 aor. system of **ἀφίημι**, § 66. τοῖς ὀφειλέταις, indir. obj. ; *sc.* τὰ ὀφειλήματα.

13. μὴ εἰσενέγκῃς, prin. parts of **φέρω**. For the construction, see § 117. ῥῦσαι (**ῥύομαι**), aor. mid. imp. τοῦ πονηροῦ may be either neut. or masc. as in 1 Jn. 2 : 13.

14. ἀφῆτε, see under **ἀφίημι**.

Luke 15.

THE PRODIGAL SON.

1. ἦσαν δὲ αὐτῷ ἐγγίζοντες = ἤγγιζον δὲ αὐτῷ. This use of the part. with **εἰμί** is a common form of participial

expression in the New Testament writers. Perhaps more
emphatic than the simple imperf. of the verb would be.
αὐτῷ, § 154.

2. συνεσθίει, note the force of συν-. What case follows
this prep.?

4. ἕκατον, § 39, a. ἀπολέσας, prin. parts of ἀπόλλυμι.
ἀπολωλός, pres. pass. sense. εὕρῃ, prin. parts of εὑρίσκω,
§ 128, for mood. αὐτό, i.e. πρόβατον.

6. συνχάρητε, 2 aor. pass. imp. of συνχαίρω. Cf. same
of φαίνω, § 58.

7. ἔσται, § 65. ἐπί, because of. μετανοοῦντι, μετανοέω.
μετά gives the idea of turning about from one stand to
another.

8. δραχμή, was a Greek coin worth about 18 cents.
οὐχί, 133, I. 3, note. σαροῖ, for the irregular contraction,
cf. δηλόω, § 59. ἕως ου, sc. χρόνου.

10. τῶν ἀγγέλων, § 152.

12. νεώτερος, see § 37, 1 and note. ἐπιβάλλον, neut.
part.; sc. μοι. διεῖλεν, di-vided; prin. parts of αἱρέω. βίον,
here, means of life, portion.

13. συναγαγών, συνάγω. The Attic reduplication is
regularly found in the 2 aor. of this verb. See note on
1 Jn. 1 : 1. Prin. parts of ἄγω.

14. δαπανήσαντος αὐτοῦ, gen. abs. 194, 10, note. ἐγένετο, γίνομαι.

15. πορευθείς, 179 and 190. ἐκολλήθη, lit. to be glued,
fastened; found in the pass. only in the New Testament,
and with the reflexive sense join one's self to.

16. ἐπεθύμει, ἐπιθυμέω. ὧν, see note on 1 Jn. 3:24.
ἤσθιον, observe the nice use of the imperf.

17. εἰς . . . ἐλθών, just as in English. ἄρτων, § 149.
λιμῷ, § 157. ἀπόλλυμαι, the action is going on.

18. ἀναστάς, see 2 aor. system of ἵστημι, § 63. ἐρῶ, a
fut. with no pres.; see under φημί. ἥμαρτον, ἁμαρτάνω.

19. ποίησον, aor. act. imp. δραμών, prin. parts of τρέχω. ἐπέπεσεν, ἐπι-πίπτω.

22. ἐξενέγκατε, ἐκ-φέρω. ἐνδύσατε, cf. ENDUE. ὑποδή-ματα, lit. *bound* (δέω) *underneath* (ὑπό).

23. φαγόντας, prin. parts of ἐσθίω. εὐφρανθῶμεν, εὐ-φραίνω, for the class of verbs, see § 82, 4.

26. συμφωνίας, SYMPHONY. For the case, see § 148. τί ἂν εἴη ταῦτα, *what this is.* εἴη is the opt. of εἰμί. For the forms of the opt. in the New Testament (and the uses of this mood), see §§ 70, 71. The optative is used instead of the indicative in indirect question when *certainty* does not exist in the speaker's mind.

27. ἀπέλαβεν, note the force of ἀπό, *back.*

28. ἤθελον, so always in the New Testament for ἔθελον.

29. ἰδού, ὁράω, 2 aor. mid. imp. ἔτη, ἔτος. παρῆλθον, observe the force of the prep. as in *trans-gress.*

30. καταφαγών, *devoured, squandered.*

31. σά is pred. ἔδει, imperf.; see **244**; *sc.* σέ or ἡμᾶς as subj. of the infinitives.

1 COR. 13.

LOVE.

1. γέγονα, γίνομαι.

2. κἂν = καὶ ἐὰν, § **13.** εἰδῶ, see under οἶδα, § **68.** μεθι-στάνειν, § **134.**

3. τὰ ὑπάρχοντα = τὰ ὄντα; *i.e. all that is, all the things I have.* παραδῶ, 2 aor. act. of δίδωμι, § **63.**

4. ζηλοῖ, cf. δηλόω, § 59.

7. στέγει first means *to cover ;* then to cover and thus *keep off* what threatens. Hence, *hold off against, endure.*

8. παύσονται, in the act. to *stop* some one ; in the mid to stop one's self. Hence, *cease.*

11. ἤμην = ἦν, mid. end. -μην; for act. -ν. Note the imperf. tense. See **78**.

12. ἐπιγνώσομαι, ἐπιγινώσκω; ἐπί adds the idea of *well* or *thoroughly*.

13. μείζων, *greater*; therefore, *the greatest*. For the case of τούτων, see § **150**.

καυχήσωμαι, v. 3, is an aor. mid. subjv. A doubtful reading where some editors give a passive form: καυθήσωμαι (-σομαι) from καίω, *burn*.

LITERAL TRANSLATION.

———◆———

CHAPTER I.

1. That-which was from beginning, that-which we-have-heard, that-which we-have-seen with-the eyes of-us, that-which we-beheld and the hands of-us handled, concerning the word of-the life, —

2. And the life was-manifested, and we-have-seen, and we-bear-witness, and we-proclaim to-you the life the eternal which (ἥτις) was with the Father, and was-manifested to-us, —

3. That-which we-have-seen and have-heard, we-proclaim also to-you, that also you fellowship may-have with us: and the fellowship truly the our with the Father and with the Son of-him Jesus Christ:

4. And these-things write we that the joy of-us may-be (having-been-filled) full.

5. And there-is this the announcement which we-have-heard from him and re-announce to-you, that the God light is, and darkness not is in him at-all.

6. If we-say that fellowship we-have with him, and in the darkness we-walk, we-lie and not we-do the truth:

7. If however in the light we-walk, as he is in the light, fellowship we-have with one-another, and the blood of-Jesus the Son of him cleanseth us from every sin.

8. If we-say that sin not we-have, ourselves we-deceive, and the truth not is in us.

9. If we-confess the sins of-us, faithful he-is and righteous that he-may-remit to-us the sins, and may-cleanse us from all unrighteousness.

10. If we-say that not we-have-sinned, a liar we-make him, and the word of-him not is in us.

CHAPTER 2.

1. Little-children of-me, these-things write-I to-you, that not ye-may-sin. And if any-one sin, an Advocate we-have with the Father, Jesus Christ righteous :

2. And he propitiation is for the sins of-us ; not for the our and only, but also for whole the world.

3. And in this we-know that we-have-known him, if the commandments of-him we-keep.

4. The-one saying that I-have-known him, and the commandments of-him not keeping, a liar is, and in this-one the truth not is :

5. Who however (ἂν) keeps of-him the word, truly in this-one the love of-the God has-been-perfected.   In this we-know that in-him we-are :

6. The-one saying in him to-abide ought just-as that-one walked also himself to-walk.

7. Beloved, not commandment new I-write to-you, but commandment old which you-had from beginning : the commandment the old is the word which ye-heard.

8. Again, commandment new I-write to-you, which-thing is true in him and in you, because the darkness is-passing-away, and the light the perfect already shines.

9. The-one saying in the light to-be, and the brother of-him hating, in the darkness is until now.

10. The-one loving the brother of-him in the light abides, and offence in him not is.

11. The-one but hating the brother of-him in the darkness is, and in the darkness he-walks, and not he-knows where he-goes, because the darkness blinded the eyes of-him.

12. I-write to-you, little-children, because are-remitted to-you the sins on-account-of the name of-him.

13. I-write to-you, fathers, because you-have-known the-one from beginning. I-write to-you, young-men, because you-have-conquered the evil-one.

14. I-wrote to-you, little-children, because you-have-known the Father. I-wrote to-you, fathers, because you-have-known the-one from beginning. I-wrote to-you, young-men, because strong you-are, and the word of-the God in you abides, and you-have-conquered the evil-one.

15. Not love-ye the world, nor the-things in the world. If any-one love the world, not is the love of-the Father in him.

16. Because every-thing the in the world, the lust of-the flesh, and the lust of-the eyes, and the vain-glory of-the life, not is out-of the Father but out-of the world is.

17. And the world is-passing-away, and the lust of-it: the-one but doing the will of-the God abides into the age.

18. Little children, last hour is; and just-as ye-heard that antichrist is-coming, even now antichrists many have-become; whence we-know that last hour is.

19. Out-of us they-went-out, but not were-they out-of us; if for out-of us they-were, they-would-have-remained (ἄν) with us: but that they-might-be-made-manifest that not are-they all out-of us.

20. And you anointing have from the Holy-One, you-know (you) all.

21. Not I-wrote to-you because not you-know the truth,

but because you-know it, and because every lie out-of the truth not is.

22. Who is the liar, if not the-one denying that Jesus not is the Christ?   This-one is the antichrist, the-one denying the Father and the Son.

23. Every-one the denying the Son, not-even the Father has : the-one confessing the Son also the Father has.

24. You that-which you-heard from beginning, in you let-it-abide.   If in you abide that-which from beginning you-heard, also you in the Son and in the Father shall-abide.

25. And this is the promise which he promised to-us, the life the eternal.

26. These-things I-wrote to-you concerning the-ones deceiving you.

27. And you the anointing which you-received from him abides in you, and not need have-you that any-one may-teach you ; but as the of-him anointing teaches you concerning all-things, and true is, and not is false, and just-as it-taught you, abide-ye in him.

28. And now, little-children, abide in him ; that if he-be-manifested, we-may-have boldness, and not may-we-be-ashamed from him in the presence of-him.

29. If you-know that righteous he-is, you-know that every-one the doing the righteousness, out-of him has-been-begotten.

TRANSLATION (Revised Version).

CHAPTER 3.

1. Behold what manner of love the Father hath be-stowed upon us, that we should be called children of God : and (such) we are.   For this cause the world knoweth us not, because it knew him not.

2. Beloved, now are we children of God, and it is not yet made manifest what we shall be. We know that, if he shall be manifested, we shall be like him; for we shall see him even as he is.

3. And every one that hath this hope (set) on him purifieth himself, even as he is pure.

4. Every one that doeth sin doeth also lawlessness: and sin is lawlessness.

5. And ye know that he was manifested to take away sins; and in him is no sin.

6. Whosoever abideth in him sinneth not: whosoever sinneth hath not seen him, neither knoweth him.

7. (My) little children, let no man lead you astray: he that doeth righteousness is righteous, even as he is righteous:

8. He that doeth sin is of the devil; for the devil sinneth from the beginning. To this end was the Son of God manifested, that he might destroy the works of the devil.

9. Whosoever is begotten of God doeth no sin, because his seed abideth in him: and he cannot sin, because he is begotten of God.

10. In this the children of God are manifest, and the children of the devil: whosoever doeth not righteousness is not of God, neither he that loveth not his brother.

11. For this is the message which ye heard from the beginning, that we should love one another:

12. Not as Cain was of the evil one, and slew his brother. And wherefore slew he him? Because his works were evil, and his brother's righteous.

13. Marvel not, brethren, if the world hateth you.

14. We know that we have passed out of death into life, because we love the brethren. He that loveth not abideth in death.

15. Whosoever hateth his brother is a murderer : and ye know that no murderer hath eternal life abiding in him.

16. Hereby know we love, because he laid down his life for us : and we ought to lay down our lives for the brethren.

17. But whoso hath the world's goods, and beholdeth his brother in need, and shutteth up his compassion from him, how doth the love of God abide in him?

18. (My) little children, let us not love in word, neither with the tongue ; but in deed and truth.

19. Hereby shall we know that we are of the truth, and shall assure our heart before him, whereinsoever our heart condemn us ;

20. Because God is greater than our heart, and knoweth all things.

21. Beloved, if our heart condemn us not, we have boldness toward God ;

22. And whatsoever we ask, we receive of him, because we keep his commandments, and do the things that are pleasing in his sight.

23. And this is his commandment, that we should believe in the name of his Son Jesus Christ, and love one another, even as he gave us commandment.

24. And he that keepeth his commandments abideth in him, and he in him. And hereby we know that he abideth in us, by the Spirit which he gave us.

VOCABULARY OF THE SELECTIONS FOR TRANSLATION INTO ENGLISH.

ἀγαλλιάομαι, *be glad.*
ἀγαπάω, *to love.*
ἀγάπη, ἡ, *love.*
ἀγαπητός, *beloved.*
ἀγγελία, ἡ, *message.*
ἄγγελος, ὁ, *messenger*, AN-
  GEL.
ἁγιάζω, *to hallow.*
ἅγιος, *holy.*
ἁγνίζω, *purify.*
ἁγνός, *pure.*
ἀγρός, ὁ, *field.*
ἀδελφός, ὁ, *brother.*
ἀδικία, ἡ, *unrighteousness.*
αἷμα, τό, *blood.*
αἴνιγμα, τό, *a dark saying*,
  ENIGMA.
αἴρω, *to take away.*
αἰσχύνομαι, *to be ashamed.*
αἰτέω, *to ask for.*
αἴτημα, τό, *request.*
αἰών, ὁ, *age*, EON.
αἰώνιος, *eternal.*

ἀκούω, *to hear.*
ἀλαζονία, ἡ, *vainglory.*
ἀλαλάζω, *to clang.*
ἀλήθεια, ἡ, *truth.*
ἀληθής, *true.*
ἀληθινός, *true, real.*
ἀληθῶς, adv., *truly.*
ἀλλά, conj., *but.*
ἀλλήλων, *one another.*
ἁμαρτάνω, *to sin.*
ἁμαρτωλός, ὁ, *sinner.*
ἁμαρτία, ἡ, *sin.*
ἄν, added to temporal and
  relative conj., not trans-
  latable ; see Greek index.
ἀναγγέλλω, *to declare.*
ἀναζάω, *live again, revive.*
ἀνήρ, ὁ, *man.*
ἄνθρωπος, ὁ, *man.*
ἀνθρωποκτόνος, ὁ, *murderer.*
ἀνίστημι, *to raise up.*
ἀνομία, ἡ, *lawlessness.*
ἀντίχριστος, ὁ, ANTICHRIST.

ἄξιος, *worthy*.
ἀπαγγέλλω, *to announce*.
ἀπέχω, *to be away*.
ἀπό, prep. w. gen., *from*.
ἀποδημέω, *to go abroad*.
ἀποκρίνομαι, *to answer*.
ἀπολαμβάνω, *to take back*.
ἀπόλλυμι, *to loose, destroy*.
ἀποστέλλω, *to send away*.
ἅπτομαι, *to touch*.
ἅπτω, *to light*.
ἀρεστός, *pleasing*.
ἀρνέομαι, *to deny*.
ἄρτι, adv., *now*.
ἄρτος, ὁ, *bread*.
ἀρχή, ἡ, *beginning*.
ἄρχομαι, *to begin*.
ἀσχημονεύω, *to act unseemly*.
ἀσώτως, adv., *dissolutely*.
αὐτός, αὐτή, αὐτό, *he, she, it*.
αὑτοῦ, *of himself*.
ἀφίημι, *to forgive*.
βάλλω, *to cast*.
βαρύς, -εῖα, -ύ, *heavy*.
βασιλεία, ἡ, *kingdom*.
βίος, ὁ, *life, sustenance*.
βλέπω, *to see*.
βόσκω, *to feed*.
γάρ, conj., *for*.
γείτων, ὁ, *neighbor*.
γεννάω, *to beget*.
γίνομαι, *to be, become*.
γινώσκω, *to know*.
γλῶσσα, ἡ, *tongue*.

γνῶσις, ἡ, *knowledge*.
γραμματεύς, ὁ, *clerk*.
γράφω, *to write*.
δακτύλιον, τό, *fingering*.
δαπανάω, *to expend*.
δέ, conj., *and, but*.
δεῖ, impers., *it is necessary*.
διά, prep. w. gen., *through*:
  acc., *on account of*.
διαιρέω, *to divide*.
διάβολος, ὁ, *devil*.
διαγογγύζω, *to murmur*.
διάνοια, ἡ, *mind*.
διασκορπίζω, *to scatter*.
διδάσκω, *to teach*.
δίδωμι, *to give*.
δίκαιος, *just*.
δικαιοσύνη, ἡ, *justice*.
διψάω, *to thirst*.
διώκω, *to persecute, follow*.
δοκιμάζω, *to prove*.
δουλεύω, *to be a servant*.
δοῦλος, ὁ, *servant*.
δύναμαι, *to be able*.
δύο, *two*.
ἐάν, conj., *if*.
ἑαυτοῦ, *of himself*.
ἐγγίζω, *to come near*.
ἐγώ, *I*.
εἰ, conj., *if*.
εἴδωλον, τό, IDOL.
εἰμί, *am*.
εἶπον, 2 aor., *I said*.
εἰρηνοποιός, *peacemaker*.

εἰς, prep. w. acc., *into, in.*

εἷς, μία, ἕν, *one.*

εἰσέρχομαι, *to enter.*

εἰσφέρω, *to bring in.*

εἴτε, *whether.*

ἐκ, prep. w. gen., *out of.*

ἑκατόν, indecl., *one hundred.*

ἐκεῖ, adv., *there.*

ἐκεῖνος, *that one.*

ἐκφέρω, *to carry out.*

ἐλεέω, *to show mercy.*

ἐλεήμων, *merciful.*

ἐλπίς, ἡ, *hope.*

ἐμός, *my.*

ἔμπροσθεν, adv., *before.*

ἐν, prep. w. dat., *in.*

ἐνδύω, *to put on,* ENDUE.

ἕνεκεν, prep. w. gen., *on account of.*

ἐνενήκοντα, *ninety.*

ἐννέα, *nine.*

ἐντολή, ἡ, *commandment.*

ἐνώπιον, adv., *before, in face of.*

ἐξ, cf. ἐκ.

ἐξέρχομαι, *to go out.*

ἐπαγγελία, ἡ, *promise.*

ἐπαγγέλλομαι, *to promise.*

ἐπί, prep. w. gen., *upon* ; w. dat., *on* ; w. acc., *to, on.*

ἐπιβάλλω, *falling to, coming to.*

ἐπιγινώσκω, *to know well.*

ἐπιθυμέω, *to desire.*

ἐπιθυμία, ἡ, *desire.*

ἐπιπίπτω, *to fall down.*

ἐπιτίθημι, *to place upon.*

ἔργον, τό, *work.*

ἔρημος, ἡ, *desert.*

ἔριφος, ἡ, *kid.*

ἔρχομαι, *to come, go.*

ἐρῶ, *shall say.*

ἐρωτάω, *to ask.*

ἐσθίω, *to eat.*

ἔσοπτρον, τό, *mirror.*

ἔσχατος, *last.*

ἔτος, τό, *year.*

εὑρίσκω, *to find.*

ἔφη, *he said.*

εὐφραίνω, *to gladden, rejoice.*

ἔχω, *to have.*

ἕως, conj., *until.*

ζάω, *to live.*

ζηλόω, *to envy.*

ζητέω, *to seek.*

ζωή, ἡ, *life.*

ἤ, conj., *or.*

ἤδη, adv., *now.*

ἥκω, *am come.*

ἡμέρα, ἡ, *day.*

ἡμέτερος, *our.*

ἠχέω, *to sound.*

θάνατος, ὁ, *death.*

θαυμάζω, *to marvel.*

θεάομαι, *to behold.*

θέλημα, τό, *will.*

θέλω, *to will.*

θεός, ὁ, *God.*

K

θεωρέω, *to observe.*
θύω, *to sacrifice.*
Ἰησοῦς, ὁ, *Jesus.*
ἱλασμός, ὁ, *propitiation.*
ἵνα, conj., *in order that.*
ἰσχυρός, *strong.*
καθαρίζω, *to purify.*
καθαρός, *pure.*
καθώς, conj., *even as.*
καί, conj., *and, also.*
Καίν, ὁ, *Cain.*
καινός, *new.*
κακός, *evil, bad.*
καλέω, *to call.*
καρδία, ἡ, *heart.*
κατά, prep. w. gen., *against*;
   w. acc., *through.*
καταγινώσκω, *to condemn.*
καταλείπω, *to leave behind.*
καταργέω, *to bring to nought.*
καταφιλέω, *to kiss.*
κατεσθίω, *to devour, squan-*
   der.
καυχάομαι, *to boast.*
κεῖμαι, *to lie, recline.*
κεράτιον, τό, the fruit of the
   Carob tree, used for the
   swine, also by poor people. Lit., *a little horn.*
κλείω, *to shut.*
κληρονομέω, *to inherit.*
κοινωνία, ἡ, *fellowship.*
κόλασις, ἡ, *punishment.*
κόσμος, ὁ, *world,* COSMOS.

κρίσις, ἡ, *judgment.*
κύμβαλον, τό, CYMBAL.
λαλέω, *to speak.*
λαμβάνω, *to take.*
λέγω, *to say.*
λιμός, ὁ, *hunger.*
λογίζομαι, *to judge, think.*
λόγος, ὁ, *word.*
λύχνος, ὁ, *lamp.*
λύω, *to loose, destroy.*
μακάριος, *blessed, happy.*
μακροθυμέω, *to suffer long.*
μακρός, *long, far.*
μαρτυρέω, *to bear witness.*
μαρτυρία, ἡ, *witness.*
μεθιστάνω, *to remove.*
μείζων, *greater.*
μένω, *to remain.*
μέρος, τό, *part.*
μετά, prep. w. gen., *with*;
   w. acc., *after.*
μετανοέω, *to repent.*
μετάνοια, ἡ, *repentance.*
μεταβαίνω, *to cross over.*
μή, *not.*
μηδέ, *neither, nor.*
μηδείς, *no one.*
μισέω, *to hate.*
μίσθιος, *hireling.*
μισθός, ὁ, *hire, pay.*
μονογενής, *only begotten.*
μόνος, *alone, only.*
μόσχος, ὁ, *calf.*
μυστήριον, τό, MYSTERY.

νεανίσκος, ὁ, *young man.*
νεκρός, *dead.*
νέος, *young.*
νήπιος, *young child.*
νικάω, *to conquer.*
νίκη, ἡ, *victory.*
νῦν, adv., *now.*
ὅθεν, adv., *whence.*
οἶδα, *I know.*
οἰκία, ἡ, *house.*
οἶκος, ὁ, *house.*
ὅλος, *whole.*
ὅμοιος, *like.*
ὁμολογέω, *to confess.*
ὀνειδίζω, *to revile.*
ὄνομα, τό, *name.*
ὁράω, *to see.*
ὀργίζω, *to anger, arouse.*
ὄρος, τό, *mountain.*
ὅς, ἥ, ὅ, *who.*
ὅστις, ἥτις, ὅ,τι, *whoever.*
ὅτε, conj., *when.*
ὅτι, conj., *because, that.*
οὐ, *not.*
οὐδέ, *neither, nor.*
οὐδείς, *no one.*
οὐδέποτε, adv., *never.*
οὐκέτι, adv., *no longer.*
οὔπω, adv., *not yet.*
οὐρανός, ὁ, *heaven.*
οὐράνιος, *heavenly.*
οὐσία, ἡ, *substance, prop-erty.*
οὗτος, *this one.*

οὕτω, adv., *thus.*
ὀφειλέτης, ὁ, *debtor.*
ὀφείλημα, τό, *debt.*
ὀφείλω, *to owe, be indebted.*
ὀφθαλμός, ὁ, *eye.*
ὄψομαι, *shall see.*
παιδίον, τό, *child.*
παῖς, ὁ, ἡ, *child.*
πεινάω, *to hunger.*
παλαιός, *old.*
πάλιν, adv., *again.*
παραβολή, ἡ, PARABLE.
παράγομαι, *to pass away.*
παραδίδωμι, *to deliver, give up.*
παρακαλέω, *to summon, com-fort.*
παράκλητος, ὁ, *advocate.*
παράπτωμα, τό, *trespass.*
παρέρχομαι, *to pass by, omit.*
παροξύνομαι, *to be provoked.*
παρουσία, ἡ, *presence.*
παρρησία, ἡ, *boldness.*
πᾶς, *all.*
πατήρ, ὁ, *father.*
πείθω, *to persuade.*
πέμπω, *to send.*
πενθέω, *grieve, mourn.*
πειρασμός, ὁ, *temptation.*
περί, prep. w. gen., *concern-ing;* w. acc., *around.*
περιπατέω, *to walk.*
περισσεύομαι, *to abound.*

περπερεύομαι, *to vaunt, boast.*
πίπτω, *to fall.*
πιστεύω, *to believe.*
πίστις, ἡ, *faith.*
πιστός, *faithful.*
πλανάω, *cause to wander.*
πλάνη, ἡ, *wandering.*
πληρόω, *to fill.*
πνεῦμα, τό, *spirit.*
ποιέω, *to do, make.*
πολίτης, ὁ, *citizen.*
πολύς, *much, many.*
πονηρός, *wicked.*
πορεύομαι, *go, come.*
πόρνος, ὁ, *fornicator.*
πόσος, *how great.*
ποταπός, *what sort of.*
ποῦ, adv., *where.*
πούς, ὁ, *foot.*
πραΰς, *gentle.*
πρεσβύτερος, *elder.*
πρό, prep. w. gen., *before.*
πρόβατον, τό, *sheep.*
πρός, prep. w. acc., *to, towards.*
προσδέχομαι, *to receive.*
προσεύχομαι, *to offer prayers to.*
προσκαλέω, *to summon.*
πρόσωπον, τό, *face.*
προφητεία, ἡ, *prophecy.*
προφήτης, ὁ, PROPHET.
πρῶτος, *first.*

πυνθάνομαι, *to learn, enquire.*
πτωχός, ὁ, *beggar.*
πώποτε, adv., *ever.*
πῶς, adv., *how.*
ῥύομαι, *to deliver.*
σαρόω, *to sweep.*
σάρξ, ἡ, *flesh.*
σήμερον, adv., *to-day.*
σιτευτός, *fatted.*
σκάνδαλον, τό, *cause for stumbling.*
σκοτία, ἡ, *darkness.*
σκότος, τό, *darkness.*
σός, *thy.*
σπλαγχνίζω, *to have compassion.*
σπλάγχνα, τά, *compassion, bowels.*
σπέρμα, τό, *seed.*
στολή, ἡ, *robe, garment.*
σύ, *thou.*
συμφωνία, ἡ, *music.*
συνάγω, *to collect.*
συνεσθίω, *to eat with.*
συνκαλέω, *to call together.*
συνχαίρω, *to rejoice with.*
σφάζω, *to slay.*
σῶμα, τό, *body.*
σωτήρ, ὁ, *saviour.*
ταχύ, adv., *quickly.*
τεκνίον, τό, *little child.*
τέκνον, τό, *child.*
τέλειος, *perfect, mature.*

τελειόω, *to perfect.*

τελώνης, ὁ, *collector of taxes, publican.*

τηρέω, *to keep.*

τίθημι, *to put, place.*

τίς, τί, *who? what?*

τις, τι, *some one, certain one.*

τοσοῦτος, *so much.*

τράχηλος, ὁ, *neck.*

τρεῖς, τρία, *three.*

τρέχω, *to run.*

τυφλόω, *to make blind.*

ὑγιαίνω, *to be well, strong.*

ὕδωρ, τό, *water.*

υἱός, ὁ, *son.*

ὑπάγω, *to go.*

ὑπάρχω, *to be.*

ὑπέρ, *prep. w. gen., for.*

ὑπόδημα, τό, *sandal.*

ὑπομένω, *to endure.*

ὑστερέω, *to lack, want.*

φαίνω, *to show, appear.*

φανερός, *plain, manifest.*

φανερόω, *make manifest.*

φέρω, *bring, bear.*

φίλος, ὁ, *friend.*

φοβέομαι, *to fear.*

φόβος, ὁ, *fear.*

φρονέω, *to think.*

φυλάσσω, *to guard.*

φυσίομαι, *to be puffed up, inflated.*

φῶς, τό, *light.*

χάλκος, ὁ, *brass, bronze.*

χαρά, ἡ, *joy.*

χαίρω, *to rejoice.*

χάριν, *used as prep. w. gen., for the sake of.*

χείρ, ἡ, *hand.*

χοῖρος, ὁ, *swine.*

χορός, ὁ, *dancing.*

χορτάζω, *to be filled.*

χρεία, ἡ, *need.*

χρηστεύομαι, *to be kind.*

χρίσμα, τό, *anointing.*

Χριστός, ὁ, *Christ.*

χώρα, ἡ, *country.*

ψεύδομαι, *lie, to speak falsely.*

ψευδοπροφήτης, ὁ, *false prophet.*

ψεῦδος, τό, *lie.*

ψεύστης, ὁ, *liar.*

ψηλαφάω, *to touch, handle.*

ψυχή, ἡ, *soul.*

ψωμίζω, *give in small parts.*

ὧδε, *as follows, thus.*

ὦμος, ὁ, *shoulders.*

ὥρα, ἡ, *hour.*

ὡς, *as.*

ὠφελέω, *to owe, be indebtea to.*

PART II. — GRAMMAR.

1. WRITING AND SOUND.

ALPHABET.

§ 1. Greek is written with twenty-four letters.

FORM.		NAME.		LATIN.	
A	α	ἄλφα	*alpha*	a	as in *father*
B	β	βῆτα	*beta*	b [1]	
Γ	γ	γάμμα	*gamma*	g	as in *get*
Δ	δ	δέλτα	*delta*	d	
E	ε (short)	ἒ ψῑλόν	*epsilon*	ĕ	as in *met*
Z	ζ	ζῆτα	*zeta*	z	
H	η (long)	ἦτα	*eta*	ē	as in *they*
Θ	θ ϑ	θῆτα	*theta*	th	as in *thing*
I	ι	ἰῶτα	*iota*	i	as in *machine*
K	κ	κάππα	*kappa*	c *or* k	
Λ	λ	λάμβδα	*lambda*	l	
M	μ	μῦ	*mu*	m	
N	ν	νῦ	*nu*	n	
Ξ	ξ	ξῖ	*xi*	x	as in *example*
O	o (short)	ὂ μῑκρόν	*omicron*	ŏ	as in *obey*
Π	π	πῖ	*pi*	p	
P	ρ	ῥῶ	*rho*	r	
Σ	σ ς	σίγμα	*sigma*	s	
T	τ	ταῦ	*tau*	t	
Υ	υ [3]	ὒ ψῑλόν	*upsilon*	y	{ French *u* or German *ü*
Φ	φ	φῖ	*phi*	ph	as in *phase*
X	χ	χῖ	*chi*	ch	as in *chasm*
Ψ	ψ	ψῖ	*psi*	ps	as in *lips*
Ω	ω (long)	ὦ μέγα	*omega*	ō	as in *tone*

[1] Letters without equivalents are pronounced as in English.
[2] σ in the middle of a word; ς at the close.   [3] See **11**, *a*.

§ 2.

TABLE OF CONSONANTS.

SEMIVOWELS.		MUTES.			DOUBLE CONSONANTS.
		Smooth.	Middle.	Rough.	
Sibilant. σ	Labials	π	β	φ	ψ from πς, βς, or φς
Liquids. λ, ρ, ν	Linguals	τ	δ	θ	ζ " " σδ or δσ
Nasals. μ (γ)	Palatals	κ	γ	χ	ξ " " κς, γς, or χς

E.g. ἄγγελος (äng-gel-ŏs), *angel.*

a. γ before κ, γ, or χ is pronounced like *ng.*

TABLE OF VOWELS.

§ 3. The vowels are α, ε, η, ο, ω, ι, υ. Of these ε, o are always short; η, ω always long; α, ι, υ are sometimes long, sometimes short.

Short vowels, ᾰ ε ῐ ŏ ῠ   *Open short vowels,* ᾰ ε ο   *Close vowels,* ι υ
Long vowels, ᾱ η ῑ ω ῡ   *Open long vowels,* ᾱ η ω

CONTRACTION OF VOWELS.

α ε η ο ω | ι υ

§ 4. The vowels before the line are *open* ; they combine with the *close* vowels after the line, and form *diphthongs* as follows :

1	2	3	4	5	6
αι	ει	οι	αυ	ευ	ου

1	2	3	4	5	6
ᾳ	ῃ (ην ων)	ῳ			

as in English *aisle* *height* *oil* *our¹* *feud* *group*,
   1   2   3   4   5   6
pronounced as in English ᾱ   ē   ō   wee

proper diphthongs,
   1   2   3
as English ᾱ   ē   ō

υι, *improper*

α ε η | ο ω

§ 5. The vowels before the line contract with those after, and the result is ω:

$$\overset{1}{αο=ω} \quad \overset{2}{αω=ω} \quad \overset{3}{(ηο=ω)} \quad \overset{4}{ηω=ω} \quad \overset{5}{οα=ω} \quad \overset{6}{ωη=ω).}$$

$$\overset{7}{εο, οε, οο=ου (Exc.)} \quad \overset{8}{εω=ω} \quad \overset{9}{(ωε=ω)} \quad \overset{10}{οα=ω} \quad \overset{11}{οη=ω} \quad \overset{12}{οο=ω}$$

α ε η

§ 6. These vowels contract, and the first vowel in long form prevails:

$$\overset{1}{αε=\bar{α}} \quad \overset{2}{αη=\bar{α}} \quad \overset{3}{ηα=η} \quad \overset{4}{ηε=η} \quad \overset{5}{εη=η} \quad \overset{6}{εα=η.} \quad \text{Exc. } \overset{7}{εε=ει}$$

CONTRACTION OF VOWEL WITH DIPHTHONG.

§ 7. When the vowel and the first vowel of the diphthong are alike, the vowel is absorbed:

$$\overset{1}{ααι=αι} \quad \overset{2}{εει=ει} \quad \overset{3}{οοι=οι}$$

§ 8. When the vowel is unlike the first vowel, the two are contracted according to the laws for contraction of vowels, and the second vowel of the diphthong, if it is ι, is retained as subscript; if not ι, the second vowel is dropped:

$$\overset{1}{αει=ᾳ} \quad \overset{2}{αῃ=ᾳ} \quad \overset{3}{αοι=ᾳ} \quad \overset{4}{εου=ου} \quad \overset{5}{(οη=ῳ)}$$

ACCENT.

§ 9. There are three kinds of accent in Greek :

The *acute ;*   as in τίς, *who ?*
The *grave ;*   "   τὶς, *some one.*
The *circumflex ;* "   αὐτῷ, *to him.*

There are two fundamental laws of accent : VERBAL, explained in **3**, *b* ; and NOMINAL (including nouns, adjectives, and participles), given in **57**.

BREATHINGS.

§ 10. Every initial vowel or diphthong has a breathing mark over it :

(᾿) is called the *smooth* breathing, and is not pronounced. ἴδιος, αὐτός.
(῾) is called the *rough* breathing, and gives the sound of *h.* ὥρα, *hōra ;* αὑτοῦ, *hautou.*

Note that the breathing is placed over the second vowel of the diphthong.

Initial ρ always has the rough breathing. ῥῆμα.

MOVABLE ν.

§ 11. Movable ν may occur at the end of the following :

1. All dative plurals in -σι(ν). πᾶσι(ν), ἀκούσασι(ν).

2. All verbs with the ending -σι. ἵστησι(ν), λύουσι(ν).

3. After -ε of the third person singular of verbs. ἔλαβε(ν), ἤκουσε(ν).

4. After ἐστί; as ἐστί(ν).

So also σ is movable in οὕτως, *thus*. Before a vowel, as οὕτως ἦν; but before a consonant, οὕτω καί.[1]

APOSTROPHE.

§ 12. In the prepositions a short final vowel may be dropped before a word beginning with a vowel. *E.g.* ἀπ᾽ αὐτοῦ, *from him;* ἐφ᾽ ᾧ, *at which;* μεθ᾽ ἡμῶν, *with us.*

Note that the elision is marked by an apostrophe, and that a smooth mute, as π, τ, changes to the corresponding rough mute, φ, θ, before a *rough* breathing.

ἀλλά, *but,* also suffers elision; as ἀλλ᾽ ἐμοί.

CRASIS.

§ 13. When two vowels, or a vowel and a diphthong, come together in two words, as καὶ ἐγώ or τὸ ἐναντίον, they are usually joined together; as κἀγώ or τοὐναντίον. This is called *crasis* (mixture), and is indicated by the *coronis* over the contracted form.

---

[1] But in the New Testament often s before a consonant.

PUNCTUATION.

§ **14**. The Greek has four punctuation marks :
the comma and the period, as in English ; the
interrogation mark (;), as the English semicolon ; and the point (·) above the line. which
equals English colon or semicolon.

---

2. ACCIDENCE.

§ **15**. Accidence treats of NOMINAL *inflexion*,
the declension of nouns, adjectives, and participles, and of the *conjugation* of verbs.

INFLEXION.

§ **16**. In Greek ALL nouns, adjectives, and participles have *inflexion ; i.e.* an ending or suffix
which is added to the stem or substantial part
of the word.   There are three sets of endings or
suffixes, and according as a noun takes one set
or the other it is said to belong to the *first*,
second, or *third* declension.

§ **17**. Nouns of the first declension have the
stem ending in -*ā*.   This is therefore called the
A-declension.

Nouns of the second declension have the stem
in -*o*.   O-declension.

Most nouns of the third declension have stems ending in a consonant, hence the term Consonant Declension is used.

GENDER.

§ 18. All nouns in Greek are either masculine, feminine, or neuter gender.

Nouns denoting *male* persons are masculine.

Nouns denoting *female* persons are feminine.

§ 19. Outside of these *sex* rules the gender may be determined very largely by the declension to which the noun belongs:

1. Nouns of the A-declension ending in *a, η, ā* are *feminine*. Those ending in -ς are *masculine*.

2. Nouns of the O-declension in -ος are mostly *masculine;* those in -ον are *neuter*.

3. In the third declension the gender varies according to the ending of the stem. See Lessons XV., XVI., XVIII., and XIX. for the discussion of these forms.

NUMBER.

§ 20. In the Greek of the New Testament there are two numbers, singular and plural, as in English.

CASE.

§ 21. There are five cases in Greek :

1. Nominative, as in English.

2. Genitive, SOURCE or WHENCE-CASE. English possessive or objective with *of*.

3. Dative, WHERE-CASE, TO or FOR which anything IS or IS DONE. English remote or *indirect* object.

4. Accusative, WHITHER-CASE. English *direct* object.

5. Vocative, case of address.

§ 22. FIRST OR A-DECLENSION.[1]

ἀρχή, ἡ, *beginning.*	σοφία, ἡ, *wisdom.*	ὥρα, ἡ, *hour.*
Stem αρχᾱ-	Stem σοφιᾱ-	Stem ὡρᾱ-

S.N.V.	ἀρχή	σοφία	ὥρα
G.	ἀρχῆς	σοφίας	ὥρας
D.	ἀρχῇ	σοφίᾳ	ὥρᾳ
A.	ἀρχήν	σοφίαν	ὥραν
P.N.V.	ἀρχαί	σοφίαι	ὧραι
G.	ἀρχῶν	σοφιῶν	ὡρῶν
D.	ἀρχαῖς	σοφίαις	ὥραις
A.	ἀρχάς	σοφίας	ὥρᾱς

δόξα, ἡ, *glory.*

Stem δοξᾱ-

S.N.V.	δόξα	P.N.V.	δόξαι
G.	δόξης	G.	δοξῶν
D.	δόξῃ	D.	δόξαις
A.	δόξαν	A.	δόξᾱς

[1] Cf. **55** for table of endings in the A-declension.

προφήτης, ὁ, PROPHET.

Stem προφητᾱ-

S.N.	προφήτης [1]	P.N.V.	προφῆται
G.	προφήτου	G.	προφητῶν
D.	προφήτῃ	D.	προφήταις
A.	προφήτην	A.	προφήτᾱς
V.	προφῆτᾰ		

a. Most nouns of this declension have the nom. in α, η, or ᾱ, and are feminine.

b. Some end in -ς, and are masc. *E.g.* μαθητής, *disciple*; νεανίας, *young man*; κριτής, *judge*.

c. γῆ, ἡ, *earth*, contracted from γέα, is declined throughout as ἀρχή, but with the circumflex accent.

§ 23. SECOND OR O-DECLENSION.

λόγος, ὁ, *word.*	δοῦλος, ὁ, *servant.*	ἄνθρωπος, *man.*
Stem λογο-	Stem δουλο-	Stem ανθρωπο-

S.N.	λόγος	δοῦλος	ἄνθρωπος
G.	λόγου	δούλου	ἀνθρώπου
D.	λόγῳ	δούλῳ	ἀνθρώπῳ
A.	λόγον	δοῦλον	ἄνθρωπον
V.	λόγε	δοῦλε	ἄνθρωπε
P.N.V.	λόγοι	δοῦλοι	ἄνθρωποι
G.	λόγων	δούλων	ἀνθρώπων
D.	λόγοις	δούλοις	ἀνθρώποις
A.	λόγους	δούλους	ἀνθρώπους

υἱός, *son.*

Stem υἱο-

S.N.	υἱός	P.N.V.	υἱοί
G.	υἱοῦ	G.	υἱῶν
D.	υἱῷ	D.	υἱοῖς
A.	υἱόν	A.	υἱούς
V.	υἱέ		

[1] See **51** and **54**.

L

δῶρον, τό, *gift*.

Stem δωρο-

S.N.A.V.	δῶρον	P.N.A.V.	δῶρα
G.	δώρου	G.	δώρων
D.	δώρῳ	D.	δώροις

a. Ἰησοῦς, *Jesus*, is Ἰησοῦ in the gen., dat., and voc.

§ 24. THE DEFINITE ARTICLE.

	Masc.	*Fem.*	*Neut.*
S.N.	ὁ	ἡ	τό
G.	τοῦ	τῆς	τοῦ
D.	τῷ	τῇ	τῷ
A.	τόν	τήν	τό
P.N.	οἱ	αἱ	τά
G.	τῶν	τῶν	τῶν
D.	τοῖς	ταῖς	τοῖς
A.	τούς	τάς	τά

§ 25. ADJECTIVES OF THE A- AND O-DECLENSION.

καλός, *good*.

S.N.	καλός	καλή	καλόν
G.	καλοῦ	καλῆς	καλοῦ
D.	καλῷ	καλῇ	καλῷ
A.	καλόν	καλήν	καλόν
V.	καλέ	καλή	καλόν
P.N.	καλοί	καλαί	καλά
G.	καλῶν	καλῶν	καλῶν
D.	καλοῖς	καλαῖς	καλοῖς
A.	καλούς	καλάς	καλά

ἴδιος, *one's own.*   μικρός, *small.*

S.N.	ἴδιος	ἰδία	ἴδιον	μικρός	μικρά	μικρόν
G.	ἰδίου	ἰδίας	ἰδίου	μικροῦ	μικρᾶς	μικροῦ
D.	ἰδίῳ	ἰδίᾳ	ἰδίῳ	μικρῷ	μικρᾷ	μικρῷ
A.	ἴδιον	ἰδίαν	ἴδιον	μικρόν	μικράν	μικρόν
V.	ἴδιε	ἰδία	ἴδιον	μικρέ	μικρά	μικρόν
P.N.V.	ἴδιοι	ἴδιαι	ἴ:α	μικροί	μικραί	μικρά
G.	ἰδίων	ἰδίων	ἰδίων	μικρῶν	μικρῶν	μικρῶν
D.	ἰδίοις	ἰδίαις	ἰδίοις	μικροῖς	μικραῖς	μικροῖς
A.	ἰδίους	ἰδίας	ἴδια	μικρούς	μικράς	μικρά

§ 26.   PRONOUNS IN -ος.   Cf. 62–64.

οὗτος, *this (one)* ; ἐκεῖνος, *that (one)* ; αὐτός, *he, himself.*

S.N.	οὗτος	αὕτη	τοῦτο
G.	τούτου	ταύτης	τούτου
D.	τούτῳ	ταύτῃ	τούτῳ
A.	τοῦτον	ταύτην	τοῦτο
P.N.	οὗτοι	αὗται	ταῦτα
G.	τούτων	τούτων	τούτων
D.	τούτοις	ταύταις	τούτοις
A.	τούτους	ταύτας	ταῦτα

a. αὐτός and ἐκεῖνος are declined like καλός, above, except the neut. sing. of each is αὐτό and ἐκεῖνο in nom. and acc.

b. αὐτός is used as the pers. pron. of the 3 pers., *he, she, it* ; but in the *oblique* cases only. When used with a noun in any case, it means *himself*, etc. ; *e.g.* ὁ ἀνὴρ αὐτός, *the man himself.* But when the art. *precedes* the pron., as ὁ αὐτὸς ἀνήρ, it means *the same (man).* Cf. 69-70.

§ 27.   RELATIVE PRONOUN.

ὅς, *who.*

ὅς	ἥ	ὅ		οἵ	αἵ	ἅ
οὗ	ἧς	οὗ		ὧν	ὧν	ὧν
ᾧ	ᾗ	ᾧ		οἷς	αἷς	οἷς
ὅν	ἥν	ὅ		οὕς	ἅς	ἅ

§ 28. CONSONANT OR THIRD DECLENSION. LINGUAL MUTE STEMS.   Cf. 127–132.

χάρις, ἡ, *grace.*   ἐλπίς, ἡ, *hope.*
    Stem χαριτ-   Stem ἐλπιδ-

S.N.	χάρις	ἐλπίς
G.	χάριτος	ἐλπίδος
D.	χάριτι	ἐλπίδι
A.	χάριν	ἐλπίδα
V.	χάρις	ἐλπί
P.N.V.	χάριτες	ἐλπίδες
G.	χαρίτων	ἐλπίδων
D.	χάρισι	ἐλπίσι
A.	χάριτας	ἐλπίδας

νύξ, ἡ, *night.*   ἄρχων, ὁ, *ruler, prince.*
    Stem νυκτ-   Stem αρχοντ-

S.N.V.	νύξ	ἄρχων
G.	νυκτός	ἄρχοντος
D.	νυκτί	ἄρχοντι
A.	νύκτα	ἄρχοντα
P.N.V.	νύκτες	ἄρχοντες
G.	νυκτῶν	ἀρχόντων
D.	νυξί	ἄρχουσι
A.	νύκτας	ἄρχοντας

§ 29. Neuter Nouns of the Third Declension. Stems in -ατ. Cf. 106.

σῶμα, τό, *body.*

Stem σωματ-

S.N.A.V.	σῶμα	P.N.A.V.	σώματα
G.	σώματος	G.	σωμάτων
D.	σώματι	D.	σώμασι

ὄνομα, τό, *name.*

Stem ονοματ-

S.N.A.V.	ὄνομα	P.N.A.V.	ὀνόματα
G.	ὀνόματος	G.	ὀνομάτων
D.	ὀνόματι	D.	ὀνόμασι

§ 30. Neuter Nouns of the Third Declension. Stems in -εσ. Cf. 135.

γένος, τό, *race.*

Stem γενεσ-

S.N.A.V.	γένος	P.N.A.V.	γένη (γένεα)
G.	γένους (γένεος)	G.	γενῶν (γενέων)
D.	γένει	D.	γένεσι

§ 31. Stems in -ι and -ευ. Third Declension.

πόλις, ἡ, *city.* Cf. 112.

Stem πολι-

S.N.	πόλις	P.N.V.	πόλεις
G.	πόλεως	G.	πόλεων
D.	πόλει	D.	πόλεσι
A.	πόλιν	A.	πόλεις
V.	πόλι		

βασιλεύς, ὁ, *king*.

Stem βασιλευ-

	S.N.		P.N.A V.	
	S.N.	βασιλεύς	V.	βασιλεῖς
	G.	βασιλέως	G.	βασιλέων
	D.	βασιλεῖ	D.	βασιλεῦσι
	A.	βασιλέα		
	V.	βασιλεῦ		

§ 32. Liquid Stems of the Third Declension.

αἰών, ὁ, *age*.   ἡγεμών, *leader*.

Stem αιων-   Stem ἡγεμον-

S.N.V.	αἰών	P.	αἰῶνες	S.N.V.	ἡγεμών	P.	ἡγεμόνες
G.	αἰῶνος		αἰώνων	G.	ἡγεμόνος		ἡγεμόνων
D.	αἰῶνι		αἰῶσι	D.	ἡγεμόνι		ἡγεμόσι
A.	αἰῶνα		αἰῶνας	A.	ἡγεμόνα		ἡγεμόνας

§ 33.   Syncopated Stems in -ερ-.

πατήρ, ὁ, *father*.   Cf. 113.

Stem πατερ-

S.N.	πατήρ	P.N.V.	πατέρες
G.	πατρός (πατέρος)	G.	πατέρων
D.	πατρί (πατέρι)	D.	πατράσι
A.	πατέρα	A.	πατέρας
V.	πάτερ		

ἀνήρ, ὁ, *man*.   Cf. 114.

Stem ανερ-

S.N.	ἀνήρ	P.N.V.	ἄνδρες (ἀνέρες)
G.	ἀνδρός (ἀνέρος)	G.	ἀνδρῶν (ἀνέρων)
D.	ἀνδρί (ἀνέρι)	D.	ἀνδράσι
A.	ἄνδρα (ἀνέρα)	A.	ἄνδρας (ἀνέρας)
V.	ἄνερ		

a. μήτηρ, *mother,* θυγάτηρ, *daughter,* and γαστήρ, *belly,* are nouns declined the same as πατήρ.

§ 34.

The following are nouns of the third declension that have irregularities of form or accent. Only forms of the New Testament are here given.

γόνυ, τό, *knee.*   Plur. γόνατα, γονάτων, γόνασι.

γυνή, ἡ, *woman,* γυναικός, γυναικί, γυναῖκα, γύναι.   Plur. γυναῖκες, γυναικῶν, γυναιξί, γυναῖκας.

θρίξ, ἡ, *hair,* τρίχα.   Plur. τρίχες, τριχῶν, θριξί, τρίχας.

κύων, *dog.*   Plur. κύνες, κυσί, κύνας.

οὖς, τό, *ear.*   Plur. ὦτα, ὠσί.

πούς, ὁ, *foot,* ποδός, ποδί, πόδα.   Plur. πόδες, ποδῶν, ποσί, πόδας.

ὕδωρ, τό, *water,* ὕδατος, ὕδατι.   Plur. ὕδατα, ὑδάτων, ὕδασι.

χείρ, ἡ, *hand,* χειρός, χειρί, χεῖρα.   Plur. χεῖρες, χειρῶν, χερσί, χεῖρας.

§ 35. ADJECTIVES OF THE CONSONANT DECLENSION.

	STEMS IN -εσ-		STEMS IN -ν-	
	ἀληθής, *true.*		ἄφρων, *foolish.*	
	Stem αληθεσ-		Stem αφρον-	
S.N.	ἀληθής	ἀληθές	ἄφρων	ἄφρον
G.		ἀληθοῦς		ἄφρονος
D.		ἀληθεῖ		ἄφρονι
A.	ἀληθῆ	ἀληθές	ἄφρονα	ἄφρον
V.		ἀληθές		ἄφρον
P.N.V.	ἀληθεῖς	ἀληθῆ	ἄφρονες	ἄφρονα
G.		ἀληθῶν		ἀφρόνων
D.		ἀληθέσι		ἄφροσι
A.	ἀληθεῖς	ἀληθῆ	ἄφρονας	ἄφρονα

§ 36. Irregular Adjectives of the Consonant Declension. Cf. 164–165.

πᾶς, *all.*   μέγας, *great.*

Stem παντ-   Stems μεγα-, μεγαλο-

S.N.	πᾶς	πᾶσα	πᾶν	μέγας	μεγάλη	μέγα
G.	παντός	πάσης	παντός	μεγάλου	μεγάλης	μεγάλου
D.	παντί	πάσῃ	παντί	μεγάλῳ	μεγάλῃ	μεγάλῳ
A.	πάντα	πᾶσαν	πᾶν	μέγαν	μεγάλην	μέγα
V.	πᾶν	πᾶσα	πᾶν	μέγα	μεγάλη	μέγα
P.N.V.	πάντες	πᾶσαι	πάντα	μεγάλοι	μεγάλαι	μεγάλα
G.	πάντων	πασῶν	πάντων	μεγάλων	μεγάλων	μεγάλων
D.	πᾶσι	πάσαις	πᾶσι	μεγάλοις	μεγάλαις	μεγάλοις
A.	πάντας	πάσας	πάντα	μεγάλους	μεγάλας	μεγάλα

πολύς, *much, many.*

Stems πολυ-, πολλο-

S.N.	πολύς	πολλή	πολύ	P.	πολλοί	πολλαί	πολλά
G.	πολλοῦ	πολλῆς	πολλοῦ		πολλῶν	πολλῶν	πολλῶν
D.	πολλῷ	πολλῇ	πολλῷ		πολλοῖς	πολλαῖς	πολλοῖς
A.	πολύν	πολλήν	πολύ		πολλούς	πολλάς	πολλά

§ 37.   Comparison of Adjectives.

1. Add -τερος for the compar., and -τατος for the superl.

ἰσχῡρός,	ἰσχῡρό-τερος,[1]	(ἰσχῡρό-τατος),
strong.	*strong-er.*	*strong-est.*

2. Add -ιων for the compar., and -ιστος for the superl.

πολύς,	πλε-ίων,	πλε-ῖστος,
much.	*more.*	*most.*

---

[1] When the penultimate vowel is short, as in σοφός, the ο is lengthened before -τερος and -τατος; *e.g.* σοφός, σοφώτερος (σοφώτατος). Cf. **225**.

§ 38.   IRREGULAR COMPARISON.

ἀγαθός, *good*	κρείσσων	κράτιστος
κακός, *bad*	χείρων	——
καλός, *good*	καλλίων	——
μέγας, *great*	μείζων	μέγιστος [1]
μικρός, *small*	ἐλάσσων	ἐλάχιστος
πολύς, *much*	πλείων	πλεῖστος

a. Comparatives in -ων are declined like ἄφρων, § 35.

§ 39.   CARDINAL NUMERALS.

	εἷς, *one.*	τρεῖς, *three.*	τέσσαρες, *four.*
N.	εἷς μία ἕν	τρεῖς τρία	τέσσαρες τέσσαρα
G.	ἑνός μιᾶς ἑνός	τριῶν	τεσσάρων
D.	ἑνί μιᾷ ἑνί	τρισί	τέσσαρσι
A.	ἕνα μίαν ἕν	τρεῖς τρία	τέσσαρας τέσσαρα

a. The cardinal numerals from 4 to 100 are indeclinable.

b. Ordinal numerals (πρῶτος, etc.) in -ος and -οι are declined like adjectives in -ος.

c. For the declension of οὐδείς (οὐδέ, *and not,* + εἷς, *one*), see 221.

§ 40.   PRONOUNS. Cf. **68** and **213**.

	ἐγώ, *I.*	*Personal.*		σύ, *you.*
S.N.	ἐγώ		S.N.	σύ
G.	ἐμοῦ, μου		G.	σοῦ
D.	ἐμοί, μοι		D.	σοί
A.	ἐμέ, με		A.	σέ
P.N.	ἡμεῖς, *we*		P.N.	ὑμεῖς
G.	ἡμῶν		G.	ὑμῶν
D.	ἡμῖν		D.	ὑμῖν
A.	ἡμᾶς		A.	ὑμᾶς

[1] Occurs but once.

Reflexive.

ἐμαυτοῦ, *myself.*   σεαυτοῦ, *thyself.*

S.G. ἐμαυτοῦ, -ῆς   σεαυτοῦ, -ῆς
   D. ἐμαυτῷ, -ῇ   σεαυτῷ, -ῇ
   A. ἐμαυτόν, -ήν   σεαυτόν, -ήν

P.G. ἡμῶν αὐτῶν   ὑμῶν αὐτῶν
   D. ἡμῖν αὐτοῖς, αὐταῖς   ὑμῖν αὐτοῖς   ὑμῖν αὐταῖς
   A. ἡμᾶς αὐτούς, αὐτάς   ὑμᾶς αὐτούς   ὑμᾶς αὐτάς

ἑαυτοῦ, *himself, herself, itself.*

S.G. ἑαυτοῦ, -ῆς   P.   ἑαυτῶν
   D. ἑαυτῷ, -ῇ   ἑαυτοῖς   ἑαυταῖς   ἑαυτοῖς
   A. ἑαυτόν, -ήν, -ό   ἑαυτούς   ἑαυτάς   ἑαυτά

§ 41. *Interrogative.*   *Indefinite.*

   τίς, *who.*   τὶς, *some one.*

S.N. τίς τί P. τίνες τίνα   S.N. τὶς τὶ P. τινὲς τινὰ
   G. τίνος   τίνων   τινὸς   τινῶν
   D. τίνι   τίσι   τινὶ   τισὶ
   A. τίνα τί   τίνας τίνα   τινὰ τὶ   τινὰς τινὰ

   a. τὶς, *some one,* is an enclitic.   Cf. 196–198.

§ 42. The indefinite relative ὅστις (ὅς, *who,* and τὶς), *whoever,* has the following forms :

   S.N. ὅστις, ἥτις, ὅ,τι.   P.N. οἵτινες, αἵτινες, ἅτινα.

§ 43.   PARTICIPLES.

λύω, *loose.*

Present Active.

S.N. λύων   λύουσα   λῦον
   G. λύοντος   λυούσης   λύοντος
   D. λύοντι   λυούσῃ   λύοντι
   A. λύοντα   λύουσαν   λῦον

P.N.V.	λύοντες	λύουσαι	λύοντα
G.	λυόντων	λυουσῶν	λυόντων
D.	λύουσι	λυούσαις	λύουσι
A.	λύοντας	λυούσᾱς	λύοντα

a. For the pres. part. of εἰμί, *am*, see **183** and **184**.

Aorist Active.

S.N.	λύσας	λύσασα	λῦσαν
G.	λύσαντος	λυσάσης	λύσαντος
D.	λύσαντι	λυσάσῃ	λύσαντι
A.	λύσαντα	λύσασαν	λῦσαν
P.N.V.	λύσαντες	λύσασαι	λύσαντα
G.	λυσάντων	λυσασῶν	λυσάντων
D.	λύσᾱσι	λυσάσαις	λύσᾱσι
A.	λύσαντας	λυσάσᾱς	λύσαντα

Perfect Active.

S.N.	λελυκώς	λελυκυῖα	λελυκός
G.	λελυκότος	λελυκυίας	λελυκότος
D.	λελυκότι	λελυκυίᾳ	λελυκότι
A.	λελυκότα	λελυκυῖαν	λελυκός
P.N.V.	λελυκότες	λελυκυῖαι	λελυκότα
G.	λελυκότων	λελυκυιῶν	λελυκότων
D.	λελυκόσι	λελυκυίαις	λελυκόσι
A.	λελυκότας	λελυκυίᾱς	λελυκότα

b. So likewise the 2 perf. act.; as ἑστώς, ἑστυῖα, ἑστός, *standing*, from ἵστημι, *to make stand*.

Aorist Passive.

S.N.	λυθείς	λυθεῖσα	λυθέν
G.	λυθέντος	λυθείσης	λυθέντος
D.	λυθέντι	λυθείσῃ	λυθέντι
A.	λυθέντα	λυθεῖσαν	λυθέν

P.N.V. λυθέντες   λυθεῖσαι   λυθέντα
   G.   λυθέντων   λυθεισῶν   λυθέντων
   D.   λυθεῖσι   λυθείσαις   λυθεῖσι
   A.   λυθέντας   λυθείσᾱς   λυθέντα

c. So likewise the 2 aor. pass.; as σπαρείς, σπαρεῖσα, σπαρέν, from σπείρω, *sow.*

§ 44. Participles in -εων and -αων contract as follows :

λαλέων [1]   λαλέουσα   λαλέον, *speaking*
become λαλῶν   λαλοῦσα   λαλοῦν
   λαλοῦντος   λαλούσης   λαλοῦντος

ζάων [2]   ζάουσα   ζάον, *living*
become ζῶν   ζῶσα   ζῶν
   ζῶντος   ζώσης   ζῶντος

§ 45. Second Aorist Participles of Irregular Verbs.

δίδωμι. — δούς, *giving.*   βαίνω. — βάς, *going.*

S.N. δούς   δοῦσα δόν   S.N. βάς   βᾶσα   βάν
  G. δόντος δούσης δόντος   G. βάντος βάσης   βάντος
         etc.   etc.

a. So the pres. part. διδούς.

τίθημι. — θείς, *placing.*   πίπτω. — πεσών, *falling.*

S.N. θείς   θεῖσα θέν   S.N. πεσών   πεσοῦσα πεσόν
  G. θέντος θείσης θέντος   G. πεσόντος πεσούσης πεσόντος
         etc.   etc.

b. So the pres. part. τιθείς.   *c.* So all 2 aor. ptcs. in -ών.

[1] See §§ 5, 8; 8, 4.   [2] See §§ 5, 1, 2; 8, 3.

ἵστημι. — στάς, *standing.*　γινώσκω. — γνούς, *knowing.*

S.N. στάς　στᾶσα στάν　S.N. γνούς　γνοῦσα (γνόν)
　G. στάντος στάσης στάντος　G. γνόντος γνούσης γνόντος
　　　　etc.　　　　　　　　　　　etc.

§ 46. All participles in -μενος are declined like καλός, § 25.

The Verb.

Voice.

§ 47. There are three voices in Greek: the active, middle, and passive. Of these the active and passive are the same as the active and passive in English.

The middle voice represents the subject as acting upon itself or in some way that concerns itself.

1. The Direct Middle where the subject acts directly upon itself; *e.g.* λούω, *I wash;* λούομαι, *I wash myself.*

2. The Indirect Middle where the subject is represented as acting in some way for itself; *e.g.* ἀγοράζω, *I buy,* ἀγοράζομαι, *I buy for myself;* νίπτω, *I wash,* νίπτομαι τὰς χεῖρας, *I wash my own hands.*

§ 48. The uses of the middle voice are numerous, and are best learned from the lexicon.

Often the sense of the verb changes in the middle; *e.g.* πείθω, *I persuade*; πείθομαι, *I persuade myself, I obey.*

Mood.

§ 49. There are five moods in Greek : the Indicative, Subjunctive, Optative, Imperative, and Infinitive. The Indicative, Imperative, and Infinitive correspond very closely to the same moods in English. The Subjunctive is most often translated by the English *potential.* The principal uses of the Subjunctive are explained in **87, 95–97, 158**. See also under Syntax.

The Optative mood is rare in the New Testament, and hence is not given with the paradigms. For the forms that occur and the uses of the same, see § **70** and § **71.**

Tense.

§ 50. The tenses of the Indicative mood are seven. The *present* and *imperfect* denote continued or repeated action ; the *aorist* and *future* denote an indefinite action ; the *perfect, pluperfect*, and *future perfect* denote completed action.

§ 51. The tenses of the subjunctive are the *present, aorist*, and *perfect;* the latter is very rare in the New Testament.

§ 52. The tenses of the Indicative are distinguished as *primary* and *secondary*.

PRIMARY: *Present, future, perfect, future perfect.*
SECONDARY: *Imperfect, aorist, pluperfect.*

§ 53. The principal parts of a Greek verb are the first person singular of the *present, future*, (first or second) *aorist,* (first or second) *perfect,* indicative active; the *perfect middle,* and the first or second *aorist passive;* e.g.

λύω, λύσω, ἔλυσα, λέλυκα, λέλυμαι, ἐλύθην
κρίνω, κρινῶ, ἔκρινα, κέκρικα, κέκριμαι, ἐκρίθην

§ 54. There is no difference in meaning nor in translation between a first aorist and a second aorist, between a first perfect and a second perfect.

§ 55. The tenses of the verb are divided into nine classes or tense systems, each having a distinct tense stem.

1. *Present*   including *present* and *imperfect.*
2. *Future*   "   *future active* and *middle.*
3. *First aorist*   "   *first aorist active* and *middle.*
4. *Second aorist*   "   *second aorist active* and *middle.*
5. *First perfect*   "   *first perfect* and *pluperfect active.*
6. *Second perfect* "   *second perfect* and *pluperfect active.*
7. *Perfect middle* "   *perfect* and *pluperfect middle* and *passive* and *future perfect.*
8. *First passive*   "   *first aorist* and *future passive.*
9. *Second passive* "   *second aorist* and *future passive.*

§ 56.   1. ACTIVE VOICE OF λύω.

		Present.	*Imperfect.*	*Future.*
INDICATIVE.	S. 1.	λύω	ἔλῡον	λύσω
	2.	λύεις	ἔλῡες	λύσεις
	3.	λύει	ἔλῡε	λύσει
	P. 1.	λύομεν	ἐλύομεν	λύσομεν
	2.	λύετε	ἐλύετε	λύσετε
	3.	λύουσι	ἔλῡον	λύσουσι
SUBJUNCTIVE.	S. 1.	λύω		
	2.	λύῃς		
	3.	λύῃ		
	P. 1.	λύωμεν		
	2.	λύητε		
	3.	λύωσι		
IMPERATIVE.	S. 2.	λῦε		
	3.	λῡέτω		
	P. 2.	λύετε		
	3.	λῡόντων or		
		λῡέτωσαν		
INFINITIVE.		λύειν		λύσειν
PARTICIPLE.		λύων,		λύσων,
		λύουσα,		λύσουσα,
		λῦον (§ 43)		λῦσον

		1 *Aorist.*	1 *Perfect.*	1 *Pluperf.*
INDICATIVE.	S. { 1.	ἔλῡσα	λέλυκα	(ἐ)λελύκειν
	2.	ἔλῡσας	λέλυκας	(ἐ)λελύκεις
	3.	ἔλῡσε	λέλυκε	(ἐ)λελύκει
	P. { 1.	ἐλύσαμεν	λελύκαμεν	(ἐ)λελύκει-μεν
	2.	ἐλύσατε	λελύκατε	(ἐ)λελύκει-τε
	3.	ἔλῡσαν	λελύκᾱσι or -καν	(ἐ)λελύκει-σαν
SUBJUNCTIVE.	S. { 1.	λύσω	[λελύκω	
	2.	λύσῃς	λελύκῃς	
	3.	λύσῃ	λελύκῃ	
	P. { 1.	λύσωμεν	λελύκωμεν	
	2.	λύσητε	λελύκητε	
	3.	λύσωσι	λελύκωσι]	
IMPERATIVE.	S. { 2.	λῦσον	[λέλυκε	
	3.	λῡσάτω	λελυκέτω	
	P. { 2.	λύσατε	λελύκετε	
	3.	λῡσάντων or λῡσάτωσαν	λελυκέτωσαν]	
INFINITIVE.		λῦσαι	λελυκέναι	
PARTICIPLE.		λύσᾱς, λύσᾱσα, λῦσαν (§ 43)	λελυκώς, λελυκυῖα, λελυκός (§ 43)	

M

2. MIDDLE VOICE OF λύω.

		Present.	*Imperfect.*	*Future.*
INDICATIVE.	S.	1. λύομαι	ἐλῡόμην	λύσομαι
		2. λύῃ, λύει	ἐλύου	λύσῃ, λύσει
		3. λύεται	ἐλύετο	λύσεται
	P.	1. λῡόμεθα	ἐλῡόμεθα	λῡσόμεθα
		2. λύεσθε	ἐλύεσθε	λύσεσθε
		3. λύονται	ἐλύοντο	λύσονται
SUBJUNCTIVE.	S.	1. λύωμαι		
		2. λύῃ		
		3. λύηται		
	P.	1. λῡώμεθα		
		2. λύησθε		
		3. λύωνται		
IMPERATIVE.	S.	2. λύου		
		3. λυέσθω		
	P.	2. λύεσθε		
		3. λυέσθων or		
		λυέσθωσαν		
INFINITIVE.		λύεσθαι		λύσεσθαι
PARTICIPLE.		λῡόμενος,		λῡσόμενος,
		λῡομένη,		-η, -ον
		λῡόμενον (§ 46)		(§ 46)

		1 *Aorist.*	*Perfect.*	*Pluperf.*
INDICATIVE.				
	S. 1.	ἐλῡσάμην	λέλυμαι	ἐλελύμην
	2.	ἐλύσω	λέλυσαι	ἐλέλυσο
	3.	ἐλύσατο	λέλυται	ἐλέλυτο
	P. 1.	ἐλῡσάμεθα	λελύμεθα	ἐλελύμεθα
	2.	ἐλύσασθε	λέλυσθε	ἐλέλυσθε
	3.	ἐλύσαντο	λέλυνται	ἐλέλυντο
SUBJUNCTIVE.				
	S. 1.	λύσωμαι	λελυμένος ὦ	
	2.	λύσῃ	λελυμένος ᾖς	
	3.	λύσηται	λελυμένος ᾖ	
	P. 1.	λῡσώμεθα	λελυμένοι ὦμεν	
	2.	λύσησθε	λελυμένοι ἦτε	
	3.	λύσωνται	λελυμένοι ὦσι	
IMPERATIVE.				
	S. 2.	λῦσαι	[λέλυσο	
	3.	λῡσάσθω]	λελύσθω	
	P. 2.	λύσασθε	λέλυσθε	
	3.	λῡσάσθων or	λελύσθων or	
		λῡσάσθωσαν	λελύσθωσαν]	
INFINITIVE.		λύσασθαι	λελύσθαι	
PARTICIPLE.		λῡσάμενος, -η, -ον (§ 46)	λελυμένος, -η, -ον (§ 46)	

3. PASSIVE VOICE OF λύω.

		Fut. Perf.[1]	1 *Aor.*[1]	1 *Future.*[1]
INDICATIVE.	S. 1.	[λελύσομαι	ἐλύθην	λυθήσομαι
	2.	λελύσῃ, -σει	ἐλύθης	λυθήσῃ, -σει
	3.	λελύσεται	ἐλύθη	λυθήσεται
	P. 1.	λελυσόμεθα	ἐλύθημεν	λυθησόμεθα
	2.	λελύσεσθε	ἐλύθητε	λυθήσεσθε
	3.	λελύσονται]	ἐλύθησαν	λυθήσονται
SUBJUNCTIVE.	S. 1.		λυθῶ	
	2.		λυθῇς	
	3.		λυθῇ	
	P. 1.		λυθῶμεν	
	2.		λυθῆτε	
	3.		λυθῶσι	
IMPERATIVE.	S. 2.		λύθητι	
	3.		λυθήτω	
	P. 2.		λυθῆτε	
	3.		λυθέντων or	
			λυθήτωσαν	
INFINITIVE.		λελύσεσθαι	λυθῆναι	λυθήσεσθαι
PARTICIPLE.		λελυσόμενος,	λυθείς,	λυθησόμενος,
		-η, -ον	λυθεῖσα,	-η, -ον
		(§ 46)	λυθέν (§ 43)	(§ 46)

[1] All other tenses of the passive voice are the same in form as the middle.

§ 57.   SECOND AORIST (ACTIVE AND MIDDLE) AND SECOND PERFECT AND PLUPERFECT OF λείπω.

	2 Aor. Act.	2 Aor. Mid.	2 Perf.	2 Pluperf.

INDICATIVE.

		2 Aor. Act.	2 Aor. Mid.	2 Perf.	2 Pluperf.
S.	1.	ἔλιπον	ἐλιπόμην	λέλοιπα	[ἐλελοίπην
	2.	ἔλιπες	ἐλίπου	λέλοιπας	ἐλελοίπης
	3.	ἔλιπε	ἐλίπετο	λέλοιπε	ἐλελοίπει(ν)
P.	1.	ἐλίπομεν	ἐλιπόμεθα	λελοίπαμεν	ἐλελοίπεμεν
	2.	ἐλίπετε	ἐλίπεσθε	λελοίπατε	ἐλελοίπετε
	3.	ἔλιπον	ἐλίποντο	λελοίπᾱσι	ἐλελοίπεσαν]

SUBJUNCTIVE.

S.	1.	λίπω	λίπωμαι	[λελοίπω
	2.	λίπῃς	λίπῃ	λελοίπῃς
	3.	λίπῃ	λίπηται	λελοίπῃ
P.	1.	λίπωμεν	λιπώμεθα	λελοίπωμεν
	2.	λίπητε	λίπησθε	λελοίπητε
	3.	λίπωσι	λίπωνται	λελοίπωσι]

IMPERATIVE.

S.	2.	λίπε	λιποῦ	[λέλοιπε
	3.	λιπέτω	λιπέσθω	λελοιπέτω
P.	2.	λίπετε	λίπεσθε	λελοίπετε
	3.	λιπόντων or	λιπέσθων or	λελοιπέτωσαν]
		λιπέτωσαν	λιπέσθωσαν	

INFINITIVE.

λιπεῖν   λιπέσθαι   [λελοιπέναι]

PARTICIPLE.

λιπών,   λιπόμενος, -η,   λελοιπώς,
λιποῦσα,   -ον (§ 46)   λελοιπυῖα,
λιπόν (§ 45, c)   -πός (§ 43)

§ **58**.   FUTURE AND FIRST AORIST ACTIVE AND MIDDLE
(LIQUID FORMS) AND SECOND AORIST AND
SECOND FUTURE PASSIVE OF φαίνω.

		Fut. Ac.	*Fut. Mid.*	1 *Aor. Act.*
INDICATIVE.	S. 1.	φανῶ	φανοῦμαι	ἔφηνα
	2.	φανεῖς	φανεῖ, φανῇ	ἔφηνας
	3.	φανεῖ	φανεῖται	ἔφηνε
	P. 1.	φανοῦμεν	φανούμεθα	ἐφήναμεν
	2.	φανεῖτε	φανεῖσθε	ἐφήνατε
	3.	φανοῦσι	φανοῦνται	ἔφηναν
SUBJUNCTIVE.	S. 1.			φήνω
	2.			φήνῃς
	3.			φήνῃ
	P. 1.			φήνωμεν
	2.			φήνητε
	3.			φήνωσι
IMPERATIVE.	S. 2.			φῆνον
	3.			φηνάτω
	P. 2.			φήνατε
	3.			φηνάντων or φηνάτωσαν
INFINITIVE.		φανεῖν	φανεῖσθαι	φῆναι
PARTICIPLE.		φανών, φανοῦσα, φανοῦν (§ 44)	φανούμενος, -η, -ον (§ 46)	φήνᾱς, φήνᾱσα, φῆναν (§ 43)

	1 *Aor. Mid.*	2 *Aor. Pass.*	2 *Fut. Pass.*

INDICATIVE.

S.
1. ἐφηνάμην	ἐφάνην	φανήσομαι
2. ἐφήνω	ἐφάνης	φανήσει, -ση
3. ἐφήνατο	ἐφάνη	φανήσεται

P.
1. ἐφηνάμεθα	ἐφάνημεν	φανησόμεθα
2. ἐφήνασθε	ἐφάνητε	φανήσεσθε
3. ἐφήναντο	ἐφάνησαν	φανήσονται

SUBJUNCTIVE.

S.
1. φήνωμαι	φανῶ
2. φήνῃ	φανῇς
3. φήνηται	φανῇ

P.
1. φηνώμεθα	φανῶμεν
2. φήνησθε	φανῆτε
3. φήνωνται	φανῶσι

IMPERATIVE.

S.
| 2. φῆναι | φάνηθι |
| 3. φηνάσθω | φανήτω |

P.
2. φήνασθε	φάνητε
3. φηνάσθων or	φανέντων or
φηνάσθωσαν	φανήτωσαν

INFINITIVE.   φήνασθαι   φανῆναι   φανήσεσθαι

PARTICIPLE.
φηνάμενος,	φανείς,	φανησόμενος,
-η, -ον	φανεῖσα,	-η, -ον
(§ 46)	φανέν	(§ 46)
	(§ 43, *c*)	

CONTRACT VERBS.

§ 59. Verbs in αω, εω, and οω are contracted in the present and imperfect. These tenses of τιμάω (τιμα-), honor, φιλέω (φιλε-), love, and δηλόω (δηλο-), manifest, are thus inflected:

ACTIVE.

Present Indicative.

S. 1.	(τιμάω) τιμῶ	(φιλέω) φιλῶ	(δηλόω) δηλῶ
2.	(τιμάεις) τιμᾷς	(φιλέεις) φιλεῖς	(δηλόεις) δηλοῖς
3.	(τιμάει) τιμᾷ	(φιλέει) φιλεῖ	(δηλόει) δηλοῖ
P. 1.	(τιμάομεν) τιμῶμεν	(φιλέομεν) φιλοῦμεν	(δηλόομεν) δηλοῦμεν
2.	(τιμάετε) τιμᾶτε	(φιλέετε) φιλεῖτε	(δηλόετε) δηλοῦτε
3.	(τιμάουσι) τιμῶσι	(φιλέουσι) φιλοῦσι	(δηλόουσι) δηλοῦσι

Present Subjunctive.

S. 1.	(τιμάω) τιμῶ	(φιλέω) φιλῶ	(δηλόω) δηλῶ
2.	(τιμάῃς) τιμᾷς	(φιλέῃς) φιλῇς	(δηλόῃς) δηλοῖς
3.	(τιμάῃ) τιμᾷ	(φιλέῃ) φιλῇ	(δηλόῃ) δηλοῖ

		τιμάω	φιλέω	δηλόω
P.	1.	(τιμάωμεν) τιμῶμεν	(φιλέομεν) φιλῶμεν	(δηλόομεν) δηλῶμεν
	2.	(τιμάητε) τιμᾶτε	(φιλέητε) φιλῆτε	(δηλόητε) δηλῶτε
	3.	(τιμάωσι) τιμῶσι	(φιλέωσι) φιλῶσι	(δηλόωσι) δηλῶσι

Present Imperative.

		τιμάω	φιλέω	δηλόω
S.	2.	(τίμαε) τίμα	(φίλεε) φίλει	(δήλοε) δήλου
	3.	(τιμαέτω) τιμάτω	(φιλέετω) φιλείτω	(δηλοέτω) δηλούτω
P.	2.	(τιμάετε) τιμᾶτε	(φιλέετε) φιλεῖτε	(δηλόετε) δηλοῦτε
	3.	(τιμαόντων) τιμώντων or (τιμαέτωσαν) τιμάτωσαν	(φιλεόντων) φιλούντων or (φιλεέτωσαν) φιλείτωσαν	(δηλοόντων) δηλούντων or (δηλοέτωσαν) δηλούτωσαν

Present Infinitive.

τιμάω	φιλέω	δηλόω
(τιμάειν) τιμᾶν	(φιλέειν) φιλεῖν	(δηλόειν) δηλοῦν

Present Participle (see § 44).

τιμάω	φιλέω	δηλόω
(τιμάων) τιμῶν	(φιλέων) φιλῶν	(δηλόων) δηλῶν

Imperfect.

		τιμάω	φιλέω	δηλόω
S.	1.	(ἐτίμαον) ἐτίμων	(ἐφίλεον) ἐφίλουν	(ἐδήλοον) ἐδήλουν
	2.	(ἐτίμαες) ἐτίμας	(ἐφίλεες) ἐφίλεις	(ἐδήλοες) ἐδήλους
	3.	(ἐτίμαε) ἐτίμα	(ἐφίλεε) ἐφίλει	(ἐδήλοε) ἐδήλου

	τιμάω	φιλέω	δηλόω
P. 1.	(ἐτιμάομεν) ἐτιμῶμεν	(ἐφιλέομεν) ἐφιλοῦμεν	(ἐδηλόομεν) ἐδηλοῦμεν
2.	(ἐτιμάετε) ἐτιμᾶτε	(ἐφιλέετε) ἐφιλεῖτε	(ἐδηλόετε) ἐδηλοῦτε
3.	(ἐτίμαον) ἐτίμων	(ἐφίλεον) ἐφίλουν	(ἐδήλοον) ἐδήλουν

PASSIVE AND MIDDLE.

† Present Indicative.

	τιμάω	φιλέω	δηλόω
S. 1.	(τιμάομαι) τιμῶμαι	(φιλέομαι) φιλοῦμαι	(δηλόομαι) δηλοῦμαι
2.	(τιμάει, τιμάῃ) τιμᾷ	(φιλέει, φιλέῃ) φιλεῖ, φιλῇ	(δηλόει, δηλόῃ) δηλοῖ
3.	(τιμάεται) τιμᾶται	(φιλέεται) φιλεῖται	(δηλόεται) δηλοῦται
P. 1.	(τιμαόμεθα) τιμώμεθα	(φιλεόμεθα) φιλούμεθα	(δηλοόμεθα) δηλούμεθα
2.	(τιμάεσθε) τιμᾶσθε	(φιλέεσθε) φιλεῖσθε	(δηλόεσθε) δηλοῦσθε
3.	(τιμάονται) τιμῶνται	(φιλέονται) φιλοῦνται	(δηλόονται) δηλοῦνται

Present Subjunctive.

	τιμάω	φιλέω	δηλόω
S. 1.	(τιμάωμαι) τιμῶμαι	(φιλέωμαι) φιλῶμαι	(δηλόωμαι) δηλῶμαι
2.	(τιμάῃ) τιμᾷ	(φιλέῃ) φιλῇ	(δηλόῃ) δηλοῖ
3.	(τιμάηται) τιμᾶται	(φιλέηται) φιλῆται	(δηλόηται) δηλῶται
P. 1.	(τιμαώμεθα) τιμώμεθα	(φιλεώμεθα) φιλώμεθα	(δηλοώμεθα) δηλώμεθα
2.	(τιμάησθε) τιμᾶσθε	(φιλέησθε) φιλῆσθε	(δηλόησθε) δηλῶσθε
3.	(τιμάωνται) τιμῶνται	(φιλέωνται) φιλῶνται	(δηλόωνται) δηλῶνται

Present Imperative.

S.	2.	(τιμάου) τιμῶ	(φιλέου) φιλοῦ	(δηλόου) δηλοῦ
	3.	(τιμαέσθω) τιμάσθω	(φιλεέσθω) φιλείσθω	(δηλοέσθω) δηλούσθω
P.	2.	(τιμάεσθε) τιμᾶσθε	(φιλέεσθε) φιλεῖσθε	(δηλόεσθε) δηλοῦσθε
	3.	(τιμαέσθωσαν) τιμάσθωσαν	(φιλεέσθωσαν) φιλείσθωσαν	(δηλοέσθωσαν) δηλούσθωσαν
		or (τιμαέσθων) τιμάσθων	or (φιλεέσθων) φιλείσθων	or (δηλοέσθων) δηλούσθων

Present Infinitive.

(τιμάεσθαι) τιμᾶσθαι   (φιλέεσθαι) φιλεῖσθαι   (δηλόεσθαι) δηλοῦσθαι

Present Participle.

(τιμαόμενος) τιμώμενος   (φιλεόμενος) φιλούμενος   (δηλοόμενος) δηλούμενος

Imperfect.

S.	1.	(ἐτιμαόμην) ἐτιμώμην	(ἐφιλεόμην) ἐφιλούμην	(ἐδηλοόμην) ἐδηλούμην
	2.	(ἐτιμάου) ἐτιμῶ	(ἐφιλέου) ἐφιλοῦ	(ἐδηλόου) ἐδηλοῦ
	3.	(ἐτιμάετο) ἐτιμᾶτο	(ἐφιλέετο) ἐφιλεῖτο	(ἐδηλόετο) ἐδηλοῦτο
P.	1.	(ἐτιμαόμεθα) ἐτιμώμεθα	(ἐφιλεόμεθα) ἐφιλούμεθα	(ἐδηλοόμεθα) ἐδηλούμεθα
	2.	(ἐτιμάεσθε) ἐτιμᾶσθε	(ἐφιλέεσθε) ἐφιλεῖσθε	(ἐδηλόεσθε) ἐδηλοῦσθε
	3.	(ἐτιμάοντο) ἐτιμῶντο	(ἐφιλέοντο) ἐφιλοῦντο	(ἐδηλόοντο) ἐδηλοῦντο

CONJUGATION OF μι VERBS.

§ 60. Verbs in μι differ from verbs in ω in the Present and Second Aorist Systems only. See Lessons XXXI. and XXXII.

§ 61. SYNOPSIS of ἵστημι, τίθημι, and δίδωμι, in the Present and Second Aorist Systems.

ACTIVE.

	Indic.	Subj.	Imper.	Infin.	Part.
Pres. and Impf.	ἵστημι ἵστην	ἱστῶ	ἵστη	ἱστάναι	ἱστάς
	τίθημι ἐτίθην	τιθῶ	τίθει	τιθέναι	τιθείς
	δίδωμι ἐδίδουν	διδῶ	δίδου	διδόναι	διδούς
2 Aor.	ἔστην	στῶ θῶ δῶ	στῆθι θές δός	στῆναι θεῖναι δοῦναι	στάς θείς δούς

PASSIVE AND MIDDLE.

	Indic.	Subj.	Imper.	Infin.	Part.
Pres. and Impf.	ἵσταμαι ἱστάμην	ἱστῶμαι	ἵστασο	ἵστασθαι	ἱστάμενος
	τίθεμαι ἐτιθέμην	τιθῶμαι	τίθεσο	τίθεσθαι	τιθέμενος
	δίδομαι ἐδιδόμην	διδῶμαι	δίδοσο	δίδοσθαι	διδόμενος
2 Aor. Mid.	ἐθέμην ἐδόμην	θῶμαι δῶμαι	θοῦ δοῦ	θέσθαι δόσθαι	θέμενος δόμενος

§ 62. PRESENT SYSTEM.

ACTIVE VOICE.

Present Indicative.

Sing.	1. ἵστημι	τίθημι	δίδωμι
	2. ἵστης	τίθης	δίδως
	3. ἵστησι	τίθησι	δίδωσι

Plur.	1. ἵστᾰμεν	τίθεμεν	δίδομεν
	2. ἵστατε	τίθετε	δίδοτε
	3. ἱστᾶσι	τιθέᾱσι	διδόᾱσι

Imperfect.

Sing.	1. ἵστην	ἐτίθην	ἐδίδουν
	2. ἵστης	ἐτίθεις	ἐδίδους
	3. ἵστη	ἐτίθει	ἐδίδου

Plur.	1. ἵστᾰμεν	ἐτίθεμεν	ἐδίδομεν
	2. ἵστατε	ἐτίθετε	ἐδίδοτε
	3. ἵστασαν	ἐτίθεσαν	ἐδίδοσαν

Present Subjunctive.

Sing.	1. ἱστῶ	τιθῶ	διδῶ
	2. ἱστῇς	τιθῇς	διδῶς
	3. ἱστῇ	τιθῇ	διδῷ

Plur.	1. ἱστῶμεν	τιθῶμεν	διδῶμεν
	2. ἱστῆτε	τιθῆτε	διδῶτε
	3. ἱστῶσι	τιθῶσι	διδῶσι

Present Imperative.

Sing.	2. ἴστη	τίθει	δίδου
	3. ἱστάτω	τιθέτω	διδότω
Plur.	2. ἵστατε	τίθετε	δίδοτε
	3. ἱστάντων or	τιθέντων or	διδόντων or
	ἱστάτωσαν	τιθέτωσαν	διδότωσαν

Present Infinitive.

ἱστάναι   τιθέναι   διδόναι

Present Participle (§ 45).

ἱστάς   τιθείς   διδούς

PASSIVE AND MIDDLE.

Present Indicative.

Sing.	1. ἵσταμαι	τίθεμαι	δίδομαι
	2. ἵστασαι	τίθεσαι	δίδοσαι
	3. ἵσταται	τίθεται	δίδοται
Plur.	1. ἱστάμεθα	τιθέμεθα	διδόμεθα
	2. ἵστασθε	τίθεσθε	δίδοσθε
	3. ἵστανται	τίθενται	δίδονται

Imperfect.

Sing.	1. ἱστάμην	ἐτιθέμην	ἐδιδόμην
	2. ἵστασο	ἐτίθεσο	ἐδίδοσο or δου
	3. ἵστατο	ἐτίθετο	ἐδίδοτο

Plur.
1. ἱστάμεθα   ἐτιθέμεθα   ἐδιδόμεθα
2. ἵστασθε   ἐτίθεσθε   ἐδίδοσθε
3. ἵσταντο   ἐτίθεντο   ἐδίδοντο

Present Subjunctive.

Sing.
1. ἱστῶμαι   τιθῶμαι   διδῶμαι
2. ἱστῇ   τιθῇ   διδῷ
3. ἱστῆται   τιθῆται   διδῶται

Plur.
1. ἱστώμεθα   τιθώμεθα   διδώμεθα
2. ἱστῆσθε   τιθῆσθε   διδῶσθε
3. ἱστῶνται   τιθῶνται   διδῶνται

Present Imperative.

Sing.
2. ἵστασο   τίθεσο   δίδοσο   or δου
3. ἱστάσθω   τιθέσθω   διδόσθω

Plur.
2. ἵστασθε   τίθεσθε   δίδοσθε
3. ἱστάσθων or τιθέσθων or   διδόσθων or
   ἱστάσθωσαν   τιθέσθωσαν   διδόσθωσαν

Present Infinitive.

ἵστασθαι   τίθεσθαι   δίδοσθαι

Present Participle (§ 46).

ἱστάμενος   τιθέμενος   διδόμενος

§ 63.   SECOND AORIST SYSTEM.

ACTIVE.

Second Aorist Indicative.

Sing.	1.	ἔστην	ἔθηκα [1]	ἔδωκα [1]
	2.	ἔστης	ἔθηκας	ἔδωκας
	3.	ἔστη	ἔθηκε	ἔδωκε
Plur.	1.	ἔστημεν	ἐθήκαμεν	ἐδώκαμεν
	2.	ἔστητε	ἐθήκατε	ἐδώκατε
	3.	ἔστησαν	ἔθηκαν	ἔδωκαν

Second Aorist Subjunctive.

Sing.	1.	στῶ	θῶ	δῶ
	2.	στῇς	θῇς	δῷς
	3.	στῇ	θῇ	δῷ
Plur.	1.	στῶμεν	θῶμεν	δῶμεν
	2.	στῆτε	θῆτε	δῶτε
	3.	στῶσι	θῶσι	δῶσι

Second Aorist Imperative.

Sing.	2.	στῆθι	θές	δός
	3.	στήτω	θέτω	δότω
Plur.	2.	στῆτε	θέτε	δότε
	3.	στήτωσαν	θέτωσαν	δότωσαν
		or στάντων	or θέντων	or δόντων

Second Aorist Infinitive.

στῆναι	θεῖναι	δοῦναι

Second Aorist Participle.

στάς (§ 45)	θείς (§ 45)	δούς (§ 45)

[1] No 2 aor. ind. act. of τίθημι and δίδωμι occurs — so the
1 aor. in -κα is given. Cf. 235, 3, note.

MIDDLE.

Second Aorist Middle Indicative.

Aor. Pass.
ἐδόθη

Sing.	1.	ἐθέμην	ἐδόμην
	2.	ἔθου	ἔδου
	3.	ἔθετο	ἔδοτο
Plur.	1.	ἐθέμεθα	ἐδόμεθα
	2.	ἔθεσθε	ἔδοσθε
	3.	ἔθεντο	ἔδοντο

Second Aorist Middle Subjunctive.

Aor. Pass. Subj.
δυθω

Sing.	1.	θῶμαι	δῶμαι
	2.	θῇ	δῷ
	3.	θῆται	δῶται
Plur.	1.	θώμεθα	δώμεθα
	2.	θῆσθε	δῶσθε
	3.	θῶνται	δῶνται

Second Aorist Middle Imperative.

Sing.	2.	θοῦ	δοῦ
	3.	θέσθω	δόσθω
Plur.	2.	θέσθε	δόσθε
	3.	θέσθωσαν	δόσθωσαν
		or θέσθων	or δόσθων

Second Aorist Middle Infinitive.

θέσθαι   δόσθαι

Second Aorist Middle Participle.

θέμενος (§ 46)   δόμενος (§ 46)

N

IRREGULAR VERBS OF THE μι FORM.

§ 64. The verbs εἰμί, *am*, ἵημι (compounded with ἀπό, σύν, ἀνά, and κατά), εἶμι, *go* (only in compounds), οἶδα, *know*, φημί, *say*, are all irregular.

§ 65. εἰμί (stem ἐσ-), *am*.

PRESENT.

		Indicative.	*Subjunctive.*	*Imperative.*
Sing.	1.	εἰμί	ὦ	
	2.	εἶ	ᾖς	ἴσθι
	3.	ἐστί	ᾖ	ἔστω, ἤτω
Plur.	1.	ἐσμέν	ὦμεν	
	2.	ἐστέ	ἦτε	ἔστε
	3.	εἰσί	ὦσι	ἔστωσαν

Infinitive. εἶναι

Participle. ὤν, οὖσα, ὄν; gen. ὄντος, οὔσης, etc. (183).

IMPERFECT.   FUTURE.

		Indicative.	*Indicative.*	*Infinitive.*
Sing.	1.	ἦν (ἤμην)[1]	ἔσομαι	ἔσεσθαι
	2.	ἦς (ἦσθα)	ἔσει, ἔσῃ	
	3.	ἦν	ἔσται	*Participle.*
Plur.	1.	ἦμεν (ἤμεθα)	ἐσόμεθα	ἐσόμενος
	2.	ἦτε	ἔσεσθε	
	3.	ἦσαν	ἔσονται	*They shall be*

[1] Cf. 78, *a.*

§ **66**.   ἀφίημι (stem ἑ-), *remit*.

The following forms of this verb occur in the New Testament :

INDICATIVE ACTIVE. — (Pres. ἀφεῖς, as though from ἀφέω) ἀφίησι, ἀφίεμεν, ἀφίομεν, ἀφίετε, ἀφίουσι.   Imperf. ἤφιε.   Fut. ἀφήσω, ἀφήσεις, etc.   Aor. ἀφῆκα, ἀφῆκας, etc.

INDICATIVE MID. AND PASS. — Pres. ἀφίεμαι.[1]   Fut. ἀφεθήσομαι.   Perf. 3 per. plur. ἀφέωνται.   Aor. pass. ἀφέθην.

SUBJUNCTIVE ACT. — 2 aor. ἀφῇ, ἀφῶμεν, ἀφῆτε.   Pass. Aor. ἀφεθῇ.

IMPERATIVE ACT. — Pres. ἀφιέτω.   2 aor. ἄφες, ἄφετε.

PARTICIPLE ACT. — 2 aor. ἀφείς, ἀφέντες.

INFINITIVE ACT. — Pres. ἀφιέναι.   2 aor. act. ἀφεῖναι.

a. In[2] compounds with σύν, the pres. ind. 3 per. plur. has συνιᾶσι, and συνίουσι.   Subjv. συνιῶσι and 2 aor. συνῶσι, and with ἀνά 2 aor. ἀνῶ.   Aor. pass. ind. ἀνέθη.

b. Pres. part. συνιείς and συνίων are found.   The former is more regular and occurs in συνιέντος, συνιέντες.   ἀνέντες 2 aor. act. part. also occurs.

§ **67**.   εἶμι (stem ι-), *go*.

But few forms of this verb occur, and always in compounds.

INDICATIVE. — Pres. -ίασι.   Imperf. -ῄει, -ῄεσαν.

INFINITIVE. — -ιέναι.

PARTICIPLE. — -ιών, -ιοῦσα, -ιόν, regular like ὤν, οὖσα, ὄν (183).

[1] Conjugated like the mid. of τίθημι.

[2] Such forms only are here given of the compounds of ἵημι as might be difficult to recognize.   The lexicon ought to be consulted for all verb forms

§ 68.   οἶδα (stem ἰδ-), *know.*

This verb is a second perfect and conjugated regularly οἶδα, οἶδας, etc.   The 3 per. plur. has ἴσασι once.   ἴστε in 2 per. plur. is also found.

IMPERFECT. — ᾔδειν,[1] ᾔδεις, etc.
FUTURE. — εἰδήσουσι.
SUBJUNCTIVE. — εἰδῶ, εἰδῶμεν, εἰδῆτε.
IMPERATIVE. — ἴστε, *know ye* (occurs once).
INFINITIVE. — εἰδέναι.
PARTICIPLE. — εἰδώς, εἰδυῖα, εἰδός, like λελυκώς (§ 43).

§ 69.   φημί (stem φᾰ-), *say.*

This verb is found in pres. ind. φημί and 3 per. sing. and plur. φησί and φασί.   Imperf. ἔφη, *he said.*

§ 70. The following forms of the optative mood occur in the New Testament:

1. *Present Tense.*
     ἔχοι, θέλοι, ἔχοιεν, εἴη, δυναίμην, δύναιντο, πάσχοιτε.

2. *First Aorist.*
     πλεονάσαι, περισσεύσαι, κατευθύναι, ποιήσαιεν, ψηλα-
          φήσειαν, εὐξαίμην.

3. *Second Aorist.*
     φάγοι, τύχοι, δῴη, εὕροιεν, ὀναίμην, γένοιτο, λάβοι.

4. *First Aorist Passive.*
     πληθυνθείη, λογισθείη.

[1] In fact a 2 pluperf., but the perf. and pluperf. have in this verb the sense of the pres. and imperf.

It may be noted (*a*) ἔχοι, θέλοι, δυναίμην, δύναιντο, πλε-
ονάσαι, περισσεύσαι, κατευθύναι, εὐξαίμην, φάγοι, τύχοι,
πάσχοιτε, ὀναίμην, γένοιτο, form the Optative by the addition of ι, which, with preceding vowel, forms a diphthong;
this diphthong is always long.   (*b*) εἴη, πληθυνθείη, λογι-
σθείη form the Optative by adding ιη; in the case of δῴη
the iota is subscript.   (*c*) ἔχοιεν, εὕροιεν, ποιήσαιεν are
also made by adding ιη, the η in the third person plural
changing to ε.   (*d*) ψηλαφήσειαν differs from ποιήσαιεν
in that ε and α have changed place.

§ 71. The following examples will illustrate the uses of the optative:

1. *The Optative of Wishing.*

   Rom. 15:5. ὁ δὲ θεὸς . . . δῴη ὑμῖν, *now may God grant unto you!*

2. *The Potential Optative.*

   Acts 26:29. εὐξαίμην ἂν τῷ θεῷ, *I could wish to God.*

3. *Indirect Question.*

   Luke 1:29. διελογίζετο ποταπὸς εἴη ὁ ἀσπασμὸς οὗτος, *she was discussing what manner of salutation this might be.*

4. *The Conditional Optative.*

   1 Cor. 14:10. εἰ τύχοι, *if it should chance.*

TENSE SYSTEMS.

§ 72. No one verb has all nine tense systems, but the following table shows the various tenses (as far as found in the New Testament) in λύω,

loose, βάλλω, *cast*, γράφω, *write*, and φθείρω, *destroy*.

Present	λυ%-	βαλλ%-	γραφ%-	φθειρ%-
Future	λυσ%-	βαλε%-	γραψ%-	φθερ%-
1 *Aorist*	λυσα-		γραψα-	φθειρα-
2 *Aorist*		βαλ%-		
1 *Perfect* . . .	λελυκα-	βεβληκα-		
2 *Perfect* . . .			γεγραφα-	

Perfect	*Perf.*	λελυ-	βεβλη-	γεγραμ-	
Mid.	*Fut. P.*	λελυσ%-			
1 *Pass.*	*Aor.*	λυθε(η)-	βληθε(η)-		
	Fut.	λυθησ%-	βληθησ%-		
2 *Pass.*	*Aor.*			γραφε(η)-	φθαρε(η)-
	Fut.				φθαρησ%-

§ 73.   PERSONAL ENDINGS.

	Active.		*Middle* and *Passive.*	
	Primary.	Secondary.	Primary.	Secondary.
S. 1.	μι	ν	μαι	μην
S. 2.	ς, (σι)	ς	σαι	σο
S. 3.	σι, τι	—	ται	το
P. 1.	μεν	μεν	μεθα	μεθα
P. 2.	τε	τε	σθε	σθε
P. 3.	νσι, ᾱσι	ν, σαν	νται	ντο

§ 74. The personal endings of the imperative are :

	Active.			*Middle* and *Passive.*		
S. 2.	θι	P. 2.	τε	S. 2.	σο	P. 2.	σθε
S. 3.	τω	P. 3.	ντων or τωσαν	S. 3.	σθω	P. 3.	σθων or σθωσαν

§ 75. The endings of the infinitive are :

Active. $\begin{cases} \text{εν, contracted with ε to ειν.} \\ \text{ναι, εναι.} \end{cases}$

Mid. and *Pass.* σθαι

§ 76. The tenses of the indicative are formed by adding to the verb theme, with certain modifications, the following suffixes.

	Pres.	*Fut.*	*Aor.*	*Perf.*	*Pluperf.*
Active :	-%-	-σ%-	-σα-	-κα-	-κει-

Middle and *Passive* have the same suffixes except in perf. and pluperf., where there is none. The aorist passive has -θε- for 1 aorist and -ε- for 2 aorist.

AUGMENT.

§ 77. 1. When the verb begins with a consonant the vowel ε is prefixed to the theme in the imperfect and aorist ; *e.g.* ἔ-λυ-ο-ν, ἔ-λυ-σα. This is called *syllabic augment.* In the perfect the initial consonant is placed before the augment ; *e.g.* λέ-λυ-κα. This is called *reduplication.* In the pluperfect the reduplicated form *may* be augmented ; *e.g.* ἐ-λε-λύ-κει-ν.

2. When a verb begins with a vowel this vowel is lengthened in all past tenses : α = η,

ε = η, ο = ω. Such an augment is called *temporal* augment; *e.g.* ἄγω, *lead*, ἦγον; ἔρχομαι, *come*, ἠρχόμην; ἀκούω, *hear*, ἤκουσα. An initial diphthong may lengthen the first vowel; *e.g.* αἰτέω, *ask for*, ᾔτησα; εὔχομαι, *pray*, ηὐχόμην.

3. Verbs beginning with two consonants or a double consonant (ζ, ξ, ψ) have the augment and *no* reduplication in the perfect and pluperfect. A mute (§ 2) followed by a liquid λ, μ, ν, ρ, is an exception to this; *e.g.* κρίνω, *judge*, has perfect κέκρικα, and καλέω, *call*, has perfect κέκληκα.

4. Verbs beginning with a rough mute φ, χ, θ, have the corresponding smooth mute π, κ, τ, in the reduplication; *e.g.* φιλέω, *love*, πε-φίλη-κα; θεάομαι, *behold*, τε-θέα-μαι.

The Eight Classes of Verbs.

§ 78. It is necessary in the study of the Greek verb to determine the *theme* or *root*, for on this, with certain modifications mostly of tense and mood signs, the various tenses are built. This theme may or may not correspond to the theme as seen in the present indicative. More frequently the present stem is a strengthened form of the theme; *e.g.* λύω, *loose*, has theme and present stem λυ- the same, while κλέπτω, *steal*, theme κλεπ-, has present stem κλεπτ-. λαμβάνω, *receive*, theme λαβ-, present stem λαμβαν-.

With reference to the relation of the theme to the present stem the verbs in Greek are divided into eight classes:

§ 79. FIRST CLASS.—*Verb stem remains unchanged throughout.* The present stem is formed by adding simply the variable vowel % to the theme:

	Theme.	Pres. stem.
λέγω, *say*	λεγ-	λεγ%
νικάω, *conquer*	νικα-	νικα%

§ 80. SECOND CLASS. — *Strong vowel forms.* Some verbs have a theme ending in a mute, § 2, preceded by a short vowel, principally ι or υ. The present theme of these verbs is formed by lengthening this vowel, ι to ει, υ to ευ, and the addition of %:

	Theme.	Pres. stem.	Fut.
πείθω, *persuade*	πιθ-	πειθ%	πεισ%
φεύγω, *flee*	φυγ-	φευγ%	φευξ%

§ 81. THIRD CLASS. — *Verbs in -πτω or the* τ-*class.* Some verbs have the theme in a labial mute π, β, φ, that form the present stem by adding τ% to the theme:

	Theme.	Pres. stem.	Fut.
κλέπτω, *steal*	κλεπ-	κλεπτ%	κλεψ%
κρύπτω, *hide*	κρυφ-	κρυπτ%	κρυψ%

a. κρύπ-τω is for κρύφ-τω.

§ 82. Fourth Class. — *Iota class.*

1. Some verbs having a theme ending in a palatal mute κ, γ, χ, add ι% to form the present stem. This ι% with the mute gives σσ%, rarely ζ% :

	Theme.	Pres. stem.	Fut.
κηρύσσω, *preach*	κηρυκ-	κηρυσσ%	κηρυξ%
πατάσσω, *smite*	παταγ-	πατασσ%	παταξ%

2. When ι% is added to a theme in δ- the present stem ends in ζ% :

	Theme.	Pres. stem.	Fut.
βαπτίζω, *baptize*	βαπτιδ-	βαπτιζ%	βαπτισ%
σώζω, *save*	σωδ-	σωζ%	σωσ%

3. A theme in a liquid, λ, μ, ν, ρ, may add ι% for the present. λι% becomes λλ% :

	Theme.	Pres. stem.	Fut.
ἀγγέλλω, *announce*	αγγελ-	ἀγγελλ%	ἀγγελε%
βάλλω, *cast*	βαλ-	βαλλ%	βαλε%

4. But with ν and ρ the ι usually passes over to the preceding vowel and with *a* or *ε* forms a diphthong :

	Theme.	Pres. stem.	Fut.
αἴρω, *take away*	αρ-	αἰρ%	ἀρε%
φαίνω, *show*	φαν-	φαιν%	φανε%

§ 83. FIFTH CLASS. — N-*class*. The present stem of some verbs is formed by adding ν% to the theme :

	Theme.	Pres. stem.
πίνω, *drink*	πι-	πιν%

1. The suffix may be -αν%.

	Theme.	Pres. stem.
ἁμαρτάνω, *sin*	ἁμαρτ-	ἁμαρταν%

2. Under this class (1) come several verbs that insert a nasal μ, ν, γ, before the final mute :

	Theme.	Pres. stem.
λαμβάνω, *receive*	λαβ-	λαμβαν%
τυγχάνω, *happen*	τυχ-	τυγχαν%

3. The suffix may be -νυμι, after a vowel -ννυμι.

	Theme.	Pres. ind.
δείκνυμι, *show*	δεικ-	δείκνυμι
ζώννυμι, *gird*	ζω-	ζώννυμι
ὄμνυμι, *swear*	ομ- (ομο)	ὄμνυμι

§ 84. SIXTH CLASS. — *Verbs in -σκω, the inceptive class*. A few verbs form their present stem by adding σκ% or ισκ% to the theme :

	Theme.	Pres. stem.
γινώσκω, *know*	γνο-	γινωσκ%
εὑρίσκω, *find*	εὑρ-	εὑρισκ%

§ 85. SEVENTH CLASS. — μι *added to simple stem.* This class includes most of the verbs of the μι-Conjugation, which form their present and imperfect tenses *without* the use of %.

	Theme.	Pres. ind.
ἵστημι, *make stand*	στᾰ-	ἵ-στημι
φημί, *say*	φᾰ-	φημί

§ 86. EIGHTH CLASS. — *Mixed class.* Verbs of this class are among the irregular verbs and form different tenses on entirely distinct stems. See the list of irregular verbs.

	Themes.		
ἐσθίω, *eat*	εσθι-	φαγ-	
ὁράω, *see*	ὁρα-	ὀπ-	ἰδ-
τρέχω, *run*	τρεχ-	δραμ-	
φέρω, *bear*	φερ-	οἰ-	ἐνεκ-

§ 87. The following verbs may be classified according to the principles laid down above.

δοξάζω, ἀκούω, ἀλείφω, τύπτω, λανθάνω, χαίρω, κράζω, στέλλω, νίπτω, ἄρχομαι, ἀγοράζω, ἀνοίγω, τίθημι, διδάσκω, ἐγείρω, ἀγγέλλω, φθάνω, ζάω, ἀποκτείνω, τηρέω, φείδομαι, ἔχω, ἐρωτάω, ῥήγνυμι, μανθάνω, ἀφίημι, ὑποτάσσω, μένω, θέλω, πυνθάνομαι, κατάγνυμι, ἐκτείνω, αὐξάνω, ἀποθνήσκω, αἰτέω, ἐντέλλομαι, δίδωμι, ἐκκόπτω, γράφω.

§ 88. The following table gives the principal parts of the most common irregular verbs in the New Testament. The aim is to give only such forms as occur. A rare compound or a variant reading may in some few cases present a form that is not given.

TABLE OF IRREGULAR VERBS.

A hyphen before a form denotes that it occurs in composition only. The second aorists and second perfects have been denoted by placing (2) after the forms.

Present.	Future.	Aorist.	Perf. Act.	Perf. Pass.	Aor. Pass.
ἄγω, lead	ἄξω	ἤγαγον (2)			ἤχθην
αἱρέω, take	αἱρήσω, -ἑλῶ	εἱλόμην¹ (2), -εἷλον (2)			ᾑρέθην
αἴρω, take away	ἀρῶ	ἦρα	ἦρκα	ἦρμαι	ἤρθην
ἀκούω, hear	ἀκούσω	ἤκουσα	ἀκήκοα (2)		ἠκούσθην
ἁμαρτάνω, sin	ἁμαρτήσω	ἡμάρτησα, ἥμαρτον (2)	ἡμάρτηκα		
ἀμφιέννυμι, clothe				ἠμφιεσμένος (part.)	
ἀναβαίνω, see βαίνω.					
ἀνοίγω, open	ἀνοίξω	ἤνοιξα, ἠνέῳξα, ἀνέῳξα	ἀνέῳγα (2)		ἠνοίχθην, ἠνεῴχθην, ἀνεῴχθην
ἀποκτείνω, kill	ἀποκτενῶ	ἀπέκτεινα			ἀπεκτάνθην
ἀπόλλυμι, destroy	ἀπολῶ, ἀπολέσω	ἀπώλεσα, ἀπωλόμην (2)	ἀπόλωλα (2)		
ἀρέσκω, please	ἀρέσω	ἤρεσα			
αὐξάνω, increase	αὐξήσω	ηὔξησα			
ἀφίημι, forgive	ἀφήσω	ἀφῆκα		ἀφέωνται	ἀφέθην

¹ In Westcott and Hort's reading, the I aor. a is often found for the 2 aor. %. E.g. εἵλατο = εἵλετο: εἶδαν = εἶδον.

Present.	Future.	Aorist.	Perf. Act.	Perf. Pass.	Aor. Pass.
βαίνω, go	-βήσομαι	-ἔβην (2)	-βέβηκα		ἐβλήθην
βάλλω, throw	βαλῶ	ἔβαλον (2)	βέβληκα	βέβλημαι	ἐβουλήθην
βούλομαι, wish					ἐγενήθην
γίνομαι become	γενήσομαι	ἐγενόμην (2)	γέγονα (2)	γεγένημαι	ἐγνώσθην
γινώσκω, know	γνώσομαι	ἔγνων (2)	ἔγνωκα	ἔγνωσμαι	ἐγράφην (2)
γράφω, write	γράψω	ἔγραψα	γέγραφα (2)	γέγραμμαι	δεχθείς (part.)
δείκνυμι, show	δείξω	ἔδειξα			ἐδεήθην
δέομαι, want					
δέρω, beat	δαρήσομαι (2 pass.)	ἔδειρα			
δέω, bind	[δήσω]	ἔδησα	δεδεκώς (part.)	δέδεμαι	ἐδέθην
δίδωμι, give	δώσω	ἔδωκα	δέδωκα	δέδομαι	ἐδόθην
δοκέω, seem		ἔδοξα			
δύναμαι, able	δυνήσομαι				ἠδυνήθην, ἐδυνήθην
ἐγγίζω, be near	ἐγγίσω	ἤγγισα	ἤγγικα		
ἐγείρω, raise up	ἐγερῶ	ἤγειρα		ἐγήγερμαι	ἠγέρθην
εἰμί, am	ἔσομαι				
εἶπον, see φημί.					
ἐκχέω, ἐκχύνω, } pour	ἐκχεῶ	ἐξέχεα		ἐκκέχυμαι	ἐξεχύθην

Present.	Future.	Aorist.	Perf. Act.	Perf. Pass.	Aor. Pass.
ἔρχομαι, *go*	ἐλεύσομαι	ἦλθον (2)	ἐλήλυθα (2)		
ἐσθίω, *eat*	φάγομαι	ἔφαγον (2)			
εὑρίσκω, *find*	εὑρήσω	εὗρησα, ηὗρον (2)	εὕρηκα		εὑρέθην
ἔχω, *have*	ἕξω, σχήσω	ἔσχον (2)	ἔσχηκα		
ζώννυμι, *gird*	ζώσω	-ἔζωσα		-ἔζωσμένος (part.)	
θάπτω, *bury*		ἔθαψα			ἐτάφην (2)
θέλω, *will*	θελήσω	ἠθέλησα			
θνήσκω, *die*	-θανοῦμαι	-ἔθανον (2)	τέθνηκα		
ἵστημι, *set*	στήσω	ἔστησα (Trans.), ἔστην (2) (Intr.)	ἔστηκα, ἔστώς (2) (act. part.)		ἐστάθην
καίω, *burn*	-καύσω	-ἔκαυσα			-ἐκαύθην, -ἐκάην (2)
καλέω, *call*	καλέσω	ἐκάλεσα	κέκληκα	κέκλημαι	ἐκλήθην
κερδαίνω, *gain*	κερδήσω, κερδανῶ (Subj.)	ἐκέρδησα, κερδάνω (Subj.)			
κλαίω, *weep*	κλαύσω	ἔκλαυσα			
κλάω, *break*		ἔκλασα			ἐκλάσθην
κρίνω, *judge*	κρινῶ	ἔκρῖνα	κέκρικα	κέκριμαι	ἐκρίθην

Present.	Future.	Aorist.	Perf. Act.	Perf. Pass.	Aor. Pass.
λαμβάνω, take	λήμψομαι	ἔλαβον (2)	εἴληφα (2)	-είλημμένος	
λανθάνω, be hidden		ἔλαθον (2)		-λέλησμαι	
μανθάνω, learn		ἔμαθον (2)	μεμάθηκώς (part.)		
μιμνήσκω, remember				μέμνημαι	ἐμνήσθην
ὄμνυμι, swear	ὀμοῦμαι	ὤμοσα			
ὁράω, see	ὄψομαι, imperf. ἑώρων	εἶδον (2)	ἑόρακα, ἑώρακα πέπονθα (2)		ὤφθην
πάσχω, suffer		ἔπαθον (2)	πέπονθα (2)		
πείθω, persuade	πείσω	ἔπεισα	πέποιθα (2)	πέπεισμαι	ἐπείσθην
περιτέμνω, circumcise		περιέτεμον (2)		περιτετμημένος (part.)	περιετμήθην
μίμπλημι, fill		ἔπλησα			ἐπλήσθην
πίνω, drink	πίομαι	ἔπιον (2)	πέπωκα		
πίπτω, fall	πεσοῦμαι	ἔπεσα, ἔπεσον (2)	πέπτωκα		
πλέω, sail		-ἔπλευσα			
πράσσω, do	πράξω	ἔπραξα	πέπραχα (2)	πεπραγμένος (part.)	ἐπράχθην
πυνθάνομαι, learn		ἐπυθόμην (2)			
ῥήγνυμι, break	ῥήξω	ἔρρηξα		ἔρρυμμαι	
ῥίπτω, cast	ῥίψω	ἔρριψα		ἐρριμμένος (part.)	
σπείρω, sow		ἔσπειρα		ἐσπαρμένος (part.)	ἐσπάρην (2)

Present.	Future.	Aorist.	Perf. Act.	Perf. Pass.	Aor. Pass.
στέλλω, send	-στελῶ	-έστειλα	-ἔσταλκα	-ἔσταλμαι	-ἐστάλην (2)
στρέφω, turn	-στρέψω	ἔστρεψα		-ἔστραμμαι	ἐστράφην (2)
σώζω, save	σώσω	ἔσωσα	σέσωκα	σέσωσμαι	ἐσώθην
τελέω, end	-τελέσω	ἐτέλεσα	τετέλεκα	τετέλεσμαι	ἐτελέσθην
τίθημι, place	θήσω	ἔθηκα, ἐθέμην (2)	τέθεικα	τέθειμαι	ἐτέθην
τίκτω, bear	τέξομαι	ἔτεκον (2)			
τρέφω, nourish		ἔθρεψα		τεθραμμένος (part.)	ἐτρέφθην ἐτράφην (2)
τρέχω, run		ἔδραμον (2)			
τυγχάνω, happen		ἔτυχον (2)	τέτευχα (2), τέτυχα (2)		
φαίνω, appear	φανοῦμαι, φανήσομαι (2 pass.)	ἔφηνα			ἐφάνην (2)
φέρω, bear	οἴσω	ἤνεγκα, ἤνεγκον (2)	-ἐνήνοχα (2)		ἠνέχθην
φεύγω, flee	φεύξομαι	ἔφυγον (2)			
φημί, say	ἐρῶ	εἶπον	εἴρηκα	εἴρημαι	ἐρρέθην
φθείρω, destroy	φθερῶ	ἔφθειρα			ἐφθάρην (2)
Χαίρω, rejoice	χαρήσομαι (2 pass.)				ἐχάρην (2)

§ **89.** To locate a verbal form at once is the most difficult thing a beginner has to learn. It is intended, therefore, that in the following pages the student shall have a special opportunity for mastering a large part of this main difficulty. Of the most common irregular verbs there are here gathered into small space the forms that occur, and by a mastery of these pages a great deal will be done towards gaining a rapid and easy understanding of the Greek, read as Greek.

After a thorough acquaintance with the paradigms and the principal parts of the irregular verbs, nothing may prove of greater profit than repeated drill on these forms.

§ **90.** ἀκούω,[1] *hear.*

ἤκουον, ἀκούουσι, ἀκήκοα, ἀκούσῃ, ἀκούσω, ἀκούσας, ἀκούων, ἀκουσόμεθα, ἀκούεις, ἀκηκόασι, ἀκουσθῇ, ἀκούετε, ἀκουσθήσεται, ἠκούσαμεν, ἀκούοντας, ἀκουσθεῖσι, ἀκούομεν, ἀκηκόατε, ἀκούσητε, ἄκουε, ἀκούσει, ἀκούσατε, ἤκουσα, ἀκούοντος, ἠκούσθη, ἀκηκοότας, ἀκούσεται, ἀκούει, ἀκουσάτω, ἀκούσωσι, ἀκούσονται, ἀκοῦσαι, ἀκου-

---

[1] The aim is to give *all* forms of these verbs, but such completeness can hardly be expected. The various editors give often a different form for the same passage, and no concordance is, as yet, published which gives W. and H's. reading.

σάτωσαν, ἀκούσαντες, ἠκούσατε, ἀκούσετε, ἤκουε,
ἀκούσεσθε, ἀκούοντι, ἀκουσάντων, ἀκούοντες,
ἀκούσουσι, ἀκούοντα, ἤκουσας, ἀκούσασι, ἀκού-
σασα, ἤκουσε, ἀκουσάντων, ἀκούειν, ἀκουέτω,
ἀκουόντων, ἀκηκόαμεν.

§ 91.   ἀνίστημι, *raise up*.

ἀνέστη, ἀναστάς, ἀναστήσεται, ἀναστῇ, ἀνίστα-
ται, ἀναστῶσι, ἀναστήσω, ἀνάστα, ἀναστῆναι,
ἀνέστησαν, ἀναστήσει, ἀναστήσας, ἀναστάντες,
ἀνίστασθαι, ἀναστήσονται, ἀνάστηθι, ἀνέστησε,
ἀνιστάμενος, ἀναστᾶσα, ἀναστάν.

§ 92.   ἀνοίγω, *open*.

ἀνοίξω, ἄνοιξον, ἠνοίχθησαν, ἀνεῳγότα, ἠνοίγη,
ἀνοίγει, ἀνοιχθῶσι, ἀνοίξαντες, ἀνεῳγμένᾱς,
ἀνεῴχθησαν, ἀνοιγήσεται, ἀνοίξᾱς, ἀνεῳγμένη,
ἀνεῴχθη, ἀνέῳγε, ἀνοίξῃ, ἀνοίγω, ἀνεῳγμένος,
ἤνοιξε, ἀνεῳγμένων, ἀνοίξωσι, ἀνέῳξε, ἠνοίχθη,
ἀνεῳγμένον, ἠνεῴχθη, ἀνεῳγμένης, ἠνεῴχθησαν,
ἀνεῳγμένην, ἠνοίγησαν, ἀνεῳγμένους, ἀνοίγων,
ἠνέῳξε, ἀνοιχθήσεται, ἀνοῖξαι, ἀνεῳχθῆναι.

§ 93.   ἀποθνήσκω, *die*.

ἀπέθανον, ἀποθνήσκων, ἀποθνήσκει, ἀποθνή-
σκωμεν, ἀποθνήσκειν, ἀποθανόντος, ἀπεθάνετε,

ἀποθνήσκουσι, ἀποθάνωμεν, ἀποθανόντες, ἀποθα-
νεῖται, ἀπέθνησκεν, ἀποθανόντι, ἀποθάνῃ, ἀποθνή-
σκοντες, ἀποθανεῖν, ἀποθνήσκομεν, ἀποθανόντα,
ἀπέθανε, ἀποθανών, ἀποθανοῦνται, ἀπεθάνομεν,
ἀποθανεῖσθε.

§ 94.   ἀπόλλυμι, *destroy, kill.*

ἀπώλεσα, ἀπολλυμένην, ἀπολέσαι, ἀπόληται,
ἀπολέσω, ἀπόλλυμαι, ἀπολομένου, ἀπολωλώς,
ἀπώλετο, ἀπολεῖται, ἀπωλέσωσιν, ἀπολέσθαι,
ἀπολέσας, ἀπόλλυε, ἀπολῶ, ἀπολλύμεθα, ἀπολέσῃ, ἀπολλύμενοι, ἀπολέσει, ἀπολέσητε, ἀπο-
λεῖσθε, ἀπολλυμένοις, ἀπώλοντο, ἀπώλεσεν,
ἀπολοῦνται, ἀπώλλυντο, ἀπολωλός, ἀπολωλότα,
ἀπολλυμένου, ἀπόλωνται.

§ 95.   ἀποστέλλω, *send.*

ἀπέσταλκα, ἀποστέλλῃ, ἀποστείλᾶς, ἀποστα-
λέντι, ἀποστελῶ, ἀπέστειλα, ἀπεσταλμένος,
ἀπεστάλην, ἀποσταλῶσι, ἀποστέλλειν, ἀποστεί-
λαντες, ἀπέστειλας, ἀποστέλλει, ἀποστείλῃ,
ἀποστείλαντι, ἀπόστειλον, ἀποστελεῖ, ἀποστέλλω, ἀπεστάλκαμεν, ἀπεστάλη, ἀπέσταλκας,
ἀπεσταλμένοι, ἀπεστάλκασι, ἀποστελλόμενα,
ἀπεστάλκατε, ἀπέσταλμαι, ἀπέσταλκε, ἀπεσταλ-
μένους, ἀποστέλλουσι, ἀπέστειλαν, ἀποστεῖλαι.

§ 96. ἀφίημι, *remit, forgive.*

ἀφήσεις, ἄφες, ἀφῆκας, ἀφίεται, ἤφιε, ἀφέωνται, ἀφῆκα, ἀφείς, ἀφιέναι, ἀφιέτω, ἀφῇ,
ἀφίησιν, ἀφήσω, ἀφῶμεν, ἀφέντες, ἀφέθησαν,
ἀφήκαμεν, ἄφετε, ἀφήσει, ἀφήκατε, ἀφῆτε,
ἀφήσουσι, ἀφεθῇ, ἀφίεμεν, ἀφῆκαν, ἀφίετε,
ἀφεθήσεται, ἀφεῖναι, ἀφεῖς, ἀφῆκες = -κας,
ἀφίουσι, ἀφίομεν.

§ 97. -βαίνω, *go, come,* ἀνα-, κατα-, ἐμ-, μετα-.

βαίνων, ἔβην, βήσεται, βαινέτω, βαίνειν, βάς,
βέβηκα, βαίνοντος, ἔβημεν, βαίνω, ἔβαινον,
βάντων, βαινόντων, βῇ, βάντι, βέβηκε, ἔβαινε,
βαίνουσι, βῆναι, βαίνουσα, βήσῃ, βαίνει, βαίνετε,
βαίνουσαν, βαίνοντας, ἔβη, βάντα, βεβηκότος,
βάν, βαίνομεν, ἔβησαν, βεβήκαμεν, βάντες,
βῆθι, βαῖνον, βάτω, βῆτε, βαίνοντες, ἀνάβα
(for ἀνάβηθι).

§ 98. βάλλω, *cast.*

βαλλόντων, βαλεῖν, βάλω, βάλλει, ἐβέβλητο,
βεβλημένος, βάλε, βεβληκότος, βάλλομεν, βαλῶ,
ἔβαλον, βάλλοντες, βέβληκε, βαλλόμενον, ἔβαλλον, βάλλεται, βέβληται, βάλετε, βληθείσῃ,
βάλωσι, βάλλουσι, βαλοῦσι, βληθῇ, βαλοῦσα,
βεβλημένον, βληθήσεται, βάλλοντας, ἔβαλε,

ἐβλήθη, βάλῃ, βληθῆναι, βάλλουσαν, ἐβλήθησαν,
βάλητε, βεβλημένην, βλήθητι, βληθέν, βληθήσῃ,
βλητέον (a verbal, Luke 5 : 38), βαλλόμενα.

§ 99.   γίνομαι, be, become.

ἐγενήθη, γενόμενος, γινόμενοι, γέγονα, γενόμενοι,
γίνονται, ἐγένοντο, γίνωνται, γένωνται, γινομένη,
ἐγένεσθε, γεγενημένον, γεγένησθε, γεγόναμεν,
γενομένων, ἐγεγόνει, γένηται, γίνου, γενομένη,
γίνεται, γεγονώς, γένησθε, γίνεσθαι, γενέσθαι,
γεγονέναι, γεγένησθαι, γενηθῆναι, γενησόμενον,
γενηθέντες, ἐγενήθησαν, γινέσθω, γινόμενον,
γενόμενον, γενηθέντας, ἐγενόμην, γένωμαι, γινώ-
μεθα, γενώμεθα, γενηθήτω, ἐγένου, ἐγίνετο,
γινόμενα, γεγόνασι, γενομένοις, γενήθητε, γενο-
μένης, γενήσεται, γινομένων, γέγονας, γενομένου,
γεγονότι, γέγοναν, γεγόνατε, ἐγένετο, γενομένην,
γενέσθω, γίνεσθε, γεγόνει, γενόμεναι, γεγονυῖα,
γενήσεσθε, γενόμενα, γεγονότες, ἐγενήθητε, γεγο-
νός, γέγονε, γενηθέντων, γένοιτο (optative, mostly
in the phrase μὴ γένοιτο, *may it not happen,*
God forbid).

§ 100.   γινώσκω, *know.*

γνωσθήσεται, γινώσκων, γνῶ, γινώσκεται,
γινώσκω, γνῶθι, γνῶσι, γινώσκειν, ἔγνωκα, γνώ-
σομαι, ἐγίνωσκον, γινώσκει, γνώτω, γνώσονται,
ἔγνωκε, γνωσθέντες, ἐγνώκατε, γινώσκετε, γινώ-

σκητε, γινώσκομεν, γινώσκωμαι, ἔγνων, ἐγνώσθη,
γνούς, γνῶτε, γνῶς, γινώσκεις, γνωσθήτω, γνῶναι,
ἔγνω, γνώσῃ, γνῷ, γνώσεται, ἐγίνωσκε, ἐγνώκειτε,
ἔγνωσται, γνόντα, γινώσκωσι, γινώσκοντες,
γνόντες, γινωσκομένη, ἔγνωσαν, γνώσεσθε, ἔγνω-
καν = -κασι, ἐγνωκέναι.

§ 101.   δίδωμι, give.

ἐδώκαμεν, διδούς, δούς, δός, δῷ, διδόασι, ἐδίδο-
σαν,[1] δώσουσι, ἔδωκαν, δῶσιν, δοθήσεται, δέδωκε,
δεδώκει, διδόμενον, δεδώκεισαν, δέδωκα, ἐδίδουν,
ἔδωκας, δίδοται, δώσω, δοθῇ, διδόναι, δοῦναι,
δοθῆναι, δῴη and δοῖ, irregular forms for δῷ, διδῶ,
δίδωμι, δῴη = optative δοίη, δώσεις, δότω, ἐδίδου,
δίδωσι, δώσῃ, δίδοτε, διδόντι, ἐδώκατε, δεδομένον,
δέδοται, δοθείσῃ, δεδομένην, ἔδωκε, δώσει, δῶμεν,
ἔδωκα, διδόντα, ἐδόθη, δοθείσης, δόντος, δώσομεν,
δῶτε, δοθεῖσαι, δίδου, δῷς, δοθεῖσαν, ἐδόθησαν,
δόντα, δέδωκας, διδόντες, δότε.

§ 102.   ἔρχομαι, come, go.

ἔλθω, ἔρχωμαι, ἔρχομαι, ἐλεύσομαι, ἐλήλυθα,
ἦλθον, ἐρχόμενος, ἤρχοντο, ἔλθῃ, ἐλθών, ἐλθοῦσα,
ἐλθέτω, ἐρχέσθω, ἐλεύσονται, ἤλθετε, ἐλήλυθας,
ἐρχόμεθα, ἔρχῃ, ἐλθεῖν, ἔρχηται, ἔρχονται, ἔλθωσι,
ἐλήλυθε, ἐλθούσης, ἔρχου, ἐλεύσεται, ἐληλύθει,
ἐλθόντος, ἦλθε, ἐλθόντι, ἐληλύθεισαν, ἐλθόντων,

---

[1] Cf. similar form in ἔχω, § 104, latter part.

ἔρχεσθαι, ἐλθόν, ἐληλυθυῖαν, ἐλθόντα, ἔρχεσθε, ἐλθόντες, ἐλθοῦσαι, ἐληλυθότες, ἤλθομεν, ἐληλυθότα, ἦλθες, ἐλθόντας, ἐλθέ, ἐρχομένη, ἔρχεται, ἐρχομένης, ἤρχετο, ἔλθῃς, ἤρχου (α commonly occurs for ʼ%ο in the 2 aor.; as ἦλθαν, ἐλθάτω. A few forms in -μενος are omitted.)

§ 103.   εὑρίσκω, *find.*

εὑρήσῃς, εὑρίσκοντες, εὕρηκα, εὑρίσκω, εὑρηθησόμεθα, εὑρέθην, εὑρεθείς, εὑρεθῶ, εὕρισκον, εὑρίσκει, εὕρῃ, εὑρεῖν, εὗρον, εὕροιεν (opt.), εὑρίσκομεν, εὑρών, εὗρες, εὑρέθη, εὑρήσεις, εὑρήκαμεν, εὗρε, εὑρέθησαν, εὑράμενος,[1] εὑρεθῶσι, εὑρισκόμεθα, εὕρωμεν, εὑρεθῆναι, εὑρίσκετο, εὑρήσουσι, εὕρητε, εὑρόντες, εὕρομεν, εὑρήσει, εὑρεθῇ, εὑρηκέναι, εὑροῦσα, εὕρωσι, εὕραμεν,[1] εὑροῦσαι, εὑρεθῆτε, εὑρήσομεν, εὑρήσετε.

§ 104.   ἔχω, *have.*

ἔχε, ἔξεις, ἔχει, ἔσχον, ἔσχηκα, σχῶ, ἔχειν, ἔχω, ἔχομεν, εἶχε, ἔσχηκε, σχῶμεν, εἶχον, ἔχῃ, ἐχέτω, ἔχωμεν, ἕξει, ἐχομένῳ, ἐσχήκαμεν, ἐχομένᾱς, ἔσχες, ἕξετε, ἔχοντας, ἔχετε, ἕξουσι, ἔχοι and ἔχοιεν (opt.), ἔχητε, ἔχουσι, ἔσχε, ἔχεις, ἐχόμενα, ἐσχηκότας, ἔχωσι, ἔχων, ἔχουσα, ἔχον,

---

[1] Cf note, p. 189.

εἶχαν, εἴχοσαν, both = εἶχον, εἴχαμεν = εἴχομεν, ἐσχηκότα (nearly all the forms of the pres. act. part. occur).

§ 105.   ἵστημι, *cause to stand.*

ἱστῶμεν, ἵστησι, στήσει, στάς, ἔστηκας, ἔστησε, ἑστώς, σταθείς, στῆσαι, στήσῃς, στήσαντες, στήσονται, στήσητε, στάντος, σταθῆναι, ἑστάναι, στῆναι, στήσετε, στῆθι, ἑστήκαμεν, ἑστηκώς, ἑστῶτος, σταθήσεται, ἔστησαν, ἑστηκότες, ἑστήκασι, σταθέντα, εἱστήκει, ἐστάθην, ἑστῶτα, σταθήσεσθε, εἱστήκεισαν, ἑστῶτες, σταθέντες, ἑστηκός, στᾶσα, σταθῇ, ἔστην, ἔστηκε, ἑστῶτας, ἑστηκότων, ἔστη, στῆτε, ἑστώτων, ἐστάθη, ἔστησαν, ἐστάθησαν, εἱστήκεσαν, στήσῃ, ἱστάνομεν, ἑστός. W. and H. give ἱστ- throughout the plupf. instead of εἱστ-.

§ 106.   λαμβάνω, *take, receive.*

εἴληφα, λαμβάνων, ἔλαβον, λαβέτω, λάβω, λαμβάνῃ, λαμβάνειν, λαβεῖν, λαμβάνω, ἐλάμβανον, λήμψεται, λάβετε, λαμβάνεις, λημψόμεθα, λάβωσι, λαμβάνετε, λαβών, ἔλαβες, εἴληφας, λαβοῦσαι, λαμβάνουσι, ἐλάβετε, εἰληφώς, λαμβάνοντες, λήμψεσθε, ἔλαβε, εἴληφε, λαβόντες, λάβῃ, λαμβάνει, λήμψονται, ἐλάβομεν, λαμβανόμενος, λαβοῦσα, λάβητε, λαμβανόμενον, λάβοι (opt.), εἴληφες = -φας.

§ 107.   πίνω, *drink.*

[πέπωκε], πιών, πίνων, πίνω, πίω, πίνει, πίεται, ἔπιε, ἔπινον, πίνετε, πίεσαι, πίητε, πίνειν, πιεῖν, πεῖν, πίνοντες, πίῃ, πίνῃ, πίνουσι, πίνωσι, πίεσθε, ἔπιον, πίε, πίωμεν, πινέτω, ἐπίομεν, πίετε, πιοῦσα, πίωσιν.

§ 107 a.   πίπτω, *fall.*

πέπτωκαν, ἔπεσα, ἔπεσον, πέσῃ, πεσών, πεσόν, πίπτει, πεσεῖται, ἔπεσε, πεσόντας, πεπτωκότα, ἔπεσαν, πέσετε, πεσεῖν, πεσοῦνται, πεσόντα, πιπτόντων, πέσητε, πεσόντες, πεπτωκυῖαν, πέσωσι, πέπτωκες (for -κας), ἔπιπτεν.

§ 108.   τίθημι, *put, place.*

τέθεικα, θείς, τιθέναι, τίθημι, θῶ, τεθῇ, ἐτίθει, θήσω, ἔθηκα, ἔθου, τεθεικώς, θέντες, θεῖναι, θήσεις, ἐτίθουν, τιθέασι, τίθησι, θῇ, τιθέτω, θέμενος, τεθῆναι, ἔθετο, θήσει, τίθεται, θῶμεν, θέσθε, τιθείς, ἔθηκαν, ἔθεσθε, ἐτέθην, τεθῶσι, τιθέντες, ἔθηκας, ἔθεντο, θέτε, ἔθηκε, ἐτέθη, τεθείκατε, ἐτέθησαν, τέθειται.

§ 109.   φαίνω, *show, appear.*

ἐφάνη, φανήσεται, φανῶσι, φαίνεται, φαίνῃ, φανῶμεν, φαίνει, φανεῖται, φαίνων, φαίνεσθε,

ἐφάνησαν, φαινομένου, φανῇ, φαινομένων, φαί-
νοντι, φαίνονται, φαινομένη, φανῆς, φαίνωσι.

§ 110. φέρω, *bear.*

ἤνεγκα, ἐνεχθείσης, οἴσει, ἐνέγκατε, ἠνέχθη,
φέρετε, ἔφερον, φερώμεθα, φέρε, φέρουσαν, φερό-
μενοι, φέρειν, φέρῃ, φέρουσι, ἔφερε, -ἠνέγκατε,
φερομένης, φέρητε, φέρει, οἴσουσι, ἐνεχθεῖσαν,
-φέρεται, ἐφερόμεθα, φέρεσθαι, -ἐνέγκᾶς, -φέρῃς,
ἤνεγκε, ἐφέροντο, -φέρονται, ἤνεγκαν, φέροντες,
φερομένην, ἤνεγκας, ἐνεχθῆναι, φέρον, φέρουσαι,
-ἐνέγκῃ, -ἐνεχθείς, -φέρωσι, -ἔνεγκε.

———◆———

3. SYNTAX.

§ 111. It is not the purpose of this introductory work to deal largely with Greek syntax.
No study, however, of the New Testament, in
the Greek, can be prosecuted without at least a
modicum of knowledge of the Greek syntax.
It is therefore within the scope of this little
work to furnish that *modicum.*

It is believed that the examples and principles here set forth will prove of great value
in assisting the beginner to keep his bearings

amidst the various forms of construction which render the Greek so rich a language, and at the same time make it appear so difficult to the learner.

The inductive study of syntax is valued by no one more highly than by the author, and I hope that the following principles may not be looked upon as *rules* that are to serve as pegs upon which the student is to hang his subjunctives, infinitives, genitives, and datives. The study of the syntax should begin with the examples and not with the principles, with the Greek text and not with a work on Greek syntax.

The New Testament, written as it was by several different persons, cannot but present the peculiarities of style that belong to these authors. This variety of style often passes over into a different syntactical expression. Accordingly, what is a very common form of construction in the writings of Paul may not be found in the Gospels, and Luke may use expressions that do not occur elsewhere.

The aim has been in the following examples to give those that are representative of the language as used by all the writers of the New Testament.

The Moods in Independent Sentences.

§ 112. The indicative in independent sentences is the natural one and needs nothing said about it here.

Subjunctive.

§ 113. The first person plural of the subjunctive, either present or aorist, may be used to denote *a command* or *exhortation*. The negative is μή (1 Cor. 15 : 32), φάγωμεν καὶ πίωμεν, *Let us eat and drink.* 1 John 3 : 18, μὴ ἀγαπῶμεν λόγῳ, *Let us not love in word.*

§ 114. The distinction between the present and aorist is that the present denotes what is *continued, extended,* or *repeated,* while the aorist denotes the fact simply without any continued or extended action. This distinction is generally true of the present and aorist in all moods except the indicative. The aorist subjunctive and imperative do not refer to *past* time, but to the present or future. The aorist infinitive may refer to past time.

115. In questions of *doubt* or *uncertainty* the subjunctive is used in the first person, rarely in the second or third. Mark 12 : 14, δῶμεν ἢ μὴ δῶμεν ; *shall we give or shall we not give ?*

§ 116. The aorist subjunctive is used with the double negative οὐ μή, to express a strong negation.   John 6 : 35, ὁ ἐρχόμενος πρὸς ἐμὲ οὐ μὴ πεινάσῃ καὶ ὁ πιστεύων εἰς ἐμὲ οὐ μὴ διψήσει, *he who comes unto me shall not hunger, and he who believes on me shall not thirst.* Note that the future indicative is thus also used.

§ 117. The aorist subjunctive may express a negative command.   Matt. 7 : 6, μὴ δῶτε τὸ ἅγιον τοῖς κυσίν, μηδὲ βάλητε τοὺς μαργαρίτας ὑμῶν ἔμπροσθεν τῶν χοίρων, *give not that which is holy to the dogs, nor throw your pearls before swine.*

Optative.

§ 118. The optative is used to express a wish that refers to future time.   Luke 20 : 16, μὴ γένοιτο, *may this not happen.*   See § 71.

In Dependent Sentences.

Subjunctive.

§ 119. *Final clauses* denoting *purpose* are introduced by ἵνα or ὅπως and take the subjunctive, more rarely the indicative; negative μή.   Mark 3 : 14, καὶ ἐποίησεν δώδεκα . . . ἵνα ὦσιν μετ᾽ αὐτοῦ καὶ ἵνα ἀποστέλλῃ αὐτοὺς κηρύσσειν, *and*

*he chose twelve in order that they might be with
him, and that he might send them to preach.*
Acts 9 : 17, ὁ κύριος ἀπέσταλκέν με . . . ὅπως
ἀναβλέψῃς καὶ πλησθῇς πνεύματος ἁγίου, *the
Lord has sent me that you might look up and be
filled with the holy spirit.*

§ **120.** *Object clauses* after verbs of *exhorting,
commanding,* and *entreating,* take the subjunctive with ἵνα, more rarely ὅπως ; negative μή.
Matt. 14 : 36, παρεκάλουν αὐτὸν ἵνα μόνον
ἅψωνται τοῦ κρασπέδου τοῦ ἱματίου αὐτοῦ, *they
entreated him that they might but touch the hem
of his garment.* Mark 13 : 18, προσεύχεσθε δὲ
ἵνα μὴ γένηται χειμῶνος, *and pray ye that it
happen not in the winter.*

CONDITIONAL SENTENCES.

§ **121.** A condition stated *simply* without anything being implied as to fulfilment has in
Greek, as in English, the simple present, future,
or past (aorist) indicative in the condition, with
the same tense in the conclusion.

Matt. 4 : 6, εἰ υἱὸς εἶ τοῦ θεοῦ, βάλε σεαυτὸν
κάτω, *if thou art the Son of God, cast thyself
down.* Matt. 26 : 33, εἰ πάντες σκαδαλισθήσον-
ται ἐν σοί, ἐγὼ οὐδέποτε σκανδαλισθήσομαι, *if
all men shall be offended in thee, I never shall be*

offended.   2 Cor. 5 : 16, εἰ καὶ ἐγνώκαμεν κατὰ σάρκα Χριστόν, ἀλλὰ νῦν οὐκέτι γινώσκομεν, *and if we have known Christ according to the flesh, yet now we know him no longer.*

§ **122.** *Conditions Contrary to Fact.* — When ἄν is added to the conclusion where εἰ appears in the condition, a non-fulfilment is implied. The same tense of the indicative is used in both parts. *If he were here I would go. a v*

§ **123.** The *imperfect* denotes *present* time, and the *aorist* or *pluperfect* denotes *past* time.

Imperfect : John 5 : 46, εἰ γὰρ ἐπιστεύετε Μωυσεῖ, ἐπιστεύετε ἂν ἐμοί, *for if you were now believing in Moses, you would now be believing in me.*   Implying that they are not believing in Moses.

Aorist or pluperfect : 1 Cor. 2 : 8, εἰ γὰρ ἔγνωσαν, οὐκ ἂν τὸν κύριον τῆς δόξης ἐσταύρωσαν, *for if they had known it they would not have crucified the Lord of Glory.*   1 John 2 : 19, εἰ γὰρ ἐξ ἡμῶν ἦσαν, μεμενήκεισαν ἂν μεθ' ἡμῶν, *for if they had been of us, they would have remained with us.*

§ **124.** *Future Conditions.* — Clauses that refer to future time are introduced by ἐάν, which is followed by the subjunctive (*rarely* the indica-

tive). In the conclusion the future indicative
occurs or the present with future sense.

Matt. 9 : 21, ἐὰν μόνον ἅψωμαι τοῦ ἱματίου
αὐτοῦ σωθήσομαι, *If I shall but touch his garment, I shall be saved.* John 15 : 10, ἐὰν τὰς
ἐντολάς μου τηρήσητε, μενεῖτε ἐν τῇ ἀγάπῃ μου,
*if ye shall keep my commandments, ye shall re-
main in my love.*

§ 125. The negative in the condition is
usually μή, in the conclusion always οὐ.

RELATIVE CLAUSES.

§ 126. Clauses introduced by relative words
as ὅς, *who*, and ὅπου, *where*, follow the same
principles as conditional clauses when referring
to present, past, or future time. The relative
word stands as the conjunction in the room of
εἰ. Where an ἐάν-construction is implied, the
relative word usually takes the place of the εἰ
and the ἄν remains, as ὅς ἄν. More rarely ὅς
ἐάν is found.

Luke 8 : 18, ὅς ἂν γὰρ ἔχῃ, δοθήσεται αὐτῷ,
whoever has, to him shall it be given. Mark
14 : 9, ὅπου ἐὰν κηρυχθῇ τὸ εὐαγγέλιον, . . . ὃ
ἐποίησεν αὕτη λαληθήσεται, *wherever the Gospel
shall be preached, that which she has done will
be told.*

P

Temporal Clauses.

§ **127.** *Temporal Clauses* introduced by ὅτε, *when,* ἕως, *until,* are followed by the same construction as relative conjunctions, § **126**; ὅτε ἄν is always written ὅταν. Mark 6 : 10, ἐκεῖ μένετε ἕως ἂν ἐξέλθητε ἐκεῖθεν, *abide there until you go out thence.* Matt. 21 : 40, ὅταν οὖν ἔλθῃ ὁ κύριος τοῦ ἀμπελῶνος, τί ποιήσει; *when therefore the lord of the vineyard cometh, what will he do?*

§ **128.** More rarely ἕως appears without ἄν. Luke 22 : 34, οὐ φωνήσει σήμερον ἀλέκτωρ ἕως τρίς με ἀπαρνήσῃ εἰδέναι, *the cock shall not crow to-day until you deny three times that you know me.*

Infinitive.

§ **129.** The infinitive is used to complete the meaning of such verbs as θέλειν, *wish;* δύνασθαι, *able;* ἐλπίζειν, *hope;* ζητεῖν, *seek.* This construction is the same as in English. If this infinitive has a subject *different* from that of the principal verb, this subject must be in the *accusative.* Hebr. 6 : 11, ἐπιθυμοῦμεν δὲ ἕκαστον ὑμῶν τὴν αὐτὴν ἐνδείκνυσθαι σπουδήν, *we moreover desire each one of you to exhibit the same earnestness.* 2 Cor. 11 : 16, μή τίς με δόξῃ ἄφρονα εἶναι, *let no one think me to be foolish* (*that I am foolish*).

§ 130. When the subject of the infinitive is *the same* as that of the principal verb, this subject is not commonly expressed, and all attributes are in the *nominative* case. Rom. I : 22, φάσκοντες εἶναι σοφοὶ ἐμωράνθησαν, *they were made foolish by declaring themselves to be wise.*

§ 131. Words of *saying* and in general expressions of thought may be followed by the infinitive with the cases as above. See last example in § 129 and in § 128.

§ 132. The infinitive may be used as a *substantive*, and in this construction may take the article in any case. This substantive phrase (while keeping its verbal force) is governed as a noun, and often takes a preposition.

I Cor. 14 : 39, τὸ λαλεῖν μὴ κωλύετε γλώσσαις, *forbid not the speaking with tongues.* Acts 14 : 9, ἔχει πίστιν τοῦ σωθῆναι, *he has faith that he will be healed,* lit. *faith of being healed.* John I : 48, πρὸ τοῦ σε Φίλιππον φωνῆσαι, *before Philip called you.*

§ 133. The infinitive is frequent after ἐγένετο, *it came to pass,* where the infinitive, with or without a subject accusative, is the subject of the ἐγένετο. Luke 6 : 1, ἐγένετο δὲ ἐν σαββάτῳ διαπορεύεσθαι αὐτόν, *it came to pass as he journeyed on the Sabbath.* Luke 3 : 21, ἐγένετο δὲ ἐν τῷ βαπτισθῆναι ἅπαντα τὸν λαὸν . . . ἀνεῳχθῆναι τὸν οὐρανὸν καὶ καταβῆναι τὸ πνεῦμα τὸ ἅγιον ἐπ' αὐτόν, *and when all the people had been baptized* (ἐν τῷ βαπτισθῆναι) *it happened that the heavens were opened, and that the Holy Spirit descended upon him.*

§ 134. ὥστε, *so that* (to be distinguished from ὥστε as an introductory word, *and so, therefore*), takes the infinitive (indicative twice), negative μή. Mark 9 : 26, ἐγένετο ὡσεὶ νεκρὸς ὥστε τοὺς πολλοὺς λέγειν ὅτι ἀπέθανεν, *he became as one dead, so that the most said that he was dead.*

§ 135. The infinitive is common after πρίν or πρὶν ἤ, *before.* Matt. 26 : 34, πρὶν ἀλέκτορα φωνῆσαι, *before the cock crows.* Acts 7 : 2, πρὶν ἢ κατοικῆσαι αὐτὸν ἐν Χαρράν, *before he dwelt in Charran.*

PARTICIPLE.

§ 136. Verbs of *hearing, seeing, knowing,* and *perceiving,* may be followed by the participle. This construction is a form of indirect discourse and is rendered by such a clause in English. Acts 7 : 12, ἀκούσας δὲ Ἰακὼβ ὄντα σιτία εἰς Αἴγυπτον, *and Jacob having heard that there was corn in Egypt.* Luke 8 : 46, ἐγὼ γὰρ ἔγνων δύναμιν ἐξεληλυθυῖαν ἀπ᾽ ἐμοῦ, *for I know that power has gone out from me.* 1 John 4 : 2, πᾶν πνεῦμα ὃ ὁμολογεῖ Ἰησοῦν Χριστὸν ἐν σαρκὶ ἐληλυθότα, *every spirit which confesses that Jesus Christ came in the flesh.* For some other examples of the participle see **190–193**.

NEGATIVES.

§ **137.** μή is the usual negative in the conditional, relative, and temporal clauses, οὐ the negative of the main clause.

§ **138.** μή is the negative of the imperative, μὴ θαυμάζετε, *marvel not.*

§ **139.** μή is used in asking questions where a negative reply is expected. John 21 : 5, παιδία, μή τι προσφάγιον ἔχετε; *little children, have ye aught to eat?*

§ **140.** οὐ is used in questions where an affirmative answer is expected. Luke 17 : 17, οὐχ οἱ δέκα ἐκαθαρίσθησαν; *were the ten not purified?*

§ 141. The *double negative* οὐ μή is used to express a *strong* negation. See § 116. Matt. 24 : 34, οὐ μὴ παρέλθῃ ἡ γενεὰ αὕτη ἕως ἂν πάντα ταῦτα γένηται. *This generation shall not pass away until all these things come to pass.*

§ 142. When a strong emphasis is desired several negatives may occur in a sentence, provided the simple negative as οὐ or μή be followed by the *compounds*, as οὐδέ, οὐδέν, or μηδέ, μηδέν. 1 John 1 : 5, σκοτία οὐκ ἔστιν ἐν αὐτῷ οὐδεμία, *no darkness is in him at all.* Mark 1 : 44, ὅρα μηδενὶ μηδὲν εἴπῃς, *see to it, speak ne'er a word to any one.* But where the negatives are simple, the effect is as in English.

§ 143. In general, οὐ is the negative of *statement* or *fact;* while μή is the negative of *conception, possibility,* or *contingency.*

USES OF THE CASES IN GREEK.

§ 144. It is supposed that the student is already acquainted with the simpler uses of the cases that have come up in the course of the lessons.

Genitive.

§ 145. Time *within which* is put in the genitive. Matt. 28 : 13, νυκτὸς ἐλθόντες ἔκλεψαν αὐτόν, *they came in the night and stole him.*

§ 146. The *agent* after a passive verb, usually a *voluntary* agent, is expressed by ὑπό and the genitive. Mark 1 : 9, ἐβαπτίσθη ὑπὸ Ἰωάνου, *he was baptized by John.* Matt. 11 : 7, κάλαμον ὑπὸ ἀνέμου σαλευόμενον, *a reed shaken by the wind.*

§ 147. The genitive may be used as a *predicate* after εἰμί. 1 Cor. 1 : 12, ἐγὼ μέν εἰμι Παύλου . . . ἐγὼ δὲ Χριστοῦ, *I am of Paul . . . and I am of Christ.*

§ 148. Verbs of *touching, begging, hearing, tasting,* and the like, are usually followed by the genitive. Luke 5 : 13, ἥψατο αὐτοῦ λέγων, *he touched him, saying.* Mark 8 : 23, καὶ ἐπιλαβόμενος τῆς χειρὸς τοῦ τυφλοῦ, *and he took hold of his hand.* Luke 5 : 12, ἐδεήθη αὐτοῦ λέγων, *he begged him, saying.* Matt. 17 : 5, ἀκούετε αὐτοῦ, *hear ye him.* John 8 : 52, οὐ μὴ γεύσεται θανάτου εἰς τὸν αἰῶνα, *he shall not taste death forever.*

§ 149. Words denoting *fulness, deficiency, plenty,* and *want,* take the genitive. John 1 : 15, πλήρης χάριτος καὶ ἀληθείας, *full of grace and truth.* Luke 1 : 53, πεινῶντας ἐνέπλησεν ἀγαθῶν, *he filled the hungry with good (things).* James 1 : 5, εἰ δέ τις ὑμῶν λείπεται σοφίας, *and if any of you is lacking in wisdom.*

§ 150. The genitive follows the comparative degree of the adjective. Mark 12 : 31, μείζων τούτων ἄλλη ἐντολὴ οὐκ ἔστιν, *no other commandment is greater than these.*

§ 151. The genitive follows verbs of *accusing, condemning,* and the like. Acts 19 : 40, καὶ γὰρ κινδυνεύομεν ἐγκαλεῖσθαι στάσεως, *for we are in danger of being called to account for the disturbance.* Mark 15 : 3, καὶ κατηγόρουν αὐτοῦ οἱ ἀρχιερεῖς πολλά, *and the high priests accused him of many things.*

§ 152. The genitive follows most adverbs, as : χωρίς, μέχρι, ἕως, ὀπίσω, ἔμπροσθεν, ἐγγύς. John 1 : 15, ὁ ὀπίσω μου ἐρχόμενος ἔμπροσθέν μου γέγονεν ὅτι πρῶτός μου ἦν, *he who comes after me was before me, because he was prior to me.*

Dative.

§ 153. The dative is used after words signifying *likeness, agreement,* or their opposites. John 8 : 55, ἔσομαι ὅμοιος ὑμῖν ψεύστης, *I shall be like you, a liar.*

§ 154. The dative follows verbs of *approaching, joining, following.* Luke 15 : 25, καὶ ὡς ἐρχόμενος ἤγγισεν τῇ οἰκίᾳ, *and as he went he*

drew near to the house. Mark 2 : 14, ἀκολούθει
μοι, *follow me.*

§ 155. πιστεύω, *believe,* and προσκυνέω, *worship,* are commonly followed by the dative.
Matt. 21 : 32, οὐκ ἐπιστεύσατε αὐτῷ, *ye believed
him not.* John 9 : 38, καὶ προσεκύνησεν αὐτῷ,
and he worshipped him.

§ 156. The dative is used after εἰμί and γίνομαι to denote the possessor. Acts 8 : 21, οὐκ
ἔστιν σοι μερίς, *no part is to you (you have no
part).*

§ 157. *Cause, means, manner, degree,* and
instrument are put in the dative; the latter
usually with a preposition. Rom. 11 : 20, τῇ
ἀπιστίᾳ ἐξεκλάσθησαν, *because of their unbelief
they were broken off.* Rom. 8 : 24, τῇ γὰρ ἐλπίδι
ἐσώθημεν, *for we are saved by hope.* Mark
10 : 48, πολλῷ μᾶλλον ἔκραζεν, *he cried much
more,* lit. *more by much.* Luke 22 : 49, Κύριε,
εἰ πατάξομεν ἐν μαχαίρῃ; *Lord, whether shall we
strike with the sword?*

§ 158. Time *when* and place *where* are in the
dative; more commonly with ἐν. Luke 12 : 20,
ταύτῃ τῇ νυκτὶ τὴν ψυχήν σου αἰτοῦσιν ἀπὸ σοῦ,
this night they ask from thee thy soul.

Accusative.

§ 159. Verbs of motion *towards* require the accusative case. The motion may be *objective* or *subjective*, still the same case occurs, and with a preposition, as εἰς, παρά, or πρός. Luke 1 : 56, ὑπέστρεψεν εἰς τὸν οἶκον, *he turned into the house*. Mark 5 : 23, πίπτει πρὸς τοὺς πόδας αὐτοῦ, *he falls at his feet*. John 1 : 1, ὁ λόγος ἦν πρὸς τὸν θεόν, *the Word was with God*.

§ 160. Extent of *time* and *space* is put in the accusative. John 7 : 33, ἔτι χρόνον μικρὸν μεθ' ὑμῶν εἰμί, *yet a little while I am with you*. John 6 : 19, ἐληλακότες οὖν ὡς σταδίους εἴκοσι πέντε, *when then they had gone about twenty-five furlongs*.

§ 161. *Two* accusatives may follow verbs of *saying* or *asking* something of some one ; also *doing* something to some one. Matt. 7 : 9, ὃν αἰτήσει ὁ υἱὸς αὐτοῦ ἄρτον, *whom shall his son ask for bread*. Matt. 4 : 19, ποιήσω ὑμᾶς ἁλεεῖς ἀνθρώπων, *I shall make you fishers of men*.

§ 162. The infinitive has the subject in the accusative. See § 131.

§ 163. PREPOSITIONS.

Genitive only.
- ἀντί, *instead of.*
- ἀπό, *from.*
- ἐκ, *out of.*
- πρό, *before.*

Dative only.
- ἐν, *in.*
- σύν, *with.*

Accusative only. εἰς, *into, to.*

Genitive and Accus.
- διά, *through.*
- κατά *down.*
- μετά, *with, after.*
- περί, *about.*
- ὑπέρ, *above.*
- ὑπό, *under.*

Gen., Dat., and Accus.
- ἐπί, *upon, at, to.*
- παρά, *from, by, to.*
- πρός, *to, at.*

§ 164. **ἀντί,** *instead of,* ὀδόντα ἀντὶ τοῦ ὀδόντος, *a tooth for a tooth.*

ἀπό denotes SEPARATION, ἀπὸ τῆς Γαλιλαίας, *from Galilee;* ἀπὸ πάσης ἁμαρτίας, *from every sin.* SOURCE, μάθετε ἀπ᾽ ἐμοῦ, *learn of me.*

διά, *genitive,* THROUGH, εἰσερχόμενος διὰ τῆς θύρας, *entering through the door.* MEANS, ὁ κόσμος δι᾽ αὐτοῦ ἐγένετο, *the world was made through him.* *Accusative,* ON ACCOUNT OF, FOR THE SAKE OF, διὰ τὸ ὄνομά μου, *for my name's sake;* διὰ τοῦτο, *on account of this.*

εἰς denotes motion toward, either real or

implied, ἀνέβη εἰς τὸ ὄρος, *he went up into the
mountain.* TIME, εἰς αἰῶνα, *for everlasting.*

Used metaphorically to denote REST or a
CONDITION, ὁ ὢν εἰς τὸν κόλπον τοῦ πατρός *he
who is in the bosom of the Father.*

ἐκ denotes motion OUT OF, where there has
been a close union, φωνὴ ἐκ τῶν οὐρανῶν, *a voice
out of heaven.* TIME, ἐκ τούτου, *after this (time).*
PLACE, ἐκ δεξιῶν, *on the right hand.*

ἐν, IN, ἐν τῇ ἀγορᾷ, *in the market-place ;* δεδομένον ἐν ἀνθρώποις, *given among men* (so often
with plural nouns). INSTRUMENT, πατάξομεν
ἐν τῇ μαχαίρῃ ; *shall we strike with the sword?*

ἐπί, with the *genitive,* UPON, with verbs of
RESTING, GOING, STANDING, ἐπὶ τῆς γῆς, *upon the
earth.* TIME, ἐπὶ Κλαυδίου, *in the time of
Claudius.*

With the *dative,* WHERE, ἐπὶ πρυμνῇ, *at the
stern ;* ἐπὶ πίνακι, *upon a charger.*

Accusative, motion toward, τιθέασιν ἐπὶ τὴν
λυχνίαν, *they put it upon a lampstand,* συνήχθη
ὄχλος πολὺς ἐπ' αὐτόν, *a great multitude was
gathered to him.*

κατά, motion FROM ABOVE DOWNWARD. *Genitive,* ὥρμησε κατὰ τοῦ κρημνοῦ, *they rushed down
the steep place.* An opinion or judgment AGAINST
any one, εἴ τι ἔχετε κατά τινος, *if you have anything against any one.*

Accusative, ALONG, THROUGH, ACCORDING TO, κατὰ τὰς χώρας, *throughout these places;* κατὰ τὸν νόμον, *according to the law.*

μετά, ASSOCIATION WITH.   *Genitive,* ὁ πατὴρ μετ' ἐμοῦ ἐστιν, *the Father is with me.*

Accusative, AFTER, denoting succession, μετὰ δὲ ταῦτα εἶπεν, *and after this he said.*

παρά, *genitive,* FROM THE SIDE OF.   FROM, always of a person, λαμβάνομεν παρ' αὐτοῦ, *we receive from him.*

Dative, BY THE SIDE OF.   Something is or is done by some one or something, παρ' αὐτῷ ἔμειναν, *they remained with him.*

Accusative, TO, CONTRARY TO, ἦλθε παρὰ τὴν θάλασσαν, *he went to the sea;* παρὰ τὴν διδάχην, *contrary to the teaching.*

περί, *genitive,* ABOUT, CONCERNING, γέγραπται περὶ αὐτοῦ, *it is written concerning him.*

Accusative, ABOUT, AROUND, περὶ δὲ ἐνδεκάτην, *and about the eleventh hour;* περὶ Τύρον, *around Tyre.*

πρό, BEFORE, πρὸ τῶν θυρῶν, *before the doors;* πρὸ καταβολῆς κόσμου, *before the foundation of the world.*

πρός, *accusative,* after verbs of motion, ἀπῆλθε πρὸς αὐτούς, *he departed to them.*   Where the motion is not objective, ἐμάχοντο οὖν πρὸς ἀλλή-λους, *and indeed they contended with one another.*

PROXIMITY, ὁ λόγος ἦν πρὸς τὸν Θεόν, *the word was with God.*   Dative, NEAR, πρὸς τῷ ὄρει, *by the mountain.*   Genitive but once, Acts 27 : 34, *for the advantage of.*

σύν, WITH, ἐπορεύετο σὺν αὐτοῖς, *he proceeded with them.*

ὑπέρ, *genitive,* FOR SAKE OF, ψυχήν μου ὑπὲρ σοῦ θήσω, *I shall lay down my life for you.*

Accusative, ABOVE, οὐδὲ δοῦλος ὑπὲρ τὸν κύριον, *nor is the servant above his master.*

ὑπό, *genitive,* always with the passive voice to denote the AGENT, ἐβαπτίσθη ὑπὸ Ἰωάνου, *he was baptized by John.*

Accusative, UNDER, ὑπὸ τὴν συκῆν εἶδόν σε, *I saw you underneath the fig tree.*

The student should by no means consider this short treatment of the prepositions exhaustive. Many of them occur more than 1000 times in the New Testament, and often with varying significance. Only the most fundamental uses have here been indicated.

In all cases constant reference should be made to the lexicon.

INDEXES.

GREEK INDEX.

Q

θε, in aor. pass., 68.
θνήσκω (θαν), only w. prep.
  ἀπο-; prin. parts, 191; class
  of verbs, 187 (bottom).
θρίξ, decl., 151.
θυγάτηρ, decl., 151 (top).

I, close vowel, 138 (3); added
  to pron. and adv., 52 (note);
  in redupl., 89; sign of the
  opt., 181.
ἵημι, see ἀφίημι.
-ιν, in acc. sing., 51 (bottom).
ἵνα, conj., construction w. final
  clauses, 206; w. object
  clauses, 207.
ἵστημι, redupl., 89; inflection
  of forms, 173; prin. parts,
  191; forms in N. T., 201.
-ιων, -ιστος, comp. and superl.,
  86.

K, for classification of mutes,
  138; before σ, 49; before μ,
  117 (top).
-κα, in verbs, 88 (note).
κακός compared, 153.
καλός compared, 153.
κατά, w. gen. and acc., 220.
κλαίω, prin. parts, 191.

Λ, 138; verbs in -λλω, 186.
λαμβάνω, class of verbs, 187;
  prin. parts, 192.
λείπω, 2 aor. of, 165.
λύω, conjug., 160.

M, 138.
μέγας, decl., 152; compared,
  153.
μετά, w. gen. and acc., 221.
μή, neg. in cond., rel., final,
  temp. clauses, 213; in wishes,
  206; w. imp., 213; w. dubi-
  tative subj., 205 (bottom);
  double neg. οὐ μή, 206 (top);
  in asking questions, 213.
μήτηρ, decl., 151 (top).

N, 138; in 5th class of verbs,
  187.
ν, case ending, 51 (bottom).
-ναι, infin., 76, 183.
-νσι, in 3d per. plur., 4.

Ξ, double consonant, 17 (top).

O, in contraction, 139; lengthened to ω, 48; to ου, 52 (132);
  connect. vowel, see under ε.
ὁ, ἡ, τό, art. decl., 146; proclitics, 21 (note).
οι, diphthong, 8, b.
οἶδα, conjugation, 180.
ὄμνυμι (ὀμ-, ὀμο-), class of verbs,
  187.
ὄνομα, decl., 42.
ὀπίσω, w. gen., 86 (note).
ὅπως, in obj. clauses w. subjv.,
  207.
ὁράω, prin. parts, 192; augment, 112 (v. 1).
ὅς, rel. pron., 33 (bottom).

ENGLISH INDEX.

See remark, page 225.

AIDS TO THE STUDY

OF

THE NEW TESTAMENT.

CONTENTS.

The asterisk before a title indicates a net price.

TEXTS.

𝔊𝔯𝔢𝔢𝔨.

*NOVUM TESTAMENTUM GRÆCE TEXTUS STE-PHANICI, A.D. 1550, curante F. H. A. SCRIVENER, M.A. 16mo. *Cambridge Greek and Latin Texts.* 90 cents. *B.*

*NOVUM TESTAMENTUM GRÆCE (Editio Major) TEXTUS STEPHANICI, A.D. 1556, curante F. H. A. SCRIVENER, M.A. With Lexicon. Bound in leather, $2.50. *B.*

1

NOVUM TESTAMENTUM GRÆCE. Antiquissimorum Codicum Textus in ordine parallelo dispositi. Accedit collatio Codicis Sinaitici. Edidit E. H. HANSELL, S.T.B. Tomi III. 8vo. $6.00.

NOVUM TESTAMENTUM GRÆCE. Edidit C. LLOYD. 16mo. 75 cents.

The same on writing-paper, with large margin. 4to. $2.75.*

THE GREEK TESTAMENT, with Critical Appendices. LLOYD and SANDAY. Printed on India paper. 16mo. $1.50.

NOVUM TESTAMENTUM GRÆCE JUXTA EXEMPLAR MILLIANUM. 16mo. 60 cents.

The same with large margin. 4to. $2.25.*

*THE NEW TESTAMENT IN GREEK, according to the Text followed in the Authorized Version, together with the Variations adopted in the Revised Version. Edited by F. H. A. SCRIVENER, M.A. $1.75.†

*GREEK TESTAMENT FOR SCHOOLS. The Text Revised by B. F. WESTCOTT, D.D., and F. J. A. HORT, D.D. 18mo. Cloth, $1.00; roan, red edges, $1.25; full morocco, gilt edges, $1.75.

An Edition, with a new Lexicon, by W. J. HICKIE, M.A., bound in leather, $1.90.

*THE PARALLEL NEW TESTAMENT, GREEK AND ENGLISH. The New Testament, being the Authorized Version set forth in 1611. Arranged in Parallel Columns with the Revised Version of 1881, and with the original Greek, edited by F. H. A. SCRIVENER, M.A. 8vo. $4.50.†

*GREEK AND ENGLISH TESTAMENT, in parallel columns on the same page. Edited by J. SCHOLEFIELD, M.A. $2.00.†

Student's Edition of above, on large writing-paper. 4to. $3.50.†

THE NEW TESTAMENT IN GREEK AND ENGLISH. Edited by E. CARDWELL, D.D. Two vols. $1.50.

*SCHOOL READINGS IN THE GREEK TESTAMENT. Edited with Notes and Vocabulary by A. CALVERT, M.A. 16mo. $1.10.

*THE CAMBRIDGE GREEK TESTAMENT FOR SCHOOLS
AND COLLEGES, with a Revised Text and English Notes.
Prepared under the direction of J. J. S. PEROWNE, D.D., Dean
of Peterborough.†

Gospel according to St. Matthew. By Rev. A. CARR. With
Maps. $1.10.

Gospel according to St. Mark. By Rev. G. F. MACLEAR.
With Maps. $1.10.

Gospel according to St. Luke. By Archdeacon FARRAR. With
4 Maps. $1.50.

Gospel according to St. John. By Rev. A. PLUMMER, M.A.
With 4 Maps. $1.50.

Acts of the Apostles. By Rev. Prof. LUMBY, D.D. With 4
Maps. $1.50.

First Epistle to the Corinthians. By Rev. J. J. LIAS. With
Maps. 75 cents.

Second Epistle to the Corinthians. By Rev. J. J. LIAS. 75 cents.

Epistle to the Hebrews. By Archdeacon FARRAR, D.D. 90
cents.

Epistles of St. John. By Rev. A. PLUMMER, M.A., D.D. $1.00.

Latin.

*NOUUM TESTAMENTUM DOMINI NOSTRI IESU
CHRISTI LATINE. Secundum Editionem Sancti Hieronymi
rec. I. WORDSWORTH, S.T.P., in Operis Societatam adsumto
H. I. WHITE, A.M. Pars I. 4to.

Fasc. I.   Euangelium secundum Mattheum. $3.25.*
Fasc. II.   Euangelium secundum Marcum. $1.90.*
Fasc. III.   Euangelium secundum Lucam. $3.25.*
Fasc. IV.   Euangelium secundum Ioannem.   (*In the press.*)

*OLD–LATIN BIBLICAL TEXTS, No. 1. The Gospel accord-
ing to St. Matthew, from the St. Germain MS. (g.). Edited
by J. WORDSWORTH, M.A. 4to. Stiff covers. $1.50.*

*OLD–LATIN BIBLICAL TEXTS, No. 2. Portions of the Gos-
pels according to St. Mark and St. Matthew. Edited by J.
WORDSWORTH, D.D., W. SANDAY, M.A., D.D., and H. J.
WHITE. 4to. Stiff covers. $5.25.*

*OLD–LATIN BIBLICAL TEXTS, No. 3. The Four Gospels.
By H. J. WHITE, M.A. 4to. Stiff covers. $3.25.*

Anglo=Saxon.

*THE HOLY GOSPELS IN ANGLO-SAXON, NORTHUM-
BRIAN, AND OLD MERCIAN VERSIONS. Edited by
the Rev. WALTER W. SKEAT. 4to. $9.00.†

*THE GOSPEL ACCORDING TO ST. MATTHEW in Anglo-
Saxon and Northumbrian Versions. Edited by the Rev. W.
W. SKEAT. 4to. $2.75.†

*THE GOSPEL ACCORDING TO ST. MARK in Anglo-Saxon
and Northumbrian Versions. Edited by the Rev. W. W.
SKEAT, M.A. 4to. $2.75.†

*THE GOSPEL ACCORDING TO ST. LUKE, uniform with
the preceding. Edited by the Rev. W. W. SKEAT. 4to. $2.75.†

*THE GOSPEL ACCORDING TO ST. JOHN, uniform with
the preceding. Edited by the Rev. W. W. SKEAT. 4to.
$2.75.†

*THE GOSPEL OF ST. MARK in Gothic. By Rev. W. W.
SKEAT. *Clarendon Press Series.* 16mo. $1.00.*

*THE GOSPEL OF ST. LUKE in Anglo-Saxon. Edited from
the Manuscripts, with an Introduction, Notes, and a Glossary,
by JAMES W. BRIGHT, Ph.D. 16mo. $1.30.*

English.

*THE HOLY BIBLE in the earliest English Versions, made by
John Wycliffe and his followers. Edited by Rev. J. FORSHALL
and Sir F. MADDEN. 4 vols., royal 4to. $16.00.*

*THE NEW TESTAMENT in English, according to the Ver-
sion by John Wycliffe, and Revised by John Purvey. 16mo.
$1.50.*

*THE CAMBRIDGE PARAGRAPH BIBLE of the Authorized
English Version, with an Introduction by F. H. A. SCRIVENER,
M.A. 4to. $6.00.†

  *Student's Edition of the above, on good writing-paper with
wide margins. Two vols., 4to. $9.00.†

*THE LECTIONARY BIBLE, WITH APOCRYPHA. $1.00.†

*THE NEW TESTAMENT SCRIPTURES in the order in
which they were written. By Rev. CHARLES HEBERT. Vol. I.
$1.00.*

* **THE CAMBRIDGE BIBLE FOR SCHOOLS AND COL- LEGES.** General Editor: J. J. S. PEROWNE, D.D., Dean of Peterborough.†

NEW TESTAMENT VOLUMES.

Now Ready. Cloth Extra, 16*mo.*

Gospel according to St. Matthew. By Rev. A. CARR, M.A. With Maps. 60 cents.

Gospel according to St. Mark. By Rev. G. F. MACLEAR, D.D. With Maps. 60 cents.

Gospel according to St. Luke. By Archdeacon FARRAR. With Maps. $1.10.

Gospel according to St. John. By Rev. A. PLUMMER, M.A. With Maps. $1.10.

Acts of the Apostles. By Rev. Prof. LUMBY, D.D. With 4 Maps. $1.10.

Epistle to the Romans. By Rev. H. C. G. MOULE, M.A. 90 cents.

First Epistle to the Corinthians. By Rev. J. J. LIAS. With Map. 50 cents.

Second Epistle to the Corinthians. By Rev. J. J. LIAS. With Map. 50 cents.

Epistle to the Galatians. With Introduction and Notes by the Rev. E. H. PEROWNE, D.D. 40 cents.

Epistle to the Ephesians. By Rev. H. C. G. MOULE, M.A. 60 cents.

Epistle to the Philippians. By Rev. H. C. G. MOULE, M.A. 60 cents.

Epistles to the Thessalonians. With Introduction, Notes, and Map by the Rev. GEORGE G. FINDLAY. 50 cents.

Epistle to the Hebrews. By Archdeacon FARRAR, D.D. 90 cents.

General Epistle of St. James. By Very Rev. E. H. PLUMP- TRE, D.D. 40 cents.

Epistles of St. Peter and St. Jude. By Very Rev. E. H. PLUMPTRE, D.D. 60 cents.

Epistles of St. John. By Rev. A. PLUMMER, M.A., D.D. 90 cents.

The Revelation of St. John the Divine. With Notes and In- troduction by the late Rev. WILLIAM HENRY SIMCOX, M.A. 80 cents.

*THE SMALLER CAMBRIDGE BIBLE FOR SCHOOLS is especially adapted to the requirements of Junior and Elementary Schools. It will include Historical Books of the Old and New Testaments, and such other portions as are suitable for school study. 18mo. 30 cents each.†

NEW TESTAMENT VOLUMES.

Now Ready.

The Gospel according to St. Matthew. With Map, Introduction, and Notes by the Rev. A. CARR, M.A.

The Gospel according to St. Mark. By the Rev. G. F. MACLEAR.

The Gospel according to St. Luke. By the Rev. Canon FARRAR, D.D.

The Gospel according to St. John. With Map, Introduction, and Notes by the Rev. A. PLUMMER, M.A.

The Acts of the Apostles. With Introduction and Notes by the Rev. Prof. LUMBY, D.D.

WORKS ON THE NEW TESTAMENT.

ABBOTT and RUSHBROOKE. — **The Common Tradition of the Four Gospels,** in the Text of the Revised Version. $1.25.

ARNOLD (MATTHEW). — **Literature and Dogma.** An Essay towards a Better Apprehension of the Bible. $1.50.

God and the Bible. A Review of Objections to 'Literature and Dogma.' $1.50.

St. Paul and Protestantism. Last Essays on Church and Religion. $1.50.

*BARRETT (A. C.). — **Companion to the Greek Testament.** 16mo. $1.25. *B.*

BIRKS (T. R.). — **Essays on the Right Estimation of MS. Evidence** in the Text of the New Testament. $1.25.

CANON MURATORIANUS : the earliest Catalogue of the Books of the New Testament. Edited by S. P. TREGELLES. LL.D. 4to. $2.75.

DAVIES (T. L. O.). — **Bible-English.** (*New Edition preparing.*)

DU BOSE (WILLIAM PORCHER). — **Soteriology of the New Testament.** $1.50.

EADIE (JOHN, LL.D.). — **The English Bible.** An external and critical History of the various English Translations of Scripture. Two vols. 8vo. $8.00.

*****HAMMOND** (C. E.). — **Outlines of Textual Criticism applied to the New Testament.** Fifth Edition, revised. *Clarendon Press Series.* 16mo. $1.25.*

*****HATCH** (EDWIN). — **Essays in Biblical Greek.** 8vo. $2.75.*

*****HICKIE** (W. J., M.A.). — **A Lexicon of the Greek Testament.** 18mo. 75 cents.

HOOLE (C. H.). — **The Classical Element in the New Testament.** 8vo. $3.75.

HORTON (ROBERT F., M.A.). — **Revelation and the Bible.** An Attempt at Reconstruction. $2.00.

*****LEWIN** (THOMAS, M.A, F.S.A.). — **The Life and Epistles of St. Paul.** 2 vols., 4to. $15.00. *B.*

LIGHTFOOT (JOSEPH B., D.D., D.C.L., LL.D.). — **On a Fresh Revision of the English New Testament.** $2.00.

*****MACLEAR** (G. F.). — **A Class-Book of New Testament History.** 18mo. $1.10.

Abridged Class-Book of New Testament History. 18mo. 30 cents.

MAURICE (FREDERICK DENISON, M.A.). — **The Unity of the New Testament.** 2 vols. $4.00.

*****MILLER** (E., M.A.). — **A Greek Testament Primer.** 16mo. 90 cents.*

Guide to the Textual Criticism of the New Testament. $1.00. *B.*

*****THE REVISERS AND THE GREEK TEXT** of the New Testament. By two members of the New Testament Company. 8vo. Paper. 75 cents.

SALMON (Dr. GEORGE). — **Non-Miraculous Christianity.** $1.75.

*SCRIVENER (F. H. A., M.A., D.C.L., LL.D.). — **The Authorized Edition of the English Bible (1611)**, its subsequent Reprints and modern Representatives. Being the introduction to the Cambridge Paragraph Bible (1873), re-edited with corrections and additions. $2.25.†

A Plain Introduction to the Criticism of the New Testament. With Forty Facsimiles from Ancient Manuscripts. 8vo. $5.00. *B.* *Out of print.*

Six Lectures on the Text of the New Testament. With Facsimiles from MSS., etc. $1.75. *B.*

STUDIA BIBLICA. Essays in Biblical and Patristic Criticism and Kindred Subjects. By Members of the University of Oxford. Vol. I. 8vo. $2.75.

Vol. II. 8vo. $3.25.*
Vol. III. 8vo. $4.00.

CONTENTS.

VOL. I.

VOL. II.

V.   The Evidence of the Early Versions and Patristic Quotations on the Text
      of the Books of the New Testament. Ll. J. M. BEBB, M.A.
VI.   The Ammonian Sections, Eusebian Canons, and Harmonizing Tables in
      the Syriac Tetraevangelium. G. H. GWILLIAM, B.D.
VII. The Codex Amiatinus and its Birthplace. H. J. WHITE, M.A.

VOL. III.

I.   The Introduction of the Square Characters in Biblical MSS., and an
      Account of the Earliest MSS. of the Old Testament. AD. NEU-
      BAUER, M.A.
II.   The Argument of Romans IX.–XI. CHARLES GORE, M.A.
III. The Materials for the Criticism of the Peshitto New Testament, with
      Specimens of the Syriac Massorah. G. H. GWILLIAM, B.D.
IV.   An Examination of the New Testament Quotations of Ephrem Syrus.
      F. H. WOODS, B.D.
V.   The Text of the Canons of Ancyra. R. B. RACKHAM, M.A.
VI.   The Cheltenham List of the Canonical Books of the Old and New Testa-
      ment and of the Writings of Cyprian. W. SANDAY, M.A.

***TEXTS AND STUDIES : Contributions to Biblical and
Patristic Literature.** Edited by J. ARMITAGE ROBINSON,
B.D., Fellow and Assistant Tutor of Christ's College.

**Vol. I. No. 1. The Apology of Aristides on Behalf of the
Christians.** By J. RENDEL HARRIS, M.A. Second edition.
8vo. $1.75.†

No. 2. The Passion of S. Perpetua. By J. ARMITAGE
ROBINSON, B.D. 8vo. $1.75.†

No. 3. The Lord's Prayer in the Early Church. By F. H.
CHASE, B.D. 8vo. $1.75.†

No. 4. The Fragments of Heracleon. By A. E. BROOKE,
M.A., Fellow of King's College. $1.75.†

Vol. II. No. 1. A Study of Codex Bezæ. By J. RENDEL
HARRIS, M.A. 8vo. $2.60.†

No. 2. The Testament of Abraham. By M. R. JAMES,
M.A. 8vo. $1.75.†

TRENCH (RICHARD CHENEVIX, D.D.). — **Synonyms of the
New Testament.** 8vo. $3.50.

WESTCOTT (BROOKE FOSS, D.D., D.C.L.). — **A General View
of the History of the English Bible.** New Edition. (*In
Press.*)

The Bible in the Church. 18mo. $1.25.

**A General Survey of the History of the Canon of the New
Testament.** Fifth Edition, revised. $3.00.

WILSON (WILLIAM, D.D.). — **The Bible Student's Guide.**
4to. $7.50.

WRIGHT (W. ALDIS). — **The Bible Word-Book.** Second Edition, revised. $2.25.

Gospels and Acts.

ALEXANDER (WILLIAM, D.D.). — **The Leading Ideas of the Gospels.** New Edition, revised and enlarged. $1.75.

BARRETT (G. S.). — **The Temptation of Christ.** 16mo. $1.25.

BIRKS (REV. T. R., M.A.). — **Horæ Evangelicæ;** or, the Internal Evidence of the Gospel History. Edited by the Rev. H. A. BIRKS, M.A. 8vo. $4.00. *B.*

CALDERWOOD (HENRY, LL.D.). — **The Parables of Our Lord.** $2.00.

*****DENTON** (W., M.A.). — **A Commentary on the Gospels.** 3 vols. 8vo. $3.50 each. *B.*

FARRAR (FREDERIC W., D.D.). — **The Witness of History to Christ.** Hulsean Lectures. Sixth Edition. $1.25.

HOOK (W. F., D.D.). — **The History of Our Lord and Saviour Jesus Christ.** In Three Parts. By W. READING, M.A. 32mo. Cloth. 40 cents. *B.*

*****JAMES** (C. C., M.A.). — **The Gospel History of Our Lord Jesus Christ in the Language of the Revised Version,** arranged in a connected Narrative, especially for the use of Teachers and Preachers. $1.10.†

A Harmony of the Gospels, in the Words of the Revised Version, with copious References, Tables, etc. $1.50.†

JEFFREY (REV. ROBERT T., M.D.). — **The Salvation of the Gospel.** A Series of Discourses. $1.75.

JOLLEY (ALFRED J.). — **The Synoptic Problem for English Readers.** 12mo. $1.25.

*****THE LIFE, TEACHING, AND WORKS** of the Lord Jesus Christ. 16mo. 75 cents.*

LIGHTFOOT (JOSEPH B., D.D., D.C.L., LL.D.). — **Essays on the Work entitled "Supernatural Religion."** 8vo. $2.50.

MALAN (S. C., D.D.) — **The Miracles of Our Lord.** 16mo. 75 cents. *B.*

The Parables of Our Lord. 2 vols. $3.50. *B.*

MOORHOUSE (JAMES, M.A.).— **The Teaching of Christ.** $1.25.

NEANDER (AUGUST). — **Life of Jesus Christ**, in its Historical Connection and Development. Translated from the German by J. McCLINTOCK and C. BLUMENTHAL. With Indexes. $1.00. *Bohn.*

RUSHBROOKE (W. G., M.L.).— **Synopticon: An Exposition of the Common Matter of the Synoptic Gospels.** Printed in colors. Complete in one vol., cloth. $10.50.

SADLER (Rev. M. F.).— **The Lost Gospel and its Contents;** or, the Author of "Supernatural Religion" refuted by himself. 8vo. $2.00. *B.*

STRAUSS. — **The Life of Jesus.** Critically examined by Dr. DAVID FRIEDRICH STRAUSS. Translated from the German Edition by GEORGE ELIOT. New and cheaper edition. 8vo. Cloth. $4.50.

TRENCH (RICHARD CHENEVIX, D.D.).— **Studies in the Gospels.** 8vo. $3.00.

VAUGHAN (CHARLES J., D.D.). — **Prayers of Christ.** $1.00.

Words from the Gospels. $1.00.

*THE VERY WORDS OF OUR LORD AND SAVIOUR **Jesus Christ.** 60 cents.*

WESTCOTT (BROOKE FOSS, D.D., D.C.L.).— **Introduction to the Study of the Four Gospels.** Seventh Edition. $3.00.

American Edition. $2.25.

WIESELER (KARL).— **Chronological Synopsis of the Four Gospels.** Translated by the Rev. Canon VENABLES. Second and cheaper Edition, revised. $1.50. *Bohn.*

WRIGHT (ARTHUR). — **The Composition of the Four Gospels.** $1.75.

———

SADLER (Rev. M. F.). — **The Gospel according to St. Matthew.** With Notes, critical and practical. With Maps. 5th Edition. 12mo. $2.00.

SLOMAN (A., M.A.). — **The Gospel according to St. Matthew.** Greek Text with Introduction and Notes. 16mo. 60 cents.

TRENCH (RICHARD CHENEVIX, D.D.). — **The Sermon on the Mount.** 8vo. $3.00.

SADLER (Rev. M. F.). — **The Gospel according to St. Mark.** With Notes, critical and practical. 4th Edition. 12mo. $2.00.

*BOND (Rev. JOHN, M.A.). — **The Gospel according to St. Luke.** Greek Text, with Introduction and Notes. 16mo. 65 cents.

*CYRILLI (ARCHIEPISCOPI ALEXANDRINI) **Commentarii in Lucæ Evangelium quæ supersunt Syriace.** 4to. $5.50.*

The same, translated by R. PAYNE SMITH, M.A. 2 vols., 8vo. $3.50.*

MAURICE (FREDERICK DENISON, M.A.). — **The Gospel of the Kingdom of Heaven.** A Course of Lectures on the Gospel of St. Luke. $1.75.

SADLER (Rev. M. F.). — **The Gospel according to St. Luke.** With Notes, critical and practical. 12mo. $2.50.

BERNARD (THOMAS DEHANEY, M.A.). — **The Central Teaching of Jesus Christ.** A Study and Exposition of the five Chapters of the Gospel according to St. John, xiii. to xvii. inclusive. $1.50.

*CYRILLI (ARCHIEPISCOPI ALEXANDRINI) **Commentarii in D. Joannis Evangelium.** Edidit post Aubertum P. E. PUSEY, A.M. Tomi III. 8vo. $11.50.*

MAURICE (FREDERICK DENISON, M.A.). — **The Gospel of St. John.** A Series of Discourses. Eighth Edition. $1.50.

SADLER (Rev. M. F.). — **The Gospel according to St. John.** With Notes, critical and practical. Fifth Edition. 12mo. $2.00.

*BISCOE (RICHARD, M.A.). — **The History of the Acts of the Holy Apostles.** Boyle Lectures. 8vo. $2.50.*

CHASE (Rev. F. H., M.A.). — **The Codex Bezæ of the Acts of the Apostles.** An Essay. 8vo. *In the Press.*

*DENTON (W., M.A.). — **Commentary on the Acts of the Apostles.** 2 vols. 8vo. $3.50 each. *B.*

PAGE (T. E., M.A.). — **Acts of the Apostles.** Being the Greek Text as revised by Drs. WESTCOTT and HORT. With Explanatory Notes. 16mo. $1.10.

SADLER (Rev. M. F.).— **The Acts of the Holy Apostles.** With Notes critical and practical. With Maps. 12mo. $2.00.

VAUGHAN (CHARLES J., D.D.). — **The Church of the First Days.** The Church of Jerusalem. The Church of the Gentiles. The Church of the World. Lectures on the Acts of the Apostles. New Edition. $2.75.

Epistles.

DAVIES (J. LLEWELYN, M.A.). — **The Epistles of St. Paul to the Ephesians, the Colossians, and Philemon.** With Notes. Second Edition. 8vo. $2.25.

*****DENTON** (W., M.A.). — **A Commentary on the Epistles.** Two vols. 8vo. $3.50 each.

EADIE (JOHN, D.D.).— **St. Paul's Epistles to the Thessalonians.** Commentary on the Greek Text. 8vo. $3.50.

KAY (W., D.D.). — **A Commentary on the Two Epistles of St. Paul to the Corinthians.** Greek Text, with Commentary. 8vo. $2.25.

*****LEWIN** (THOMAS, M.A., F.S.A.). — **The Life and Epistles of St. Paul.** Two vols. 4to. $15.00. *B.*

*****LIGHTFOOT** (JOSEPH B., D.D., D.C.L., LL.D.). — **Dissertations on the Apostolic Age.** Reprinted from editions of St. Paul's Epistles. 8vo. $3.50.

*****St. Paul's Epistle to the Galatians.** Tenth Edition, revised. 8vo. $3.25.

*****St. Paul's Epistle to the Philippians.** Ninth Edition, revised. 8vo. $3.25.

*****St. Paul's Epistles to the Colossians and to Philemon.** Eighth Edition, revised. 8vo. $3.25.

MAURICE (FREDERICK DENISON, M.A.).— **The Epistles of St. John.** Second and Cheaper Edition. $2.00.

MAYOR (JOSEPH B., M.A.).— **The Epistle of St. James.** The Greek Text, with Introduction, Notes, and Comments. 8vo. pp. 220–248. $3.50.

> "It is a work which sums up many others, and to any one who wishes to make a thorough study of the Epistle of St. James, it will prove indispensable." — *Scotsman.*

RENDALL (FREDERIC, M.A.). — **The Epistle to the Hebrews in Greek and English.** With Notes. $2.00.

    The Epistle to the Hebrews. New Translation, with Commentary. Together with an Appendix. $2.25.

SADLER (Rev. M F.). — **The Epistle to the Romans.** With Notes critical and practical. Second Edition. $1.75.

    The Epistle of St. Paul to the Corinthians. With Notes critical and practical. $2.00.

    The Epistle of St. Paul to the Galatians, Ephesians, and Philippians. With Notes critical and practical. $1.75.

    The Epistle of St. Paul to the Colossians, Thessalonians, and Timothy. With Notes critical and practical. $1.75.

    The Epistle of St. Paul to Titus, Philemon, and the Hebrews. With Notes critical and practical. $1.75.

*THEODORE OF MOPSUESTIA'S Commentary on the Minor Epistles of St. Paul. The Latin Version with the Greek Fragments, edited by H. B. SWETE, D.D. 2 vols. 8vo. $3.50 each.†

TRENCH (RICHARD CHENEVIX, D.D.). — **Commentary on the Epistles to the Seven Churches in Asia.** 8vo. $2.25.

VAUGHAN (CHARLES J., D.D.). — **Lectures on the Epistle to the Philippians.** New Edition. $2.00.

    St. Paul's Epistle to the Philippians. With Translation, Paraphrase, and Notes for English Readers. $1.50.

    St. Paul's Epistle to the Romans. The Greek Text, with English Notes. Fifth Edition. $2.25.

    The Epistle to the Hebrews. With Notes. $2.25.

WESTCOTT (BROOKE FOSS, D.D., D.C.L.). — **The Epistles of St. John.** The Greek Text, with Notes and Essays. $3.50.

    The Epistle to the Hebrews. The Greek Text, with Notes and Essays. Second Edition. 8vo. $4.00.

Apocalypse.

MAURICE (Frederick Denison, M.A.). — **Lectures on the Apocalypse.** Second Edition. $2.00.

MILLIGAN (William, D.D.). — **Lectures on the Apocalypse.** $1.50.

    Discussions on the Apocalypse. $1.50.

VAUGHAN (Charles J., D.D.). — **Lectures on the Revelation of St. John.** Fifth Edition. $2.75.

The Fathers.

*APOCRYPHAL GOSPEL OF PETER. The Greek Text of the Newly Discovered Fragment. 8vo. 35 cents.

*THE GOSPEL ACCORDING TO PETER, AND THE REVELATION OF PETER. Two Lectures on the Newly Recovered Fragments, together with the Greek Texts. By J. Armitage Robinson and Montague Rhodes James. 12mo. $1.25.

*THE AKHMIM FRAGMENT OF THE APOCRYPHAL GOSPEL OF ST. PETER. With an Introduction, Notes, and Indices. By Henry B. Swete, D.D., Litt.D. 8vo. $1.60.

CRAMER. — Catenæ Græcorum Patrum, in Novum Testamentum. Edidit J. A. Cramer. Tomi VIII. 8vo. $11.00.

CUNNINGHAM (Rev. W., B.D.). — **The Epistle of St. Barnabas.** The Greek Text, the Latin Version, and a New English Translation. $2.25.

DONALDSON (James, LL.D.). — **The Apostolical Fathers.** . A Critical Account of their Genuine Writings, and of their Doctrines. $2.00.

FARRAR (Frederick W., D.D.). — **Lives of the Fathers.** Church History in Biography. 2 vols. Large 12mo. $5.00.

*JACOBSON (William). — **Patrum Apostolicorum** S. Clementis Romani, S. Ignatii, S. Polycarpi, quæ supersunt. Tomi II. Fourth Edition. 8vo. $5.25.*

*LIGHTFOOT (Joseph B., D.D., D.C.L., L.L.D.). — **The Apostolic Fathers.** Part I. S. Clement of Rome. Revised Texts, with Introductions, Notes, Dissertations, and Translations. 2 vols. 8vo. $10.00.

*Part II. S. Ignatius to S. Polycarp. Revised Texts, with Introductions, Notes, Dissertations, and Translations. Two volumes, bound in three. 8vo. New Edition. $16.50.

*The Apostolic Fathers. Abridged Edition. With Short Introductions, Greek Text, and English Translation. 8vo. $4.00.

The Early Church.

EUSEBIUS. — Ecclesiastical History according to the Text of BURTON. With an Introduction by BRIGHT. $2.25.

Ecclesiastical History of Eusebius Pamphilius, Bishop of Cæsarea. Translated from the Greek by Rev. C. F. CRUSE, M.A. With Notes, a Life of Eusebius, a Chronological Table of Persons and Events mentioned in the History. Index. $1.50. *Bohn.*

NEANDER (AUGUST). — History of the Planting and Training of the Christian Church by the Apostles. Together with the Antignostikus, or Spirit of Tertullian. Translated by J. E. RYLAND. With Indexes. 2 vols. Each $1.00. *Bohn.*

VAUGHAN (CHARLES J., D.D.). — The Church of the First Days. New Edition. $2.75.

VERBUM DEI. The Yale Lectures on Preaching, 1893. By ROBERT F. HORTON, M.A., author of "Revelation and the Bible," etc. 12mo. $1.50.

"We thank him heartily both for the fresh, true thought and the strong, right spirit which he has striven so earnestly and with such fascinating power of conviction to communicate." — *Advance.*

REVELATION AND THE BIBLE. An Attempt at Reconstruction. By the same Author. 8vo. Cloth. $2.00.

"Broad in learning and rich in religious feeling, he himself in these pages is proof that Christianity has nothing to fear and everything to gain by the frankest recognition of proved facts, however revolutionary they appear. His book will greatly promote the era of good understanding between scholars and church-pastors." — *New World.*

THE MACMILLAN COMPANY,

66 FIFTH AVENUE, NEW YORK.